ANN MORROW

HIGHNESS

The Maharajahs
of India

GRAFTON BOOKS
A Division of the Collins Publishing Group

LONDON GLASGOW
TORONTO SYDNEY AUCKLAND

Grafton Books
A Division of the Collins Publishing Group
8 Grafton Street, London W1X 3LA

Published by Grafton Books 1986

British Library Cataloguing in Publication Data

Morrow, Ann
Highness: the maharajahs of India.
1. India—Kings and rulers   2. India
—Social life and customs
I. Title
954.03'0880621   DS423

ISBN 0-246-12664-7

Photoset in Linotron Bembo by
Rowland Phototypesetting Ltd
Bury St Edmunds, Suffolk
Made and printed in Great Britain by
William Collins Sons & Co Ltd, Glasgow

Contents

Acknowledgements

IN PRINCELY India, my thanks to the Maharajah of Baroda, a wise friend and mentor, the Yuvaraj of Bharatpur; the Maharajah of Bikaner and the Maharawal of Dungarpur, to the Rajmata of Jaipur; Maharao of Kotah and Maharajkumar Arvind Singh of Udaipur for great kindness; to Charles Allen who introduced me to his princely network; to Raj Puri, an unofficial prince whose ability as a raconteur of affectionate stories about the princes prompted the book.

For their guidance and help, thank you to Sir George Abell, Jaya Advani, Connie Alexander, Princess Ayesha – Begum of Hyderabad, Lord Avebury, Adrian Ball, C. H. Barry, Eric Bean, Maharajah of Benares, Lady Betjeman, the Begum of Bhopal, Maharajah of Bikaner, Lady Birdwood, Podge Brodhurst, Maurice Burn, Herbert and Helen Butt, Alan Campbell-Johnson, Lady Carnworth, Colonel Carroll-Leahy, Winifred Charles, Michael Charlesworth, Elizabeth Collins, T. R. Cookson, Lawrence Copley-Thaw, J. P. Das, Sandra and Roy Dickens, Sharada Dwivedi, Maharawal of Dungarpur, Dr Dutt George Eaton, Giles Eyre, Virigina Fass, Dr and Mrs Gaye, Jack Gibson, Lord Glendevon, Sir Percival Griffiths, Lady Pamela Hicks, Carmen Hill, Sir Owain Jenkins, Maharajah of Kapurthala, Dr Kautaria, M. M. Kaye, Peter and Sheila Lawton, Rita Marshall, Philip Mason, Avril Mollison, Lord Monckton, Sir Penderel Moon, Derry Moore, Lady Audrey Morris, the

Nawab of Palanpur, the Nawab of Pataudi, Aditya Patanker, David Preston – Rolls-Royce, Antony Ramsay, Lalit Sen – Rajah of Suket, Dr Karan Singh – Maharajah of Kashmir, Angus Stirling, Pearson Surita, Andrew Sutton, Edmund Swinglehurst, Trevor Turner, Maharajkumar Mohendra Singh of Udaipur, Itsik Vaknin, Muriel Watson, John Williams, Philip Ziegler.

Thank you to all the people who responded so generously to an appeal for photographs – especially Her Highness Annabella Singh of Udaipur – and, in trust, lent their family albums; also to Air India, to Alan Fernandes, Vice-President, Marketing, of the Oberoi Hotel Group and to the staff at the London Library.

I owe Richard Johnson at Grafton Books, Mike Shaw of Curtis Brown and Janice Robertson most special thanks; Anne Charvet for her contribution to the manuscript and Marianne Taylor for the photographs; to Terry Keeler for his help; and Angie Montfort Bebb, my assistant who charmed the most reticent maharajahs.

And for G, whose support never faltered, this book is for him.

Picture Credits

Black and White

Jam Shri Vibhaji of Nawanagar with his successor – *Popperfoto*
Maharajahs in the making – *Topham Picture Library*
Unusual view of 1911 Durbar – *Royal Commonwealth Society*
Boy Maharajah of Bharatpur – *Topham Picture Library*
A visit from the Viceroy – *India Office Library*
Lady Reading with other guests in Simla – *India Office Library*
Gracious lady sahibs enjoy a hop – *India Office Library*
Mir Allahdad Khan after a shoot – *India Office Library*
Maharajah of Bharatpur with guests after a shoot
Maharajah of Alwar with a tiger at his feet – *India Office Library*
Maharana of Udaipur (Mewar) with wife and Rolls Royce – *Singh Mewar Private Collection*
Maharajah of Kapurthala on his tricycle – *BBC Hulton Picture Library*
Wedding of Maharajah of Jaisalmer – *from the Private Collection of the Rajmata of Jaisalmer*
Maharajah and Maharani of Jaisalmer – *from the Private Collection of the Rajmata of Jaisalmer*
Uniformed *chaprassi* with baby prince – *Doris Martin*
Maharajah of Baroda with showgirl 'lovelies' – *Topham Picture Library*
Sita Devi being helped into her necklace – *Topham Picture Library*
Prince Sayajirao with his mother – *Topham Picture Library*
Maharani of Cooch Behar – *Popperfoto*
Maharajah of Jaipur, Gayatri Devi and their son – *Popperfoto*
Maharajah of Bharatpur's sons – *India Office Library*
Maharajah of Jaipur and family at Bognor – *Doris Martin*
The Jaipur royal children – *Doris Martin*
Nanny and children rowing – *Doris Martin*
Nanny and children riding – *Doris Martin*

Colour

Introduction

ONCE THERE WERE 565 Princes in India. They were bewitching, wanton, cruel, exotic, mischievous, imperious, generous, lovable, ascetic, subtle, charming and hedonistic. They claimed descent from the sun, the moon, from Aryan tribes dating back five hundred years before the time of Christ. Swimming pools were filled with champagne to celebrate their birth, some were sons of village women born in huts on mud floors. Their babies were rocked in cradles of gold, their titles included the Lord of the Umbrella. Some had states the size of France, others were scarcely bigger than a pocket handkerchief.

They were like Renaissance Princes, they ruled over one-third of India and were gods to their people. They were hated by the pale Nehrus, who thought them, with their moats and palaces, fortresses, elephant armies, court musicians, poets and artists, 'gilded and empty-headed', an invention of the Raj.

Carpets of ivory, pearls and gold, coffers of diamonds and rubies, emeralds as big as goose eggs, jewels designed by Cartier were taken for granted. Their marble palaces were filled with Aubusson tapestries, cigar boxes playing minuets, Fabergé clocks, paintings by Landseer and Rembrandt and gaudy posters, 'Love Me, Love My Dog'. Nowadays a box of gold tiddly-winks may be all that is left of an inheritance.

Opposite 'Occupation' in their red passports, it said 'Ruler'.

They loved dhoom-dham, the ceremonial, the gun salutes. In
the Punjab, there was an Officer for the Trousers.

Beneath the veneer of Western civilisation, life behind the
arras was medieval and full of intrigue. Some sat all day in iced
baths, drinking gimlets, playing mah-jong and being showered
with rose petals, or they built canals, turned deserts into grana-
ries, and educated their people.

Their eyes were as dark as the Medicis'; they made dynastic
marriages with princesses of twelve. Their women grew into
stately matriarchs in purdah guarded by rippling-skinned eunuchs. There was an Inspector General for Dancing. Concubines
were wheeled to their beds so that silken skin would not be
sullied with perspiration, and might be thrown to the crocodiles
if their breasts were not like Alfansa mangoes. Crushed diamonds were their aphrodisiac.

In their palaces today your bath stopper may be tied with
wire or made of gold shimmering against green marble; attar of
roses mingles with the acrid smell of the bearers' bidi cigarettes;
cardamom competes with Cardin; modern white ceramics are
next to ancient blue Persian tiles.

They travelled by elephant or gold Rolls-Royce; their carts
had solid gold wheels. Barefoot, they led their people on spiritual pilgrimages and believed in their astrologers. Tigers were
reduced to rugs, then hunters became conservationists.

Mocking clichés refer to 'cruel-lipped Princes' and their
'dusky slim-hipped girls'. They could be lascivious yet prudish;
a maharajah shocked by a vicereine's décolletage remarked, 'She
is not a very gentlemanly lady.'

They were autocratic; Lewis Carroll's 'No, no. Sentence first,
verdict afterwards' could have been written with them in mind.
In their libraries, *Twinkle Toes* sat beside Tod's scholarly *Annals
of Rajasthan*.

They aped the West with cocktail bars, and their radiograms
had tiger's-paw feet. They had a dedication to self-indulgence:
palaces were modelled on Versailles and on gloomy Scottish
baronial castles. They took dancing lessons to perform a
quadrille at a Simla Viceregal Ball and later the foxtrot as their

own eight-piece bands played 'Happy Days Are Here Again'.

They went to English public schools – one boy brought his panther – and as grown men kept in touch with their headmasters, writing 'Dear Daddy'. Like true aristocrats, they were completely lacking in snobbery. They spoke beautiful English, were invited to Balmoral and ate omelette Arnold Bennett. Every telegram sent by the Nizam of Hyderabad ended with 'Rule Britannia'.

Never raising their voices, they were languid, but people who displeased would simply disappear. They cared deeply about their religion and their ancestors, talking about fifteenth-century Mogul warriors as if they were cousins.

Royal India was powerful; it spread over half a million square miles and a quarter of the 300 million population lived in Princely States. At its peak, the British Raj still only controlled three-fifths of India.

During the Mutiny in 1857, the loyalty of some of the Princes was in doubt. The Crown took over from the East India Company and Queen Victoria became first Empress of India. The maharajahs' armies were taken away and they no longer had any say in foreign affairs. They could not go abroad without permission from the Viceroy and were really under the most civilised form of house arrest.

But princely dignity was not impaired because they always believed the Viceroys were their friends. Far from feeling dominated by an imperial power, they were flattered by meaningless pomp. The Princes who had long enjoyed exotic honorifics, Hindu Maharana and Maharawal, and Jam Saheb, Moslem Nizam and Nawab, were now called Highness as well. They were honoured by gun salutes graded according to their wealth, which made them bicker like children. The lowest was a Rajah with nine while a select few, a Nizam and four Maharajahs, had 21; still a long way from the Viceroy's 31 and the King's 101.

They were given foolish crests and coats of arms; instead of dragons, boars and fleurs-de-lis, they had monkeys, camels and elephants as supporters. The British had fallen back on the best remedy they knew and tried to create an Indian aristocracy. But the Princes were eastern potentates. They could never be a hybrid of English eighteenth-century aristocracy and muscular Christianity.

Under the influence of the Raj, the Rulers became divorced from their people. Some were brilliant; the Barodas, the Mewar dynasty of Udaipur, Bikaner, Patiala and Bhopal all had vision. They were the law-givers, the road builders, the enlightened Princes who fought to abolish purdah and suttee. But they were not heeded by the other Princes and thought slippery by the British.

Lord Linlithgow paid the Hindu Maharajah of Bikaner the compliment of saying he had a Western mind. But when he disagreed with the Viceroy, he was described as 'unreliable'. The British were happier dealing with the Moslem Princes whose people made ideal biddable soldiers. The Moslems had the solid virtues, but none of the mental athleticism of the Hindus, always looking for ways to bend the rules.

When Lord Kitchener, known as Lord of the Battles, asked one of his turbaned men how he was getting on, '*raza bazy*', he replied. It sounded like 'easy peasy' but was Hindi for 'happy and contented'. And in that sunny mood they went to war.

Close to the British Crown, the Rulers responded fulsomely in both world wars. Indian casualties in World War I amounted to 121,598 men, 'fighting side by side with Tommy Atkins against the hordes of the Kaiser'. There was nothing to match this courage. Kings in miniature won the Military Cross for gallantry, faithful feudatories.

But at home, once the responsibility of power had gone, there was stupendous dissipation amongst the few who could not face up to the shame of no longer being a warrior Prince. Ruled by British Residents, guardians and tutors, and with their own mothers keeping sinister sway by indulging the Crown Princes, they became infantile, apathetic and impotent in the oblivion of harem sex and drugs. By the 1920s and 1930s they were going abroad. The subtle corruption of their own heritage meant confusion between the cultures of East and West. At home they made dynastic princely unions; in Europe they married flamenco dancers and balloonists.

When the British Resident rebuked a Prince of Rajnangow for squandering all the family money on women, planes, cars and drugs, he replied: 'You have taught me all I know.' They came back from British universities in Savile Row suits and in the twenties said to their wives 'You must bob your hair.' But the women remained in purdah and became guardians of the culture as the British had no access to them.

An élite pampered by the British, the Rulers were bewildered in 1947 when they were abandoned in a newly independent India. It is touching to look back and see how they believed that they were special to the Crown. The Maharajah of Dholpur felt so close to the royal family, he sent a telegram giving his blessing to Edward VIII and Mrs Simpson.

The English had a love affair with Greece, after Missalonghi; the divorce happened somewhere after Cyprus. The love affair with India ended in 1947. They say the good the British did in India has never been sung, that they left behind two great gifts, scepticism and irrigation. But the blow the Princes have never recovered from was dealt not by Mountbatten but by India's leading daughter Indira Gandhi, when she smashed their titles, took away their purses and secretly wondered afterwards if she had been too harsh.

Some were utterly destroyed; others like rare delicate birds fluttered and hovered in the cold air; some still remained detached, like eighteenth-century bishops; others are selling off their heritage, European furniture and *objets d'art*; a few run their palaces as hotels and guests excitedly write 'In the name of Allah the Almighty I am very delighted to have spent time here' in the register. A few were appointed ambassadors; some are conservationists, working to save the tiger, another endangered species.

The Princes may be crushed, yet they do not invite pity. They never posed; they were never ordinary, untrue to themselves or mediocre. They remain unique.

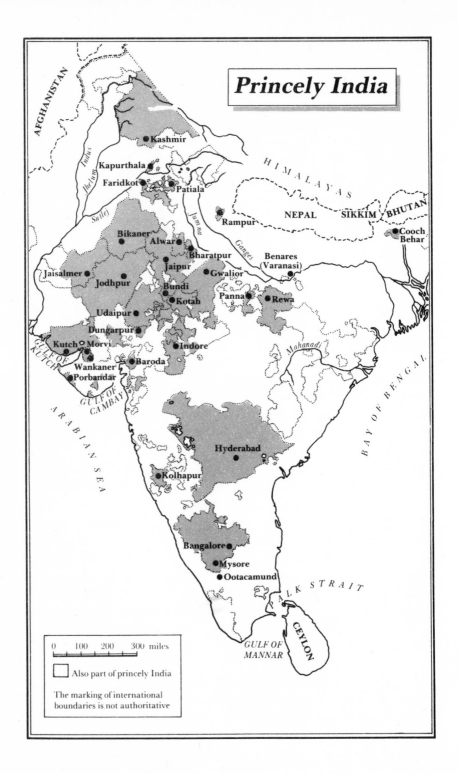

Princely India

AFGHANISTAN

Indus

Jhelum

Sutlej

HIMALAYAS

NEPAL   SIKKIM   BHUTAN

●Kashmir

Kapurthala●
Faridkot●   ●Patiala

Jumna

Rampur●

Ganges

●Cooch
Behar

Bikaner●   Alwar●
   ●Bharatpur
Jaipur●
Jaisalmer●   ●Gwalior
Jodhpur●   Bundi●
   ●Kotah

Benares
(Varanasi)
●

Panna●   ●Rewa

Udaipur●

Dungarpur●
Kutch○ ●Morvi
Wankaner●   ●Baroda
●Porbandar
   ●Indore

Mahanadi

GULF OF
KUTCH

GULF OF
CAMBAY

ARABIAN   SEA

BAY OF BENGAL

Hyderabad
●   ○

Kolhapur●

Bangalore●

●Mysore
●Ootacamund

PALK   STRAIT

CEYLON

GULF OF
MANNAR

0   100   200   300 miles

☐ Also part of princely India

The marking of international
boundaries is not authoritative

⊰ 1 ⊱

Highness Has No Power

ON 25 July 1947, the Maharajahs met their Viceroy, Lord Louis Mountbatten. The Princes were at their most languid and splendid in their white silk trousers, ornate brocade jackets and turbans studded with jewels, hair smooth with Rowlands Macassar Oil, the gold stopper removed from the cut-glass bottle by a valet. Many had come to Delhi on the same flying boat from Cannes and Deauville. The air was heavy with eau-de-Cologne and attar of roses; dark eyes flickered world-weary greetings; podgy fingers picked monogrammed cigarettes from gold cases to ease the *longueurs*.

Some were worried about how many Persian rugs should be laid down in the tents during the next tiger-shoot, should the swimming pool be filled with dry or sweet champagne – the British always liked a Brut bubble – and would the specially made fridges studded with diamonds ever arrive? Others had little more than country houses and an adequate number of servants.

The great rulers like Hyderabad, Gwalior, Baroda and Indore held power of life and death in their States. Some had Dewans who acted brilliantly on their behalf. These were the Prime Ministers who spent their lives intriguing, using the art of flattery with great subtlety, loving the Florentine web of intrigue surrounding their masters. King George VI never quite understood their significance and once earnestly asked the Indian

Service administrator Sir Conrad Corfield why the Princes were always changing their 'divans'.

In 1921, the more serious, enlightened Rulers had formed the Chamber of Princes which was inaugurated by the Duke of Connaught on behalf of King George V. Known as the Princes' Trade Union, it took off haltingly and grudgingly for they squabbled amongst themselves, each one an autocrat, often surrounded by sycophancy, impoverished relatives telling him what he wanted to hear.

Then in 1935, with the Government of India Act, a Federation Committee was set up. The Maharajahs of Bikaner, Jaipur, Jodhpur, Patiala and Gwalior believed in the new independent India. They were practical and hardheaded enough not to support the foolish dream of a separate princely India. But others ignored the turbulent murmurings of Independence. The Maharajah of Alwar, though a highly intelligent man, epitomised the attitude of many. 'If the people wish to live in hell, one should not compel them to live in paradise,' he told Mountbatten, like a profligate Marie Antoinette suggesting cakes for the starving, rebellious French mob.

Now Mountbatten stood before them. Refreshed by a cold bath, the Viceroy was an impressive figure, never a hair out of place. (One of his ADCs always had a comb handy.) Beside him stood the handsome Chancellor of the Chamber of Princes, the six-foot-four Maharajah of Patiala, an impressively bearded Sikh.

Some of the Princes stirred, smiling slightly; after all, Mountbatten was a personal friend of Bikaner and Dholpur, had enjoyed shooting tiger in Gwalior and fishing in Mysore. Both he and the Maharaj Rana of Dholpur had been ADCs for the Prince of Wales's visit to India in 1921. Many of them thought of him simply as 'Dickie – one of us'.

The red carpet showed off his admiral's white dress uniform with its orders and decorations, ice cool in the drenching heat. 'Do you think I should go just in sort of plain clothes and arrive as Viceroy like that?' he asked Woodrow Wyatt before leaving for India. 'After all, aren't they very left-wing?' But Wyatt had advised, 'Good Lord no, put on your best admiral's uniform and all your medals; do the lot.' Mountbatten cheered visibly. 'Oh good,' he said. 'I'm so glad,' because he loved uniforms. And appearances did matter to the Princes. Few Englishmen could compete with their glittery-diamond presence, but Mountbatten's bearing and flamboyance, vital on this day, could sway most of them. He always spoke well. One of his staff recalled his first meeting with Pandit Jawaharlal Nehru, 'Mountbatten did all the talking and Nehru nearly all the thinking.' Now he spoke to them with urgency and a disarming frankness, at his most persuasive for it was a matter of pride for him to achieve Independence on the date set. Despite his own *Almanach de Gotha* descent he had no fundamental sympathy for the Princes and had even referred to them privately as 'this bunch of nitwits'.

The Princes leant back, hands clasped, the flared brocade of their coats just touching their knees and the tight beginnings of their silk leggings. There were 25 important Rulers and 74 States representatives. They were like plump, velvet cattle, their large, sad, calm brown eyes fixed trustingly on their herdsman – who was about to tell them the best way to the abattoir.

Mountbatten spoke without notes to an audience whose mood he had gauged intuitively. They were much impressed by this and his good-looking presence, with its peacock 'look at me' aura. Sir George Abell once said Mountbatten was rather like a high-spirited horse: 'I can't think of anyone more glamorous with that blend of ingenuity and presentation.'

His message was simple. India was moving inexorably towards Independence. The Princes must make their peace with the Congress leaders and decide whether they would be integrated with Pakistan or India. After 15 August, they must no longer think of him as their Crown representative; he would remain sympathetic, of course, but would be powerless to help them. At present two Indias were administered from Delhi, British India and the Princely States. Gandhi and Nehru – with

Jinnah speaking for the embryo Pakistan – wanted both Indias
delivered up. For their own sakes, the Princes must learn to live
with the infant democracy and sign the Instrument of Accession.
'Instrument of Execution', Dungarpur snorted, irritated by
his unthinking, impulsive colleagues who seemed unable to
understand their loss. Others were reconciled to Independence
but feared a complete breakdown of authority. One Maharajah
predicted that after Independence, not a virgin or a rupee would
be left in the Punjab. A laughable thought as its Rulers were
Patiala and Kapurthala, two of the most libidinous Princes.
Others were increasingly afraid of the Congress Party. 'Fifteen
or twenty of them got me in a corner, they were desperate, on
the edge of a precipice,' Sir George Abell recàlled. The good-
looking, towering figure of Sir George, a Cambridge Blue and
now Mountbatten's Private Secretary, struck the Princes as a
'no-nonsense kind of a fellow' who could reassure them. But he
shook his head. 'Make your peace with Jinnah and Nehru;
identify with their wishes for Home Rule, do it quickly,' he
advised.

After Mountbatten had spoken, the meeting was thrown
open. There was something appealingly childlike about some
of the Rulers. They could be maddening, obtuse, incredibly
gullible and yet devious. They asked all sorts of silly questions
– would they have exclusive rights to tiger-shoots and what
about their gun salutes? Other Princes listened to it all then
went away.

One Prime Minister was not prepared to say whether his
master would sign. 'I do not know my Ruler's mind,' he said
and added that he was on a cruise. Quick-thinking and subtle,
Mountbatten picked up a heavy glass paperweight saying, 'I
will look into my crystal ball.' With great solemnity he turned
it in his hand with the reflective air of a fortune-teller, then
paused for about ten seconds. 'I see your Prince; he is sitting at
the captain's table and he says, "Yes, what is it?" Now he says,
"Yes, sign the Act of Accession."' There were gales of laughter
but in retrospect the story is sad and says something about the
Viceroy's opinion of his audience.

Tough and unflinching, Sardar Vallabhbhai Patel was the seasoned politician who presided over relations with the Princes for the government which would rule the new independent India. He wanted every single Prince to accede, no inertia or shillyshallying, saying bluntly to Mountbatten, 'It's got to be everybody. If you can bring me a basket filled with every apple off the tree, I'll buy it. If it hasn't got all the apples, I won't.' He was not the sort of guest who would have much enjoyed princely hospitality where silver trains carried the port and brandy and Rolls-Royces the visitors; where gold taps sprinkled attar of roses on hands and wrists.

Patel knew just how to handle them. Many believed that they were not rulers but agents for the deity who ruled. Travancore was one of these and his Prime Minister, Sir Ramasamai Iyer, said, representing him, 'Highness has no power to make such a decision.'

'This is a unique problem which requires deep thought,' Patel said. Next day the wily Patel revealed with awe that in his sleep he had a talk with Almighty God who had told him Travancore must sign. It worked.

The Princes had turned to their great ally Sir Conrad Corfield, the Viceroy's Political Secretary, and the social conscience of a missionary's son made him fight desperately to save them. He suggested to Lord Listowel at the Foreign Office, when he flew to London on their behalf, that after Independence the powers they originally surrendered to the Crown should be returned. The idea was designed to give the Princes the choice either of siding with India or Pakistan, or of being independent. All Corfield achieved was his own removal from India, but he did the Princes a great favour before he left for he destroyed all papers relating to their peccadilloes.

If the behaviour of some of the Princes seems quirky today, it is salutary to remember that the records relating to their more outlandish activities were burnt in this act of inspired kindness. No official trace remains of those meticulous private reports written by oil-lamp, in a tent, by exasperated British civil servants, often with stomach upsets. Reluctantly they recorded in manila folders their failure to put a stop to the more outrageous princely frolickings. But they have their memories and some have kept their diaries and letters home. They still smile as they recall happenings they were duty bound to report.

There was the difficulty of impressing the subtleties of English administration on the Maharajah of Bharatpur, who liked to cavort in a shallow pool filled with lotus flowers and forty giggling naked girls bearing lighted candles held in a most erotic spot. 'Come and join us, we are having madcap fun.' The British visitor to Bharatpur declined but noticed that the beauty who kept her candle alight longest after a dance in the water was rewarded with an invitation from her master to join him later for more high jinks. In this skittish mood, it was impossible for the Resident to go on about tax reforms. 'Your Highness, if I may say, sir, this is a stepping stone for the Princely States,' was met by a helplessly foolish smile as the Maharajah devoured the winner with his eyes.

On 28 July there was a reception for over fifty Ruling Princes. This was designed to gauge who was refusing to sign and how many would side with Nehru and how many with Jinnah's Moslem Pakistan.

Mohammed Ali Jinnah, pale, icy and imperious, European in outlook, was barely Moslem at all. The *Illustrated London News* was more his reading than the Koran. He had no Urdu and found India dreadfully hot and crowded.

He had been born in Kathiawar, coincidentally close to Gandhi, and he, too, ate his dinners at the Inns of Court and dedicated a fine legal mind to freeing India of the British. He had himself once worked for the Hindu-Moslem Congress Party but Gandhi had streaked ahead of him. Wherever Jinnah looked there were posters and photographs of the Mahatma: Gandhi walking, Gandhi leading the salt march, Gandhi praying, Gandhi smiling, Gandhi being followed through monsoons and heat by adoring Hindus.

Lady Reading remembered Jinnah coming to dinner in the twenties, 'with his pretty, fascinating wife who had less clothes and more golden skin showing than I have ever seen before.'

All the men raved about her while 'Mr Jinnah was prowling around like a leopard.' It was not unexpected when this first marriage failed.

But Jinnah had touches of de Gaulle in his single-minded pursuit of a Pakistan for the 90 million Moslems. What he once thought an 'impossible dream' had got to the first stage on 3 June 1947, when Mountbatten agreed that India should be divided. Gandhi was having his feet massaged with a stone by one of his acolytes after his bath and was heartbroken when he heard the news. Mountbatten remembered how Gandhi came to see him and sat crumpled up in his chair 'like a bird with a broken wing'.

For the Princes, trooping up the steps of Viceroy's House in New Delhi, Edwin Lutyens's creation in pink Dholpur sandstone, that last gathering at the end of July was unbearably poignant. They were greeted, importantly as always, by columns of ramrod-straight, scarlet-liveried Imperial Bodyguard, shoulders back and almost touching the white marble walls. The butler glided amongst them with chota gins and whiskies and champagne while whiffs of orange blossom and frangipani brought back wistful memories of banquets and State Balls.

A succession of Viceroys had entertained them, gold plate had sparkled, the servants splendid in crimson and gold while the band played 'The Roast Beef of Old England'. After dinner they would stroll out from the teak-panelled dining room in mellow mood, enduring music hall solos of 'My Old Dutch' and 'Lady of Laguna', rather a contrast to the sensuous Indian love songs and rolling eyes of their Indian *chanteuses*. Some had been the toddler Maharajahs chosen to carry the Viceroy's train for an investiture.

The Bodyguard stood smartly to attention along the corridors pillared in yellow porcelain as the Viceroy and his pages glided into the Durbar Hall. A fanfare of trumpets, the signal of panoply, made the hearts of those waiting skip. The Princes remained solemn as some six hundred people gingerly watched their step on the shimmering purple and white porphyry floor, bowing low before the Viceroy and the two impressive thrones draped in crimson velvet.

The sophisticated were uneasy about the future, filled with foreboding; only the most foolish could have been unaware. But the Princes were still pathetically divided by dynastic squabbles. The air of unreality and refusal to face up to their future was fuelled by their own courtiers, sycophants who would say anything to please. At this time of crisis there were anxieties, not about the workings of the new Congress Party, but about their own precedence. God help the ADC who got it wrong.

Most stood around in a semi-circle, three deep. Others were wandering about 'like letters without a stamp', as one Dewan remarked. After a 'friendly' talk with each, Mountbatten introduced them to Patel who waited to gather them into his basket. 'Who's HE getting to work on now?' one of the older Princes joked as the Viceroy tried to persuade a Ruler to agree to sign.

Mountbatten was pleased; after intensive lobbying he told his daughter Patricia: 'I have been making unbelievable progress with the Princes . . .' although he did not delude himself that they were all happy. Sir Penderel Moon summed it up well: 'In the end the Princes were bullied.'

There was an air of penitential calm as Prince after Prince came to Viceroy's House to sign. Some were like sad children who had been told that they must change tutors for their own good, give up the old aristocrat who liked parties and treats and have a new socially conscious one who would insist on their pocket-money going to good causes.

The flamboyant young Maharajah of Jodhpur signed but at considerable cost to V. P. Menon, Mountbatten's subtle constitutional adviser and the only non-Briton in a senior role on the Viceroy's staff. The Hindu Jodhpur had been intriguing with Jinnah and Nehru, playing one off against the other because his state was so close to Pakistan. But though he had already negotiated rather good terms and was acceding to India, he threatened the appalled Menon with death. 'If you betray the starving people of Jodhpur you will be shot like a dog,' the

excitable Maharajah cried angrily, flourishing a .22 pistol which
had been disguised as a fountain pen and causing the civil
servant's air of weary calm to vanish as quickly as the gun had
appeared. Mountbatten, also a conjuring enthusiast and fellow
member of the Magic Circle, treasured the confiscated pistol
and later presented it to the magicians' club.

But Jodhpur got an even more terrible revenge. He forced
the prudish vegetarian Menon to drink champagne and whisky
and then insisted on flying him back to Delhi in his private
plane, rocketing him about and wildly looping the loop as he
clutched the Accession document to his dhoti.

The Maharajah of Indore sent his signed Instrument of Accession by post, tormenting the viceregal team who had no idea
whether this was a joke or not.

It was particularly painful that some of Mountbatten's special
friends amongst the Maharajahs should be the ones who were
refusing Patel's blandishments. They still believed that perhaps
they alone might get special terms from their friend. One
was the Moslem Nawab of Bhopal, whom Mountbatten liked
enormously – a 'charming and high-principled man'. But Bhopal, who wanted to keep his state independent, felt betrayed by
Mountbatten. He listened to all the arguments and signed in the
end but insisted it should be kept secret for ten days. He never
saw Mountbatten again although, with elaborate royal courtesy,
he wrote that, throughout the weeks of agonising, 'I have been
treated with consideration and have received understanding and
courtesy from your side.' *Toujours la politesse.*

The Maharajah of Gwalior, signing at Viceroy's House in
Delhi, left 'in a very sad state', thought Elizabeth Collins, one
of Edwina Mountbatten's secretaries. Equally mournful was
the gentle Maharaj Rana of Dholpur who liked to wear a pink
turban. Not very robust, scarcely taller than Gandhi, he claimed
descent from the moon and had a mystical belief in his role as
Ruler.

He was a particular friend of the Mountbattens and their
daughter Lady Pamela Hicks remembers how gentle he was
with animals. He became emotional about the ending of links

with Britain and only Hindu fatalism could stem the tears. Dholpur was not an important state but the Viceroy took the trouble to write his old friend a letter of concerned friendship and somewhat contrived flattery: 'If you accede now you will be joining a Dominion with the King as Head . . . I know that His Majesty would personally be grieved if you elected to sever your connection with him whilst he was still King of India.'

Subtly he added that he felt it would be sad if the illustrious family of the Rana should have to travel without diplomatic privileges, adding, 'unless Your Highness were able to set up legations or consulates in various parts of the world . . .' Very unlikely for this tinpot Jat state of 1,200 square miles which only merited a 15-gun salute.

No amount of clubby blustering or flattery could persuade the Nizam of Hyderabad to accede. Not only was he the richest man in the world, he was the Moslem ruler of the largest state in India, almost the size of France, with a population of sixteen million, nearly all of them Hindus. He had been attracted by Jinnah's fanatical promises and wanted to be part of Pakistan.

The Nizam had the money and wisdom to employ the finest legal brains. The English lawyer Sir Walter Monckton was his Constitutional Adviser, believed to have been costing him £1,000 a day. His son, Lord Monckton of Brenchley, remembers to this day how some of the Nizam's courtiers came to stay at his father's house at Ightham and placed their prayer mats in the right direction. Allah was in Kent also.

One of the Viceregal team was sent to Hyderabad in a last attempt to persuade the Nizam to accede and could hardly believe his eyes when he first met His Exalted Highness. 'I was staggered by his threadbare appearance . . . dressed most shabbily in what looked like a thin white cotton dressing-gown and white trousers with caramel-coloured slippers and light brown socks lying loosely about his ankles, a brown fez perched on top of his head. I thought he was a servant at first.'

The most telling moment was when the Nizam said, 'Young man, there is no one to whom I have to pay courtesies.' Hyderabad was the leading sovereign state in the heart of India;

he was one of the last of the great Mogul Princes, had known George V and presented squadrons of Hurricanes and Tornadoes to the British war effort.

Patel was determined that there would be no question of Hyderabad's being a dissident state or acceding to Pakistan but, in the end, it was force and not persuasion which hurled this final apple into his basket.

Time does not have the same relevance in India as in the West. Steeped in a mythology and culture centuries old, the recalcitrant Princes were in no hurry and were much amused by the frantic British officials shuttling between their states. Lassitude and sycophancy were princely evil demons. Mountbatten's aides from Delhi had to pay a courtesy call on the Nizam's heir, the worthless Prince of Berar, who was later disinherited by his father because of his ne'er-do-well, decadent way of life.

Conversation turned to praise of Mountbatten's dynamism, energy and decisiveness. A fawning Private Secretary called Samader Yar Jung bowed low to the Prince and, in a hoarse whisper, subserviently suggested, 'In these respects he may be said to have the same characteristics as Your Highness.' But the Prince was worried about the royal tonsils and anxious to get to London to have them treated.

While his team tried to cope with the Nizam's obstinacy, Mountbatten went to Kashmir. His task there was to persuade the Hindu Maharajah to accede his mainly Moslem state to Pakistan, while Nehru, who was a Kashmiri Brahmin, was emotional about his home State and determined that it should remain part of India. Not a devious man, the Maharajah, who had been blackmailed in London in what became known as the Mr A case, dithered for a long time. He hated the idea of acceding to anyone, Hindu or Moslem, and had a touching belief that he could stand out against all advice. A little inertia, he thought, would make the problem go away.

Mountbatten was beautifully entertained. It was June and he was exasperated to be sent off on long fishing trips in the Trika, water bouncy-fresh and sparkling from the Himalayan snow.

The air was exhilarating for the palace was near Srinagar, the capital, 7,000 feet high, overlooking lakes and houseboats and gardens which are even today full of English flowers with notices saying 'No plucking'.

But Mountbatten had phenomenal energy and never needed this sort of restoring break. Even more annoying for him, because he was competitive, he did not catch a single fish; all the golden trout went to his ADC. He shocked the palace servants by sunbathing in the nude.

By mistake he pressed a bell under the table which the Maharajah had specially installed. This was to have been the signal for the band, telling them to play 'God Save the King' towards the end of the State banquet. But when the Viceroy's toe wandered everyone had to jump to their feet halfway through the main course, which was lamb tandoori. Dr Karan Singh of Kashmir, then the Yuvaraj or heir apparent, thought it hilarious but his father was affronted and all thoughts of accession receded. 'Besides,' his son recalls, 'my father still did not believe that the British would actually leave.'

Mountbatten had to return to Delhi cheated of a meeting with the Ruler, who at the last minute found he had a severe attack of colic. In the end Kashmir acceded to India, but only when Pakistan invaded this vital strategic area six weeks after India got her freedom. A broken man and outraged by this indignity, the Maharajah had lost the will to act. He complained that his home was commandeered and he had lost everything just because he procrastinated.

His Roman-Emperor insouciance put him in real danger from the Pakistan raiders, for when the capital was about to fall, he decided to have a splendid lunch. Afterwards he told one of his ADCs, rather loftily, 'I am expecting some of the Indian army to rescue me. Tell them I am having a siesta.' As he was walking away he turned, 'Oh, by the way, if they are not here by three, please shoot me. But now I'm going to sleep.' 'He was saved in the nick of the time,' an aide recalls, 'but we had to admire the fellow's cool.'

In 1949, Nehru intervened and the heir apparent, a brilliant eighteen-year-old boy, was appointed Regent of Jammu and Kashmir. He writes lyrical poetry, part love, part spiritual, and was one of the few Princes to be impatient with those who struggled against the loss of their titles in 1972.

Dogs were the great passion of the Maharajah of Junagadh, who thought nothing of spending £22,000 on a wedding for two of his favourites. His state, which was founded by Afghan marauders, was 82 per cent Hindu while he was a Moslem. He had wanted to remain independent along with the great states of Hyderabad and Kashmir, both vast compared with his little stretch of 3,337 square miles, but he left the State for a social engagement and in his absence the people decided by referendum that Junagadh would accede to India.

Everything had to be divided in Partition; the fate of 400 million people had to be decided, the Army reorganised, and the Kennel Club. This last was of considerable concern to the Princes; it went to India.

By early August all the apples were gathered in except for Kashmir, Junagadh and Hyderabad. Trying to drive the point home, an aide told the Nizam quite forcefully that the British were really on the point of departure. Hyderabad bounced up in his seat and with a gleeful grin said, 'You mean I can do then as I like?'

In 1949, two years after the transfer of power, the Indian Army marched into his State and there was a five-day occupation. The estranged wife of the present Nizam's father remarked that it was typical of her husband, the Prince of Berar, to absent himself from the battle but be present for the surrender.

When Mountbatten chose 15 August 1947 as the date for India's freedom, he clashed with the astrologers who said the day was not auspicious. There was a compromise; it would be at the stroke of midnight when the 15th was just an emerging dot. Mountbatten spent his last hours that evening sitting at his desk in a serene mood of almost unreal calm. That Germanic efficiency meant there was not a paperclip out of place. As his daughter Pamela recalls, 'My father had done everything and he looked at the ceiling and thought, in the exhilaration of

Independence creeping nearer, I wonder what I could still do in these last few hours as Viceroy. I know, I'll make my old friend Iqbal's wife a Maharani.' The Nawab of Palanpur had married an Australian and she had never been given a title.

In the streets of Delhi hysterically happy crowds of nearly 600,000 gathered. They garlanded their heroes with marigolds and ate special biscuits decorated with orange peel, pistachio and white sugar, India's national colours. They chanted 'Pandit Mountbatten' as well as 'Long Live India' and at midnight they went to temples twinkling with oil-lamps where the air was scented with scatterings of rose petals and saffron-robed priests marked their foreheads with sandalwood paste.

In Bombay that night, the Mountbattens stood up in an open Rolls for the triumphal sweep round the crescent shore by the Arabian Sea and a policeman put a large sign outside the whites-only Bombay Yacht Club which said 'Closed'. Grinning boys linked arms; girls with wide-eyed babies raced alongside the lucky owners of bicycles; caparisoned elephants lumbered through the streets and it was as if everyone were going to an Indian wedding.

In Residencies and palaces, formal, slightly awkward parties were taking place. The Princes wore their decorations with sad dignity and British men were in formal white tie and tails. In Lucknow the engraved invitations to a midnight flag-raising at the Residence stressed, 'National Dress: Dhotis will be suitable'. Indians working at the Residency as part of the ICS team were slightly shocked, none would ever have dreamt of wearing ethnic clothes to work. One of them, Rajeshwar Dayal, suddenly felt light-spirited after fourteen years in a suit.

The Nizam of Hyderabad gave a sombre farewell banquet for the British administrators. He never worried about dhotis, just pulled on his loose tattered trousers and a little before midnight proposed a toast to his outgoing King-Emperor. A sad moment which touched Lord Monckton: 'It is horrible that we should have encouraged the Rulers to believe in our promises up to such a short time ago and should then leave them without the resources to stand comfortably on their own feet.'

Mountbatten, who became Governor-General upon the stroke of midnight, announced that he would be leaving India in less than a year. To stay, he thought, would be bad for India and bad for him. In fifteen months they had entertained 7,605 guests to lunch, 8,313 to dinner and 25,287 to tea and garden parties. They had employed 5,000 servants including a pin wallah and one to turn the blotter each day. Another was in charge of the mongoose. Now at this moment of his greatest personal triumph Mountbatten wrote his wife a note acknowledging all her support throughout those hectic months, ending with an endearingly simple, 'Thank you, my pet.'

As a reward for 'a job supremely well done', the new Governor-General was raised from the rank of Viscount. The Princes instructed their private secretaries that their friend had a new title, Earl Mountbatten of Burma. They were to learn that titles were fragile when they lost theirs, their privileges and their privy purses less than twenty-five years later at the hands of Nehru's daughter.

Meanwhile, however, in return for giving up their powers, abandoning any claims to independence and acceding to the Indian Union, the Princes would keep their palaces, immunity from arrest and the right to British decorations. They would receive either compensation or an annual privy purse. In addition to their existing titles they were promised some daft new ones, like Rajpramukh, or Governor, which was quite meaningless.

The Princes' champion, Sir Conrad Corfield, could not stomach their inevitable humiliation. He flew home to England, confessing to 'a feeling of nausea, as though my own honour had been smirched and I had deserted my friends'.

Dungarpur was one of the Princes who understood the realities throughout. 'I went to see Mountbatten,' he recalled, 'and had a long talk with him but then I got up in complete disgust. I said to him, "Your Excellency, I think it is best to disagree. Why not quit at once and leave us to our fate?"'

Shortly after the Princes had signed away their kingdoms Dungarpur was forced into another meeting with Mountbatten, to receive the Companionship of the Indian Empire for his work

during the war. He vividly remembers saying, 'It is a kiss with
a kick' as his hand was shaken. Mountbatten dissembled and
agreeably suggested, 'Come and have a glass of champagne
with Edwina and myself.' It was 11.30 am, which Dungarpur
thought early for a glass, and the Mountbattens were normally
abstemious. 'They pressed me to stay for lunch,' he recalled,
'but I said, "No, Your Excellency, I have an engagement" and ·
I left feeling down and broken-spirited.'

There are many of the Raj who still feel guilty about the
treatment of the Princes in 1947. 'The Princes did feel let down,'
the distinguished Indian Civil Servant Sir Percival Griffiths
recognises. 'We had given them assurances it wasn't humanly
possible to carry out. We had let them somehow feel that the
British Government was behind them whereas it was not.'

The daughter of a British Resident, Lady Vere Birdwood,
echoes this ache of conscience. 'I should not like to meet a Prince
today,' she says. 'We broke treaty after treaty.'

2

A Beastly People

THE TENTACLES of the British Empire first touched India in the autumn of 1600, when an enterprising group of London merchants set up the East India Trading Company to compete with the Dutch. Queen Elizabeth I, always acquisitive, granted the twenty-four entrepreneurs a royal charter allowing trading beyond the Cape of Good Hope. One hundred and twenty-five shareholders put up the initial capital of £72,000 and there never was a better investment.

William Hawkins sailed to Bombay to meet the most powerful man in India. He set off for Agra to meet the Emperor Jehangir, a potentate who ruled over 70 million people. Although Hawkins was hardly a diplomat in the mould of Sir Philip Sydney, he impressed the Fourth Great Mogul by speaking to him in Turkish. An agreement was signed allowing the East India Company to trade in the area around Bombay.

Hawkins did extremely well for his Queen and country, securing the embryo of the Raj which was to control India for nearly three hundred years. He stood before the Mogul throne and noticed '. . . the master hangman . . . accompanied by forty hangmen wearing . . . a certaine quilted cap; others with all sorts of whips being there, readie to do what the King commandeth'. Hawkins was offered something special from the Emperor's harem and was made a member of the royal household. There was no gift he could offer in return for treasure which was to so enrich a damp little island in the English Channel.

By the mid-nineteenth century, claims by traders and the military that they were simply obeying orders from London and not being acquisitive were as transparent as netting over rosy red strawberries ready for eating. One by one, Baroda, Hyderabad, Gwalior, Travancore, Mysore and later the princely states of Rajasthan and the Punjab with its fertile land, all succumbed. The British wanted the whole of India; it had become irresistible and trade, philanthropy or teaching military skills were no longer needed as a cover.

In 1857 the Mutiny, or the first Indian War of Independence as it is now officially known in India, gave the British a sharp shock. They had nearly lost India through giving the traders too free a hand. So it was decided that the Crown would rule India. The East India Company was dissolved on 12 August 1858 by royal decree and plausible officials persuaded the Princes to sign individual paramountcy treaties recognising Britain as the supreme power. The Viceroy was acting, the Princes were assured, on behalf of their good friend Queen Victoria. But they lost control of defence and any say in foreign affairs. If they had any administrative worries then one of the 2,000 Indian Civil Servants would be delighted to help. If there was any little anxiety about an attack on their state, what else were the 60,000 solid British soldiers there for, but to make princely territories secure? Indeed their own countrymen, 200,000 of them, had joined the Indian Army, with 10,000 British officers keeping a benevolent eye.

Polished envoys from England got the unwitting Princes to agree to the removal of their teeth and claws. Impeccable British Presidents taught them the skills of social behaviour and diplomacy. India had become a 'vast system of outdoor relief for Britain's upper classes' thought John Stuart Mill.

The British attitude to the Empire was that they had 'an inalienable right to rule'. The Princes had a simple, unassailable faith in the great British Imperial family ruled by Queen Victoria. Indeed, many of their subjects thought she was immortal, and it is not unusual in India today to be asked by a taxi driver, 'Madam, how is Lord Canning?'

To save face, the Princes were told that within their own states they had total authority over their people although, of course, they had lost all real power. They were now like big tame cats meriting occasional affectionate pats from a visiting viceroy as they padded about aimless and overweight from lack of exercise.

Many of them were not very sophisticated and only a few had travelled, but a grave and cruel error was continually to sound the call that the treaties they had made were, and would remain, inviolate. As late as 1946, Lord Wavell, a man of total integrity, was rather belatedly moved to propose that there should be much less harping on the sanctity of these treaties, to try to warn the Princes that with Independence they would be in the hands of their own young Congress government.

In fairness, it was not always easy to get the Princes to be serious. It was difficult for the earnest, well-meaning British Resident to advise some of those who could be at best trying, if not downright childish. When there was a tremendous invasion of locusts in Kapurthala, the administrator was shocked by the attitude of the Maharajah, who said airily, as giggling girls swayed around him in swirling, see-through harem pants, 'Let the locusts dance, we are going to dance in Paris.'

The Maharajah of Patiala had to be persuaded to give up the custom of walking naked through the streets once a year wearing nothing but a breastplate of 1,001 blue-white diamonds while showing a priapic acknowledgement of his subjects' cheers.

One hard-pressed Resident, Sir Bertrand Glancey, had travelled hundreds of miles to talk to one of the Princes about a problem. He was very put out to be told that Highness could not be disturbed. He protested that he had come a long way and eventually the Maharajah appeared. 'Ah, Sir Bertrand,' he said in a state of some excitement, 'we are having a very urgent Cabinet meeting.'

The Resident, appreciating this sort of priority, was suitably impressed.

'Yes,' went on the Maharajah. 'There is a most interesting item on the agenda; we have three canaries and we are trying to decide which one sings best.'

Another political agent paying his regular visit to Rajputana found the Prime Minister of the little state sitting gloomily by the side of the road. When asked what was the matter, he mournfully replied that the State elephant had eaten his budget.

One of the most important warning signs for the British that their presence was unwelcome occurred at Amritsar in the Punjab in April 1919. There was a riot in which four Englishmen were killed and the civil authorities found themselves unable to restore order. It was then that the zealous Brigadier-General R. E. Dyer did for them all with his plan of attack. As Amritsar's Commander, he took charge and his fifty soldiers fired 1,650 rounds of ammunition into a relatively peaceful crowd of several thousand men, women and children gathered in the Jallianwalla Bagh, leaving hundreds of dead and injured piled one upon another. In those six minutes, Dyer felt that he had acted decisively and 'done a jolly good thing'. Churchill, however, considered his action one of 'quite un-English frightfulness'.

Dyer's action was clearly indefensible and Amritsar was a turning point for many members of the Congress Party. Nehru's father, Motilal Nehru, had not previously been anti-British but this incident turned him into an enemy, as it did his son. By a strange irony, his grand-daughter, Indira Gandhi, would lose her life because of troubles in Amritsar. As Prime Minister, she had ordered troops to storm the Golden Temple which had been occupied by zealots determined to turn the Punjab into the independent Sikh state of Khalistan. The following year, in November 1984, Mrs Gandhi was assassinated by two of her Sikh bodyguards.

As far as the Princes were concerned, Sir Penderel Moon, former Private Secretary to the Governor of the Punjab, thought they had been 'treated with excessive generosity; their peccadilloes and failure to manage their estates properly were overlooked.' But much depended on who was Viceroy.

Lord Curzon was very strict; in Minto's time the reins were more relaxed and there was much more latitude. Lord Linlithgow, a viceroy unkindly described by Nehru as 'heavy of body and slow of mind', pampered the Princes and did not take the threat of a seceded Pakistan too seriously. He was the Viceroy who declared India at war with Germany in 1939 without consulting a single Indian. This high-handed decision stabbed the truth home to Indian leaders, though he was merely exercising his constitutional right.

The next Viceroy, Lord Wavell, sensitive to the mood of India, was stung into openly writing to Churchill 'The vital problems of India are being treated by His Majesty's Government with neglect, sometimes even with hostility and contempt.' For Churchill had never been sympathetic to India, once confiding to India's Secretary of State, Leopold Amory, 'I hate Indians, they are a beastly people with a beastly religion.' India's trouble was that she had the caste system and so many religions, Sunni and Shia Moslem, Hindu Brahmin and Sikh; while in several states the Ruler's faith was not that of his people.

All the same it had been a good partnership, but the honeymoon between Imperial Britain and India was nearly over. Only the Princes and some British went on cherishing the illusion of a lasting relationship held within a web of treaties. These few were blithely unaware of the cataclysmic events which would soon overtake them.

One of those who did see the times changing was the Maharawal of Dungarpur. His palace in Rajasthan with its pale blue walls set beside a lake has a sad beauty. It is run down and sweepers ineffectually chase squirrels and monkeys out of the marble courtyards. He is a man of innate aristocratic elegance, slim and lithe in his typically English loose brown cardigan and with the day's newspapers tucked under his arm. Like many an elderly aristocrat, he is devoted to the worn slippers in which he shuffles towards a tray of dusty crystal glasses in the drawing room. Some of these have handles for hot brandy, 'awfully popular with the young subalterns', if they were not having half a dozen gin slings before lunch after a hard morning's shooting or some sets of tennis.

Dungarpur was once the darling of the viceregal set and was a great admirer of the old order. But that was before Independence in 1947 and the crumbling of all but the brightest Princes. He still loves London and never tires of bacon and egg. The waiter comes to the table and says, 'And to follow, Sir?' and the Maharawal always replies, 'To follow? Bacon and egg again, of course. It is much the best.'

India has always been predominantly Hindu with a quarter of the population Moslem. In the great days of the Mogul kings, the Moslems ruled. But that was before the arrival of the British, when the Hindus, bright, and intuitively quick, learnt to adapt to Western ways while the Moslems, even in Bengal and the Punjab where they were in the majority, tended to be slower. They were popular with the Raj and made good soldiers and farmers but did not shine in British institutions like the Civil Service or the law courts.

The Moslems and Hindus have never mixed. Hindus worship the cow, Moslems eat it. The Moslems revere the Koran in Arabic; Hindus think it is pagan.

After World War II India was impatient for Independence and on the brink of anarchy. 'Operation Madhouse' was how Lord Wavell, a sensitive, perceptive man, described the task of trying to achieve harmony between Moslem and Hindu. Clement Attlee, Britain's post-war Labour Prime Minister, decided that Britain must quit fast and in a brilliant moment chose Lord Louis Mountbatten to preside over the end of British rule in the sub-continent. Looking back Lord Louis' handling of Partition may seem to resemble the driver of a rickety train hurtling over the points in a pitch-black tunnel but he felt, as Lloyd George once suggested, that you cannot jump over a precipice in two stages.

Dungarpur, however, was appalled at the indelicate speed with which Independence was achieved and the indignity suffered by this fellow Princes. 'I was,' he said, 'in no doubt that Mountbatten wanted to scuttle the Empire.'

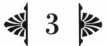

He Simply Fell in Love With Her

ONCE SHE WAS one of the world's most beautiful women, and now everyone is waiting for her to appear. It is her party, at Lilypool, but the Maharani of Jaipur was never on time, even in the old days for the grand occasions.

As a child she coped gracefully with five hundred servants, and was blasé about the national anthem being played every time she left her grandfather's palace in Baroda. When she grew up there was a fairytale marriage to one of India's most personable Princes; she was the darling of the social set; no party was complete without the golden Jaipurs. It seemed too perfect to last.

Lilypool is a comfortable, stockbrokerish house in Jaipur, with cream carpets, photographs of the Queen and Prince Philip and one of the Maharani by Cecil Beaton capturing the elusive quality which has held men in thrall. There is an air of anticipation. Nobody is really concentrating on conversation. White-coated waiters move smoothly amongst the guests, keeping them happy for an hour or so. Suddenly the low buzz of conversation stops, and all eyes turn as the hostess flutters into the room.

Gayatri Devi is sixty-seven, and is wearing a blue-green gauzy chiffon sari, no jewellery apart from two large diamond rings. She is svelte, exotic and compelling, and there is a moment of absolute quiet. Then the silence dissolves and the atmosphere zings. She flits round, chats about 'the ball in New Orleans', her fillies 'at the stud farm' in America and the Arc de Triomphe, wafting about in a flirty conspiracy of fun.

There is a full length de Laszlo portrait of her mother, 'Ma' Cooch, over the mantelpiece, a sandal slipping off a wanton foot. Widowed when she was only thirty, Ma had all the fragile delicacy of an Indian butterfly, a worldly twenties socialite whizzing round London and Paris with characters who could have been created by Evelyn Waugh or Nancy Mitford.

Her admirers included the Prince of Wales and Man Singh, the Maharajah of Jaipur, who embarked upon a passionate and long-running affair with the tiny and deliciously languid princess. He found her irresistibly frolicsome. He liked to tweak the tails of his advisers, who were unremittingly gloomy about the relationship. 'This lady,' they warned, 'is going to ruin him as she has done a good many before.'

Ma slept in an ivory bed and always refused to live on the women's side of the palace. Her bathroom was marble, the steam-bath disguised as a chaise-longue; her toes snuggled in a 14-skin leopard rug designed by Schiaparelli. Her maid was Swiss, Ma spoke excellent French and her shoes came by the hundred from Ferragamo in Florence.

Life at Woodland's, Ma's home in Calcutta, was one long houseparty. For successive winter polo seasons, the Maharajah of Jaipur was a welcome guest. He arrived in a green Rolls-Royce and with sixty polo ponies. He was flirtatious and women loved his drawling English.

The head butler, Jaffar, was a regular Jeeves. He mixed potent Alexanders, getting the vermouth and crême-de-cacao with a wave of whipped cream on top just right for houseguests who did not drink champagne. At dusk, as guests chatted, servants moved softly on the other side of the rose-quartz and jade studded Chinese screen in the drawing room shaking silver urns of incense.

There was international cuisine and a table always formal with gold and silver settings, in the middle a crystal bowl of roses and frangipani. The Maharani dragged one of her bemused

Indian cooks to Alfredo's in Rome so that he could learn how to cook lasagne properly. Her flamboyant Russian chef, who had been in the Tsar's army, could be exceedingly capricious. Once, in a fit of temperament, he foxed an entire dinner party by presenting food quite different from that printed in French on menu cards embossed with the Cooch Behar crest. The dogs drank only Evian water.

In the heady, fairytale atmosphere of yet another polo victory party for 'Jai', Ma, delectable in chiffon and diamonds, shimmied across the room to him, waves of French scent drifting from the folds of her silk sari. Like a goddess in Greek mythology garlanding the hero, she looked up at him and asked, with outstretched jewelled hand, 'What would you like? You can have anything you want . . . anything.'

To her credit, she did not flutter an eyelash when he asked, with that charming smile she knew so well, if Ayesha, her thirteen-year-old daughter, might come to the celebration dinner being given that night at Firpo's, Calcutta's smartest restaurant. 'Yes,' Ma answered in that worldly way of hers. 'Why not?'

Ayesha was already beautiful, with a mane of dark hair, a voluptuous mouth and a hint of mystery. She was spirited, and a shade wild. Jai simply fell in love with her.

She was called Ayesha after the heroine in a Rider Haggard novel which Ma had been reading during her pregnancy, though her daughter had been christened Gayatri.

Even at thirteen this was no simpering, nervous, inarticulate schoolgirl. As a five-year-old in London, in the family's Knightsbridge House, she used to give her nanny the slip and go across to Harrods to order delectable goodies, saying, 'Put it on the Cooch Behar account.'

Cooch Behar was famous for its elephants and Ayesha raced them round the sandstone paths and great borders of roses, sitting calmly between their cabbage leaf ears. When her grandfather's ashes were brought to the station, the elephants were lined up and they trumpeted in unison as tears trickled down their grey cheeks.

With a little jasmine tucked in her hair, she was a sporty slip of a girl who shot her first panther when she was twelve, played tennis and rode well. At the end of the day, she slept in gossamer light sheets. Her schoolgirl dream was to be changed by a wave of a fairy wand from a princess into a girl groom. Then she could look after the Maharajah of Jaipur's polo ponies.

'I never heard such sentimental nonsense,' the Maharani expostulated when told by Man Singh, Maharajah of Jaipur, that he wanted to marry her daughter when she had grown up, though secretly she was pleased.

Still a schoolgirl, Ayesha was now infatuated with this glamorous figure. When she was sixteen, she escaped watchful eyes and went by arrangement to the Dorchester where Man Singh picked her up in his Bentley. Driving round Hyde Park, his favourite run, he proposed and Ayesha said 'Yes' in a flat voice. He was rather taken aback. 'You don't have to say "Yes" if you don't mean it,' he said, distinctly worried. But she did mean it and it was this very unpredictable, airy insouciance which he found so intriguing.

Later when the same wilful spirit drove her to play a dangerous game politically, he supported her. He doted on her and his roving eye would proudly settle on this third Maharani, at Ascot holding top-hatted admirers in thrall, presenting a cup at a polo match, or campaigning in a peppermint green sari in a dusty village in Rajasthan. It was a great love story, as golden and legendary in India as the inseparable gods Vishnu with his discus and conch shell, and Lakshmi, his lady, who sprang from the waves like a glorious Indian Venus.

The new Maharani of Jaipur was twenty-one. They had been unable to marry until 1940 because of the war. She was appalled by purdah and her apartments, freshly decorated, were put next to the Maharajah's. Like her mother, she did not sleep in the women's quarters.

The Maharajah had been a poor farmer's son from a small village, but of the right caste and chosen to ensure the succession. He was educated by English tutors and bear leaders, growing up to become Sawai Man Singh II, the glamorous, polo-playing

'Jai', last ruling Maharajah of Jaipur. In 1949 Jaipur was merged into the new state of Rajasthan. He was discreet about his wealth, not wildly intellectual, so he did not agonise over the future and remained much loved.

He had become the first Indian ever to get a commission in the Household Cavalry, and was Indian ambassador to Spain. One of the best polo players in the world, with a handicap of nine, he was known to the Queen and Prince Philip simply as Jai. Prince Philip in mellow mood said he had met many people who could be described as charming, 'but few, if any, had quite Jai's special brand of kindly charm and gentleness of character.'

At the age of ten, he was formally engaged to two Jodhpur princesses. One was his own age, the other, her aunt, was twenty-two. The boy and his British guardians were horrified by the age difference, but had to swallow the package. On 30 January 1924, a hoped-for dynastic marriage between the houses of Amber and Jodhpur took place; he married the aunt.

This first wife, the Princess Marudhar Kanwar of Jodhpur, gave birth to a daughter Princess Prem Kumari, 'Mickey', in Simla in 1929. But it could never have been called a love match although First Her Highness, as she was called, was intelligent, but orthodox and anti-British. Her young husband was a smiling soldier and sportsman, not a questing politician. In 1931 she gave him the longed for heir, 'Bubbles', whose true name was Bhawani Singh.

The Maharajah was a kind man, but he had little in common with the mother of his children and was now spending more time in Europe. When he was asked what he did in London, he would reply, 'Oh parties, of course.' Man Singh had all the *Tatler* graces, and could even be a bit of a Hooray Henry – a Jeremy Jaipur tearing round Hyde Park in his Bentley, being chased by policemen as he darted into Knightsbridge Barracks, claiming diplomatic immunity. But he loved being a soldier and took it seriously. His set included Sir Harold and Lady Zia Wernher, Sir Robert 'Bobby' Throckmorton and a clutch of young sprigs from the Household Brigade.

Top hostesses like Mrs Ronnie Greville found the young

Maharajah a social catch. He would turn up at their parties, and they thought him 'too divine' in his brocade, jewels and turban, and always with his own half bottle of Bollinger. He loved London and he thought 'the girls . . . heaven'. Sparkling favourites were actress Virginia Cherryl, who was to marry first the Earl of Jersey and afterwards the film star Cary Grant, and the peer's daughter Joan Eyres Monsell who later married writer Patrick Leigh Fermor and lives in Greece. These were of a very different calibre from the telephonists, dancers and night-club singers seen gadding about Mayfair on the arms of more gullible fellow Princes.

He was too mature and responsible ever to think marriage to a European could really work. Biddably, he was married a second time in 1932 to his wife's niece, the young Jodhpur princess, Kishore Kanwar, 'Jo Didi'. Traditional though he was, he declined to suck the breasts of the oldest woman in the harem, the custom when a prince was getting married. He settled for a speedy swig at his mother's instead, outraging the zenana houris.

His second wife was more decorative, and much younger than her aunt. But purdah tradition had been too strong in Jodhpur; she could never be a companionable, social wife for him. She gave birth to two more sons, Jai Singh in 1933 and Prithviraj Singh in 1935, and the marriage was over.

When Jaipur married a third time, and for love, Second Her Highness could only peer through the latticed verandahs as the fun couple swished off again in the Rolls to the airport to fly to Buenos Aires or London, making the large type in Jennifer's Diary and other gossip columns. Training since birth to accept other wives may have helped the second Maharani, but in her increasing loneliness Jo Didi relied ever more on the blanketing power of alcohol and died when she was forty-two in 1958.

The Maharajah was sensitive about the atmosphere in the palace, '. . . it must be pretty awful for you,' he wrote, a year after their marriage to Ayesha, 'at home shut up and surrounded by evil thoughts all the time'. At first, the young chatelaine did find Jaipur, with its 400 servants, chillingly formal after the frisky socialising at Woodlands. Often described as India's answer to Jacqueline Kennedy, she brought the same glamour to Jaipur, and a sense of economy. She cut household expenses by half at the palace believing too much had been spent on food and drink. But drinks still went on being served as dinner was never before ten. Finding her altogether too haughty and gracious in those early days, there was an outburst from her good-looking, easygoing brother Indrajit when he was visiting Jaipur: 'Who the hell do you think you are?' he asked. 'Queen Mary?'

But soon the new Maharani was a relaxed hostess presiding with confidence at the creamy glistening Rambagh Palace. There was always that air of ineffable distinction, whether it was tea on the lawn beside marble lotus fountains; on horseback; showing the Queen the Jaipur collection of exquisite Indian miniatures, or dancing till dawn when the sky was pink and gold and the scuttling peacocks were shrieking morning calls from the English herbaceous borders.

The Jaipurs were tremendously popular. Social climbers who did not know them at all would talk knowledgeably about 'Jai and Ayesha'.

Even the events of 1947 did not alter the fairy story. The handsome Prince worked conscientiously for a smooth integration of Jaipur with independent India, and afterwards became Rajpramukh of Rajasthan. This spell as Governor was not spectacular, but he stayed out of trouble. He was weighed in silver at the time of his silver jubilee in 1947 and was rich enough to carry on with the same princely way of life, but discreetly. Unlike his wife and many of the Princes, he did not seethe with resentment about the socialist Congress Party. His decision to turn his Rambagh Palace into a hotel in 1958 was seen as a wise populist move.

Under Shastri's government he became ambassador to Spain. But the headstrong Gayatri Devi had no time for the harmless demands of life as a diplomat's wife, hosting trade delegations and never being provocative. In 1961 she raced back from

Madrid to join the new, right-wing, Swatantara party to attack socialism.

Not everyone was enchanted by Gayatri Devi's beauty. Some saw her as a latterday Rani of Jhansi, a particularly savage princess killed when fighting the British during the Indian Mutiny in 1857. There are princely families who feel her political stance did the Jaipur family a grave disservice. Her husband was so besotted by her, he had to agree to this recklessness whatever the consequences in this still immature, prickly democracy.

'Long Live our Maharani', the villagers chanted during the 1961 elections as she campaigned in her 1948 Buick, bringing her own sheets and cooking pots. They garlanded her with marigolds and smothered her in petals. 'I've got terrible hay-fever,' she sniffed as they pushed heavy coconut sweetmeats into her mouth seven times in ritualistic welcome.

The village women could hardly believe that this beautiful princess had come to talk to them. Hidden by their bamboo purdah screens, they heard her: 'I want to tell you, my sisters . . .' The Maharani won the Jaipur seat with the highest majority in any democratic election in the world, making the *Guinness Book of Records* with her 157,692 votes out of a total of 192,909.

In 1970 the Maharani's beloved 'Jai' died. He seemed to have a premonition about his death, saying before they left Jaipur for England, 'You know, I won't be coming back.'

His heir, the present Maharajah, Colonel Sawai Bhawani Singh, still known as 'Bubbles', remembers how it was a typical May day in England, drizzling, grey and rainy. 'My stepmother and I were sitting in the car watching polo at Circencester when suddenly my father just keeled over backwards. St John Ambulance rushed to him, but it was too late; he died on the field.'

A small red light flashing on top of a glossy, navy-blue Mercedes as it swishes through the streets of old Jaipur indicates that the opulent and amiable Bubbles is on his way home. There is a whiff of incense and the heavy, smoky sweetness of joss sticks in the bazaar.

The shouts of the embroiderers and the jewellers with their silver and gold ornaments for the ears, ankles, neck and navel, echo to the pink-frescoed walls of the Palace of the Winds. This was where the royal women sat behind the cool trellis watching the processions. A couple of years ago, a memorial to a dog was found in the palace grounds. It had performed a very special task, carrying *billets doux* to the zenana in a special pouch round its neck. It would wait quietly and then trot back with a time fixed for the evening's tryst.

The heavy crested gates of the City Palace swing open. The royal apartments, like a Russian doll, are in the smaller Moon Palace, rising like a creamy confection with gold studs above the Mogul City palace with its terracotta fretwork and delicate lacy white borders.

The House of Amber, as the Jaipurs were known in their old hill capital, were the first of the Rajputs to give in to Mogul blandishments. So Jaipur became rich and beautiful as the great ruler and astronomer Jai Singh II created the Pink City of Jaipur in 1728 in a dried-up river bed seven miles from their palace fort.

Amber still has an enchantment. An old court musician still plays a haunting royal fanfare on a flute, walking up the hill beside tourists on elephants. 'Hello, little man,' they say, and he is not sure whether they are talking to him or to the Hanuman monkeys.

Highness's car appears and warrior guards who have been leaning back against the carved elephants spring to attention, dust down their scarlet and cinnamon jackets and white churridas and salute. As the gates close they drift back to the 'at ease' position, flopping crosslegged against marble columns.

Everything is perfect on the seventh-floor pearly terrace of the pink eighteenth-century Moon Palace. But the staff still rush about, fussily rearranging the white wickerwork chairs, the English newspapers and magazines, and laying out silver goblets beneath the coloured umbrellas swaying in the soft breeze. A little grey monkey playfully shakes the gold weathervane, making the bells tinkle. The monkeys risk electrocution by disconnecting the fairy lights when there is a party; they also like to get at women guests' dressing tables and make themselves up with lipstick and blusher.

Jaipur is a phlegmatic figure who moves like the soldier he once was, shoulders back, arms slightly curved at the elbows, courteous and guarded in repose like a benevolent glossy panther. He looks affably at the monkey; it has the best view of Jaipur, the City of Jewels, of the Amber Fort, and of his stepmother's home Moto Doongri, a perfect replica of a Scottish castle.

'Bubbles' seems much too frivolous a name for this reticent 56-year-old who was a professional soldier for twenty-one years and won the DSO for gallantry during the Indo–Pakistan war. He modestly forgets to tell you that he commanded the Para Commandos in 1971, the equivalent of the SAS. He has lived with the skittish nickname ever since he was born in 1931, when the marble palace fountains flowed with champagne. 'I was the first legitimate male child born to a Jaipur Prince since a holy man had cursed the family three generations before, so an English friend of my father's said we must celebrate.'

Ten years before his birth, when Madho Singh II, the old Maharajah of Jaipur, died, there was no direct heir. His successor, Jai, came from a different family because Madho Singh had been told by a soothsayer that if he ever had a child by a proper wife he would die. So he married nine princesses for the good dynastic purpose of putting them aside, never going to bed with them. He amused himself with an incredible 7,000 concubines. But there were only 107 children so perhaps most were for titillation and anticipation.

Colonel Singh seems such a westernised maharajah, and of course strictly speaking all these former Rulers are plain 'Mr' now. But the people ignore Mrs Gandhi's decree and when Jaipur is dressed in traditional brocade and turban, with his full lips and shy brown eyes which crinkle when he laughs, he becomes the exotic Mogul. Then he belongs to the City Palace which exudes gold, where chandeliers are Baccarat and you take your shoes off for a 300-year-old carpet made of shot silk thread. The ceiling is gold too, becoming a crazy multicoloured starlit sky as its emerald and coral stones twinkle riotously in the mirrored walls.

The City Palace has 1,500 oleander-pink-and-white rooms, filled with Benares brocade, carpets of rose gold, inlaid ivory violins, silver embroidery and shawls made from the silken beards of Kashmiri goats, so fine they can pass through a wedding ring. An old man at the palace does his trick, undoing his magenta turban and showing how quickly it can be rewound again. He brings out a huge red cummerbund, 'cummer' means waist and 'bund' tie. It is vast enough to have belonged to the third Maharajah of Jaipur, who was over seven feet tall and proportionately built. 'We Hindus say small feet, no good, big feet, gentleman.'

The Maharajah, who has a devout Hindu wife and one daughter who likes American pop music, owns three palaces, two hunting lodges and a hillside of jewels. It is a tradition in the Jaipur family that once in his lifetime the Ruler's heir is taken to the Fort on the hill which is guarded by a strange, gipsy tribe. He is allowed to look at the treasure and choose something from the gold urns and jars, diamonds and emeralds, gold statuettes and swords encrusted with jewels. Bubbles' father chose a golden bird with ruby eyes and an emerald in its beak, but now the emerald has disappeared.

Stories of curses and legends and holy men seem more like fairytale make-believe coming from the lips of this unexcitable army officer in Italian casual clothes. But he is very serious when he tells you about his miraculous origins as a direct descendant of the Sun God. 'This means that each morning after my bath, I choose nine jewels which will be auspicious for the day.'

The luncheon table is Lalique with silver edges, enormous for two. Diamonds, pearls, sapphires and rubies glitter from the Colonel's wrist as he dips his paratha into one of the seven traditional silver bowls.

In 1975 a questing Mrs Gandhi, who had always thought the Jaipurs far too wealthy, sent in her tax officials who pounced on the Rajmata at Moti Doongri. This was the beginning of a nasty twist in the fairytale lives of the Jaipurs.

The taxmen found intriguing maps and secret chambers of gold coins, gold bars they could hardly lift, diamonds, paintings and jewels. They pulled down ceilings and ripped paintings apart:

'We have found gold,' they crowed.

'Mind you count it properly,' retorted the Dowager Maharani.

It was a mistake to be so high-handed. This disdain only confirmed their worst prejudices. She refused to let them picnic on her lawn and was irritated by the woman inspector rummaging through her saris and cosmetics.

The gold, then worth three or four million pounds, was from Man Singh II's personal treasury and had been meticulously declared. What would incriminate Gayatri Devi was a laughable amount of sterling found on her dressing table. But for the time being, this was February, instead of showing the humble respect the taxman needs when he takes the trouble to call on you, she imperiously dismissed them and told them not to come back.

But they did, seven months later, with a warrant for her arrest. Bubbles, staying with his stepmother at the time, thought it must be a joke, went out to see what was happening, and got arrested too. The charge against the Maharani was Contravention of Foreign Exchange Regulations and Prevention of Smuggling Activities. Those nineteen spare pounds on the dressing table should have been converted to rupees.

Bubbles, born to command, quickly sorted out the prison form in Tihar jail and got a verandah room with washing facilities. His elegant stepmother was pushed into a smelly cell with a rusty tap some way down a murky corridor. She only avoided having to share a cell with the devout Rajmata of Gwalior by cleverly pleading that their prayers might conflict: religion being the only acceptable plea.

Mrs Gandhi's spleen would have been further enlarged had

she realised that jars of Beluga caviar and copies of *Vogue* and *Tatler* were winging their way to Gayatri Devi, sent by friends in England. The Prime Minister was not a frivolous woman and it is too easy to say that she was jealous of the two beautiful dowagers now being humiliated in one of her prisons. It is more likely that she was irritated by their political views and their silliness in her eyes. It was a political vendetta but also a sop to the hard left in the Congress party.

There were raised eyebrows when Bubbles managed to be released after only two and a half months. His stepmother struggled on, incarcerated in the foul Tihar, delicately avoiding cockroaches and rats and enduring the ever-present flies and mosquitoes. She spent her time amusing the children in the jail, teaching them exercises and talking to their mothers, who were in on charges of murder, prostitution and robbery. Lord Mountbatten and friends from the golden days pressed for the Maharani's release. Then, after five and a half months, a lump was discovered on her breast and after tests in hospital, she was released.

Today the mane of black hair is streaked with grey, and her face is tired, but there is a compassion about those large eyes, a humour about the soft mouth. Gayatri Devi, looking at the work of her interior designer in Lilypool, says drily, 'I would never hold grudges. Besides, I would have been most insulted if she hadn't thought me important enough to put in jail.' When Mrs Gandhi's son Sanjay was killed in a flying accident in 1979 near Delhi, the Rajmata telephoned to sympathise, but the olive branch was refused.

The bond which had been exceptionally warm and close between Gayatri Devi and her stepson Bubbles has gone. You never meet them at each other's homes in Jaipur, though each is always curious to know if you have seen the other. Now Gayatri Devi's son, Jagat Singh, has taken legal action over the division of property in the family. He has alienated his step-brother Colonel Bhawani Singh, in what promises to be another bitter, long-drawn-out Indian princely family feud. This evening the mood as hostess is airy, everything is fun. In London on an earlier occasion it was weary, a little distracted, so much to do, the new house in Berkshire and the book for Doubleday which she is writing with Jackie Kennedy.

'Let us speak of the lighter side. No, of course I never thought of myself as particularly beautiful. I was one of four, in a family you are always being ragged.' These days she is no longer in politics, though the people still come to her and say 'Maharani, we were happy in your time.' And secretly the Rajmata agrees. 'We are the real India,' she will say privately. 'The people trusted us for so long.' In Jaipur she loves going to the two schools she has started, one forty years ago to break purdah and another more recently named after her husband, Sawai Man Singh. This is where the Maharani is often to be found sitting on the steps reading Dickens to the children or taking them off in her chauffeur-driven car.

In the dining room at Lilypool, the lights are soft, it is late. At the head of the long table the Rajmata sits surrounded by young polo players unable to take their eyes off her. The talk is intense, an ebb of laughter and then the serious murmur again.

As the cars shoosh up to the door, it is as if she does not want anyone to leave. 'See you in Washington', 'My love to Boopoo', and then a very urgent aside, 'Now mind you go to my school tomorrow, promise, and do look at the Jaipur blue pottery.' Then suddenly she has vanished. In the morning she is leaving for Paris to mesmerise the French.

4

As Plentiful as
Blackberries

THEY SCATTERED PEARLS as confetti, they played marbles with
emeralds as large as panther's eyes. When Barbara Hutton wore
her treasured black pearl necklace to dinner in Hyderabad, the
Nizam merely smiled and showed her boxes full of them among
diamonds, rubies and emeralds belonging to the last Tsar of
Russia. They put rubies in their navals and diamonds in their
noses; they owned 'The Light of the World', the Timur ruby.
The elephants at Baroda had anklets of solid gold. Maharajah
Ranjit Singh's stallion wore an emerald girdle and a princely
welcome home was a 21-gun salute fired from a solid gold
cannon.

The Maharajah of Dholpur, an ascetic man, had a nine-row
necklace of pearls as big as gulls' eggs. The Baroda collection
included a coloured diamond necklace given by Napoleon III to
the Empress Eugenie as a wedding present and a seven-stringed
Baroda pearl necklace.

The pearl carpet made in Baroda was offered as a canopy for
the tomb of Mahomet at Medina. This arabesque tapestry was
believed to be 'the most wonderful piece of embroidery ever
known'. The centre was an open, blossomy flower studded
with soft gold, mounted with a rosette of diamonds. Jewelled
palms and flowers sprang from delicate stems and around it were

crescents of iridiscent seed pearls, cabochon rubies, sapphires, emeralds and lasque diamonds. When it was finished the devout Mullahs said that it could honour the Prophet's Tomb, but then they would cut it up and give small pieces away to other mullahs and Very Important Pilgrims.

The Maharajah of Baroda refused. Embroiderers and master jewellers had worked on this carpet for over three years. In 1911, a panel was decorously exhibited in the Victoria and Albert Museum during the Coronation. But nobody knows where the carpet is now, or whether it came to the undignified end planned for it by Islam.

There was an insouciance amongst the Princes about their jewels; rather as the English take Tudor architecture for granted. When John Kenneth Galbraith was American ambassador to India he complimented a princess on her necklace of fifty good-sized rubies and diamonds. 'Oh,' she said, surprised, touching her neck, 'it's just an old piece from the south.'

A duchess may treasure her tiara, but there was something very fetching about the Maharani of Jodhpur in an exquisite little head-hugging cloche made of diamond solitaires and her blue diamond disc pendant. Eyebrows of diamonds held delicately over her ears were witty and intriguing. Sometimes the ethereal eighteen-year-old Maharani could not stand without help from two of her attendants for her jewels were more than her own weight. In Jaipur temples even the goddesses wore 70-carat diamonds and canopies were of strung pearls.

But such elegance had its own price. The Maharajah of Jaipur had been holding an audience in white brocade, a frock coat with diamond buttons, silk trousers tight around the calves, pearls and diamonds in his turban. Getting up from his silver-plated throne, he was weary and almost apologetic about the finery. 'I have to put them on. My people like them and the people must have what they want.'

The Maharajah of Mysore wore a candystriped turban with osprey feathers springing like a fountain from an aigrette of diamonds. The Princes' love of multistranded necklaces which covered the whole of the chest started the vogue for the 1920s hip-length ropes of pearls worn by the flappers. They were blasé about their treasure but finally tired of acquisitive Vicereines admiring a piece of jewellery and expecting it to be passed on as a gift.

The Maharajah of Nawanagar, who had his own pearl fishery, let them be used for Hindu medicine. He had an unrivalled emerald collection and his daughter remembered that a black servant was employed at the palace solely for the texture of his velvet skin. His only task was to wear the six-rope pearl necklace to keep its lustre.

A jeweller called in to advise the Nizam of Hyderabad felt giddy when he first saw the cascading glitter of unset jewels spilling from trunks which had been undisturbed in the palace vaults for decades. The Jacob diamond, which weighs 162 carats, forty more than the Koh-i-Noor, was found in the toe of an old slipper belonging to the sixth Nizam. His son just mounted it on a gold filigrée base and used it as a paperweight.

The Nizam decided one day that it was high time his pearls were sorted out. 'I want them all graded,' he instructed the horrified courtiers in charge of the treasury. For hours they 'pulled out buckets and buckets and buckets of pearls of all shapes and sizes'. The pearls were washed in boric acid and graded. When they were laid out to dry on the palace roof there was not an inch between them. For a few hours the palace had a minaret to minaret pearl carpet.

Next to Hyderabad, the Baroda jewellery was the most impressive. Sayaji Rao III, a discerning ruler whose passion was jewellery, commissioned Jacques Cartier to reset his collection in platinum, in the early days when its chic was overtaking gold.

When the 262-caret Star of the South diamond was brought to Laxmi Vilas it was honoured by being placed on a saddled, caparisoned giraffe. It was the largest diamond found by a woman, an African slave in the Brazilian mines in 1867. It had a delicate pink glow and was to sit on the young throats of Baroda princesses in a necklace of pear- and tear-drop diamonds. The slave was given her freedom and a pension.

The Punjab Princes, Kapurthala and Patiala, handsome, upright Sikhs, were exotic with their black beards tucked under
turbans held with ruby, diamond and sapphire turahs. Jagatjit
Singh Kapurthala's favourite was a clip of three thousand diamonds and pearls winking in his tea-rose-pink turban, while
on his belt he wore a huge deep-golden topaz, one of the biggest
in the world. He was a besotted Francophile and at the Paris
Opera Ball of 1922, Princess Karam of Kapurthala wore a tiara
with Persian harem pants and was escorted by a troop of Persian
slaves.

Patiala was even more striking. He was six feet tall, and had
a preference for a daffodil yellow or jet black turban held with
a cluster of emeralds. He tended to wear white buckskins, a
long tunic of scarlet trimmed with gold and thigh-high black
leather boots.

On a ceremonial day in Delhi, he would not be wearing less
than four ropes of pearls to the waist, and the fashion was to
string emerald beads snuggled between each pearl. Around his
waist he wore a belt of diamonds, and a gold lamé scarf was
held by a four-inch emerald. Five necklaces of diamonds and
emeralds were tiered like a vineyard round his neck with a collar
of diamonds in platinum at the top. He carried a jewelled sword.

European jewellers from London, Paris and Amsterdam set
out on long sea voyages in the hope of doing business with the
Princes. They could wait for months without seeing a maharajah
but would be taken on tiger-shoots and sightseeing around
marble temples in Rolls-Royces.

The man from Garrard, the Crown jewellers, who was staying in the Jodhpur Palace in 1926, noted with some superiority
that his rival from Boucheron was put in the dak bungalow.
But even on a third visit to India, he had the greatest difficulty
persuading the Maharajah to have platinum mounts. 'He is
afraid he will be seen as a silver prince and not a gold one.'

Generations of Cartier sons served the aesthetic needs of the
maharajahs. Jacques Cartier, who died in 1942, was a precise,
fastidious man who lived in Woking. His chauffeur drove him
in his Rolls-Royce to Bond Street each morning at 10 o'clock

and he invariably took afternoon tea at the nearby Ritz. Each year he went to India with trunkfuls of exotic ideas and designs. The maharajahs used to stay at his house in Surrey where they all played golf. He redesigned their jewels and excited them about new trends; art deco brooches, chinoiserie, mystery clocks, Fabergé, panther motifs on gold watches and crystal furniture. In 1928 Baroda asked him to be his sole adviser on jewels.

In their quiet, orderly homes in the Home Counties, the jewellers absorbed the Mogul culture and studied Indian miniatures. Soon the mango leaf, the Kashmir palm, the lotus flower and Hindu deities – pronounced DTs by their Indian guides – were appearing on waistbands and chokers and turban tassels.

They interpreted the Mogul emperors' love of flowers and designed white jade roses set with pearls, rubies and bunches of emerald grapes. They made hathpuls, which were wedding bracelets. For one, 223 pearls were drilled and stretched over the back of the bride's hand, linking the fingers in a delicate tracery. As painstakingly as they created diamond bow brooches, chokers, pearl studs and enamelled miniatures for European royalty, they turned their talents east. They fashioned bracelets, armlets and naths – nose rings – in diamond, ruby, sapphire and emerald. The Maharajah of Kashmir liked to wear handsome pearls around his ankles. Another Prince who insisted his wife should wear a chastity belt only got his way by having it made of diamonds.

The ledger for 1 April 1853 records an ordinary day at Garrard: 'Repair clasp to diamond brooch, setting and finishing 15 opals,' and so on until Docket 38819. There the meticulous hand, using a fine nib and blue-black ink, states simply: 'Her Majesty the Queen' and, underlined, 'Setting the Koh-i-Noor'. The cost was £60,000, paid by the people of India.

But it had never been their gift to the royal family. It came to Queen Victoria from the East India Company, 'with humble duty', in 1851, when they deposed the Lion of the Punjab's son, the Maharajah Dhuleep Singh.

The jewel was handed for safekeeping to John Lawrence, one

of the Company's administrators in Lahore, who promptly
forgot all about it. Eventually, reminded that the Queen was
enquiring about her gift, Lawrence raced to his bungalow and
asked an old servant to unwrap it from the raggy piece of cloth
in which it was kept. 'Sahib, there is nothing here but a bit of
glass.' The Koh-i-Noor, the Mountain of Light, was safe. It sat
securely on Queen Victoria's parted hair in a brilliant tiara of
2,000 diamonds.

The diamond was to sit on a succession of royal heads,
beautiful Queen Alexandra, stately Queen Mary, the appealing
and sympathetic Queen Elizabeth the Queen Mother and her
daughter the present Queen. When the Duke of York became
King George VI the original tiara, a circle of roses, was broken
up and used for the Queen Mother when she was crowned
Queen in 1937. The present crown has the Koh-i-Noor with
eight horseshoes of diamonds and, as it is believed to be unlucky
for male rulers, it will be seen on the fair hair of the Princess of
Wales on the day she becomes Queen.

Necklaces for the Indian Princes were heavy with fringes of
emerald berries and leaves of sapphires, rubies and pearls. Queen
Victoria may have been robust enough to carry such stomachers
with doughty aplomb but not her beautiful, fluttery daughter-
in-law Princess Alexandra, who was almost sixty when she
became Queen Consort. She was not given access to the royal
jewels until her mother-in-law's reluctant departure to join her
beloved Albert in 1901.

Six months after Queen Victoria's death, Pierre Cartier was
summoned to Buckingham Palace to convert an ornate Indian
necklace into something the new queen could wear. He used 94
emeralds, 17 pearls and 13 cabochon rubies from the sumptuous
piece and created an Edwardian jabot. This was the celebrated
collier résille which looked superb with the Queen's high
cheekbones and upswept hair. Alexandra longed to visit India.
'I was not allowed to go when I wished it so very, very much,'
she told her son George V, and she never forgave Edward VII
for going without her in 1875 when he was Prince of Wales. It
was hardly his fault for Queen Victoria did not like either

of them out of her sight. Only with the greatest reluctance did she allow him off for six months to check the Indian Empire.

In 1876 the future Edward VII brought back an embarrassment of riches from his tour of India. In holy Benares, cynically called City of Burning, City of Learning, he was given a large double bed of solid silver, a silver palanquin lined with ubiquitous red satin and trimmed with gold, a solid silver bath and in Gwalior another bed of solid gold. The Barodas gave him a solid silver tea service in a blackwood cabinet, a pearl necklace with a vast emerald pendant set in gold for Queen Victoria, a diamond brooch for Princess Alexandra and a diamond ring for himself. The House of Oudh gave him a pearl and diamond crown with pearl drops.

Instead of silver salvers, in those days the equerries organised gold snuff boxes. But the tiny Gaekwad of Baroda got a sword which almost came up to his shoulder. He was nine at the time and he never did grow very tall. He was also given a gold watch, a medal, and a book of engravings of Windsor Castle and, of course, portraits of the royal family. But on the whole, the Prince of Wales gave dictionaries, walking sticks, flasks, field glasses and riding crops.

So the irresponsible 'Bertie' brought back tangible proof of the Maharajahs' devotion to their mother, the Empress of India: emeralds, diamonds, pale pink rubies, sapphires, a serpent bracelet which the present Queen finds a little spooky, a gold crown hung with emerald drops; in all three trunks of jewellery. Solid gold drinking cups, swords with gold scabbards, silver swords and armour inlaid with gold were all loaded at Bombay aboard HMS *Osborne* and HMS *Serapis* for the long voyage home.

Ladies-in-waiting had her portmanteaux of gifts from the Indian Princes brought to the Queen's private sitting room. A very feminine woman, the Queen warmed to her dear Maharajahs even more as her little hands unclasped one case after another of jewels. Out poured torrents of diamonds and sapphires; indeed her palms could not hold the ruby necklaces, the diamond bracelets, pearl chokers, diamond rings and belts with emeralds the size of greengages.

She put them on her head, on her wrists and on her chubby fingers at a New Year's Day banquet at Windsor Castle in 1877, but her suites of Indian jewellery have never been seen since.

'Diamonds,' sniffed one observer on the Prince of Wales's tour in 1875, 'seem as plentiful in India as blackberries in England.'

❊ 5 ❊

Who is Baby Jesus?

ENGLISH NANNIES, those smiling, wholesome girls who became firm, motherly women, were as important a status symbol to the Indian Princes as the Rolls-Royce. Personal maids could come from France or Switzerland, but Nanny and later the male guardians had to come from England.

They went out to India with their copies of *Home Education*, determined to teach the Victorian virtues of Regularity, Obedience, Independence, Courage, Precision, Industry and Delicacy and embroidered mottoes like 'The Key to Pleasure is Hard Work' on lace pillow cases. They coped with the hierarchy of princely wives, the intrigue and jealousy, and taught their charges English manners.

They wore calico aprons with square bibs, plain cambric Peter Pan collars, summer tussore dresses and bonnets trimmed with silk. Even in the tropics they believed in Cow and Gate, Farley's Rusks and rose-hip syrup. Grubby toys were cleaned with fuller's earth, furry animals with hot bran and rocking horse saddles came up beautifully with an old banana skin.

They slept under mosquito nets and, like their charges, had white painted beds. They were surprised by the excellent fish in India, the good lemonade and ginger pop. They did not bother too much with Indian folklore and instead read *Hansel and Gretel* and *Alice in Wonderland* to their charges. 'Ah, how Nanny used to read to us,' sighs the Maharajah of Bikaner, a

large man and an Olympic shot who recollects Nanny Edith
Dent with such affection that he gets quite overcome.

Grown men's faces suddenly light up with a smile of childlike
sweetness at the mention of Nanny Dent, Nanny Bartlett,
Nanny Fisk, remembered as gentle creatures dressed in grey,
watching bearer pushing their charge in a Dunkley Duchess
pram round the Palace grounds.

At Patiala, there were ninety-six prams, each with its own
Nanny, crunching the gravel under archways of bougainvillaea.
When their feet ached in spite of their sensible shoes, they rested
by a marble fountain instead of beside Frampton's statue of
Peter Pan in Kensington Gardens.

Travelling in India was a bit exhausting, even on royal trains.
They did long journeys and all through the night heard the
dismal cry 'baksheesh, baksheesh'.

'Oh, the heat, the dust and the dirt . . . how one longed to
see England after the stubble of India.' Bath water on the train
flowed from taps shaped like gold dolphins and there was a
form of air conditioning which kept them cool. 'We used to
have an enormous thing like a baptismal font made out of solid
silver on which you could put a great block of ice, a vast thing,
brought on by a coolie at each station with his head bowed. He
never looked at you, just came hurrying on and put this thing
down and hurried out again. It was really an enormous iceberg
in a tin with a fan to circulate the air.'

'I really thought I should dislike seeing the natives about
everywhere but I found it quite fascinating, so picturesque.
The coolie babies are sweet,' thought Kathleen Austin. It was
difficult to keep children amused for two whole days and nights
on a train, so traditional English standbys were trotted out.
'What do we say when we see the milkman?' and a tiny maharajah and his brothers and sisters would shout back . . . 'Coo . . .
eee!' Nanny endlessly puffing out her cheeks and reaching a
crescendo of 'chuff chuffs' palled, as Indian trains stop and start
so often, but 'the little travellers' looked polite. The royal
children loved these stops of an hour or more.

The Rajmata of Jaipur remembers how 'men would come

selling charming, funny painted toys that I have seen nowhere except on Indian station platforms: elephants with their trunks raised to trumpet, lacquered in grey and scarlet, caparisoned in gold; horses decked out as though for a bridegroom; camels, cheetahs, tigers, all stiff and delightful with wide painted eyes and endearing, coquettish smiles.' The children raced round the platforms chased by nannies, governesses and tutors. The treat was not to have to eat off gold plate, but in the railway dining room, lamb and vegetables, 'Railway curry' which could not offend either the Moslem or the Hindu passenger.

After the meal princesses in jewels and princes in miniature turbans and brocade listened attentively to more tales of Alison Uttley's *Little Grey Rabbit*. If they were going to cooler weather, they wore regulation blue coats with velvet collars, shoes from Daniel Neal in Kensington High Street and white ankle socks.

They were much less inclined to be rowdy or misbehave than their English charges. However, a Prince in Hyderabad disliked his nanny and one evening dosed her beloved cat with castor oil, knowing it always slept in her bed.

Indian children seemed terribly pampered, lying around being indolent and carried up and down the palace steps. At the palace in Udaipur, Arvind Singh, the Maharana's younger son, remembers with disgust how his fat cousin was still being carried around when he was seven, and 'the nanny was always panting, such a skinny creature'. The Maharajah of Dhrangadhra's feet never touched the ground until he was two.

Three generations of royal children thought of Mrs Edith Dent as an exceptionally warm and loving nanny. She was 'a mother to all of us'. Life in the nursery was much the same as for any aristocratic family in England, not so much life behind the green baize as the ivory door. Edith Dent worked first for the Bikaners, the sophisticated desert family in Rajasthan.

When the future Ruler of Udaipur married a Bikaner princess, guests included fourteen reigning Princes, each with an entourage of between 200 and 600 servants. The railway station at Bikaner was jammed with private princely trains. Jaipur and

Jodhpur flew in their own planes to the sandy strip outside the city.

The streets were decorated with bunting and fairy lights; troops lined them during the wedding procession, when white oxen in red, saffron and purple blankets pulled solid silver carts and caparisoned elephants carried honoured guests in gold and silver howdahs. Instead of the usual white horse, the bridegroom was carried by a bull elephant which had silver ornaments on its legs and a coverlet of gold under a gold howdah. The bride was hidden under magenta silk and her attendants wore silver. There was a banquet for three hundred guests who ate from solid gold plates.

But when the time came for the bride to leave for her honeymoon, sitting in the gold and cream royal train, watched by all the guests, she suddenly burst into tears and asked for Nanny. Her young husband, the Maharana of Udaipur, was helpless. The train was waiting and guests heaved a sigh of relief when Edith Dent appeared on the platform, bustling along urgently, 'smiling, reassuring'. There was a tearful scene in the carriage, she mopped her charge's eyes and the honeymoon was on again. Goodbye Nanny.

But Nanny was with her in Udaipur for the birth of her first child, Mohendra, and stayed to look after the other two, a boy and a girl.

The Udaipur children did not know the taste of Indian food until they were twelve or thirteen. They were weaned on the spoon and pusher regime, and had rice pudding or custard at four o'clock. 'Nanny Dent could be strict,' Arvind Singh of Udaipur grins. 'She would tap our elbows with a fork. "No uncooked joints on the table, thank you, Master Arvind."' He emptied his bowls of custard over the marble balustrades of the palace, where a small yellow heap was discovered one day. Even the grey pigeons, normally so greedy, baulked at this English nursery fare.

Distances were so great, nannies often did not get a chance to swop tips, unless they had jobs together in a palace. Nevertheless there were confidences, 'Well, I am having very little success with prayers. "Who is Baby Jesus?" they ask.' Then there were those bad habits which 'make children nervous and excitable'. 'I make his little Highness fold his hands on the pillow.'

One of the nannies was bound to have brought with her a Nurse Galton's Ear Cap made of silk net, ideal for correcting sticking-out princely ears that might present a problem in the future with turbans. Tapes attached helped keep the ears perfectly flat. And they cuddled and cosseted their charges although India is not a tactile country. When one of the Princes was asked his name, he replied with the solemnity of a Lord Fauntleroy, 'I am called Darling Sweetheart . . . You see, I have an English name.'

The influence of the English nanny was imperative as 'native nannies' were often too sycophantic. Honoria Lawrence, wife of Sir Henry Lawrence who was killed while defending the Residency of Lucknow during the Mutiny, was shocked when she heard her tiny son called 'Lord and Protector of the Poor', by his ayah and being told, with a sibiliant hiss, 'When you are a man you will flog the black people and please yourself.'

There was a subtle hierarchy and the nursery governess felt superior to nanny. These genteel, fairly well-educated girls who went abroad with ingrained notions about their social standing were often cruelly disappointed although they tried earnestly to keep up standards. In Australia, in the early days, they complained of living in broken down shacks, scrubbing, driving horse-drawn wagons and teaching children who were as wild as unbroken colts. Many of them could not afford to come home. But in India, in the princely families, they got the recognition they felt they deserved.

One of these girls, Doris Martin, was twenty going on twenty-one when she went to work for the Jaipur family. Her father was a hill farmer on the fells of Cumbria and their home was not far from Beatrix Potter's house in Sawrey, where the rhododendrons bloom five shades of pink in the spring and the meadows are filled with apple blossom.

A close friend of the Jaipurs, Lady Zia Wernher, had spotted Doris when she was working for Lady Astor. 'Lady Alice was

a bit capricious, always changing her mind about the children's
clothes,' and even though there were trips to America on the
Aquitania, 'it was time for a change.' So, assured by Lady Zia
that she would be safe in Jaipur, Doris Martin packed sheets
and pillowcases and sailed to India. She had been sent decent
travelling expenses from Jaipur, 'and I was well paid.'

The journey out on the RMS *Cathay* in 1936 took three
weeks. Doris Martin's photograph album is full of pictures
showing a leggy girl in shorts leaning against the rail and being
ogled by young Bulldog Drummond figures with moustaches
and pipes, showing lots of hair oil and confidence. Captions in
white ink on the dark paper mark the inevitable picture in Port
Said and another, 'Tangiers snake charmer'.

In Bombay Doris stayed at the Barodas' house on fashionable
Malabar Hill, a headland in the Arabian Sea. Her only memory
of this city, given as a present to Charles II by the Portuguese
and then leased to the East India Company for £10, is of the
lepers. But she also saw the dhows and the old fishing boats as
the chauffeur drove along the road that curves round the bay
shoreline known as the Queen's Necklace. And she laughed at
a comical billboard with a letter missing – Air India and Sipping
Corporation. It is a city of poverty and parks where signs tell
you 'It is prohabated to sleep in the gardens or bring in eatables'
and entertainments offered include 'a formal function and then
an interesting programme of facial distortions'. Nowadays fairy
lights highlight the Directorate of Family Planning.

After a couple of days, Doris Martin travelled to Jaipur with
an English chauffeur and a babu who were going to the palace
too. Two splendid Warrant Officers, Sgt Majors McGann and
Welsh, met her at the station in Jaipur. She remembers how
'they vied with each other' to take this young girl out. McGann
used to go to the Indian club and get a bit tight, 'But there was
nothing else to do.' Until now she had been taken care of like
a VIM – a very important memsahib – and felt a little let down
when she got to Jaipur.

Presiding over coffee, Doris, now Mrs Humber, a neat,
sprightly woman, remembered being shocked by her accommo-

dation. 'I was put in a hotel and this upset me. I was not very happy. I slept in a net with lizards running up the bed. There was a lady's maid there also, Elsa, a Swiss person, and a tennis pro came from Baroda called Eric Fenton. I was there for three weeks.'

But soon she was moved into the palace and the nursery wing, finding a hornet's nest of intrigue in the zenana where the four children were brought up with their mothers. The Maharajah's two wives were aunt and niece. Bubbles and a daughter, Mickey, were the children of First Her Highness. 'The first and older wife was very traditional,' Doris recalls, 'and sometimes would travel out of the palace in an old bullock cart with the other half-wives and concubines of the previous ruler. When the women came back to the palace, as soon as they got to the zenana, there would be great shouting and the doors would open and there would be the eunuchs, for whom it was an honour to be given this job.'

But the trouble and uneasiness lay with Second Her Highness, who had fashionably bobbed hair, wore nail varnish and was the mother of two smalls boys, Pat and Joey. She lived in the zenana too. Her sitting room was quite European but she used the purdah car with its smoked blue glass. The zenana was pretty, with latticed windows and enclosed courtyards shaded by trees. But she was beginning to be acutely aware that her husband was falling in love with Gayatri Devi, the lovely Cooch Behar Princess, and was most unhappy.

Ruling the nursery wing was Nanny Barnes. 'Barnsey' was very much on the side of the second wife and was rather bossy and prickly with the new nursery governess who seemed to be having such a good time. 'I think she was a bit jealous of me because I could wear shorts,' Doris Martin says.

The Comptroller at the Rambagh Palace had already warned her about the whispering intrigues, so she tried to keep busy. And while it lasted, Doris found her stay at Jaipur was an introduction to a delightful way of life. She went out riding every morning at six and her tennis improved with excellent coaching. There was lots of hunting – 'Mr Leach, the huntsman, was English' – badminton on the rooftops and swimming. On special occasions there was 'HH's trooping, but instead of bearskins, his troops wore gold saffras, turbans which are about ten yards long.'

Food was wonderful, English or Indian, and the cooks were Goanese. 'There were top men handling everything; there was even someone in charge of the water. You could drink it without any worries although we did have our own doctors and dentists. We wore evening dress even for the cinema; there were garden parties, receptions, picnics and marvellous polo, you never had to lift a finger. I remember the Untouchables were not allowed even on the carpets, so they crept round the side of the room on the marble to go and clean the lavatories.'

And the work? 'Oh, the work, I gave the children their first lessons and of course we all spoke English. Two chapprassis would push the prams, so we never had to do anything like that. There were a couple of dhurzies with Singer sewing machines and if we wanted a button sewing on, it was done in minutes, they just sat outside. You just had to give them a picture and in the afternoon it was made up. Bubbles wore silk tops with button-down frilly collars.'

The children had ponies called Tarzan and Snowball and as soon as they could ride they were trained for polo. There were two fabulous swimming pools, one in the zenana where the children swam, although occasionally the crocodile got out of his tank nearby and slithered up the steps. At Christmas Santa Claus arrived by elephant.

There were lots of dogs. Servants, who all wore gold cummerbunds and high turbans which looked like starched wings or fans, would walk the St Bernards, Great Danes, Scots terriers and poodles. It was auspicious to put liver in a silver container (or brass for the younger ones) and pass it over the heads, not of the dogs, but of the children, at least six or seven times. Then the liver would be thrown away and the vultures would swoop down, often wanting to pick up one of the little dogs on the palace lawns as well.

'Occasionally the Maharajah would come into the nursery

and throw Bubbles in the air and take his hat off and keep it just out of reach,' and then dine in the women's quarters, wonderfully innocent about the emotional havoc he was leaving behind. Doris Martin thought him 'a charming man', easygoing even when the nursery governess was toppled on the marble floor in the palace by his little girl Mickey, who had crept up behind to jump on her, saying 'be an elephant'. Doris fell backwards on top of the child, breaking her leg and her own arm. 'His Highness was very good about it and I think was rather amused.' He was a caring father but a little remote with his children. Conversation was not easy even later on when the boys were home from Harrow.

In 1937 the nursery and household sailed to England for the Coronation, but the children and nusery staff did not stay in London: 'We were bundled off to stay in the Selsden Park Hotel while they were somewhere glamorous like Claridges.' There are photographs of the children in tweed coats on their way to Bognor, to the rented house, 'while the Maharajah enjoyed himself racing round to Deauville and places. I now realise he was seeing Gayatri Devi at this time . . . in London.'

'If it were not for Barnsey, I might have been in charge of that whole nursery wing, but she made life too uncomfortable for me. A girl of twenty-one could not cope with all that scheming in the zenana so I came home.'

They have a theory in India that if you can get someone to stay for three days, they will come back and Doris returned to see her charges in Jaipur in 1983. 'Bubbles took me round to parties and Gayatri Devi was very kind. Unfortunately Joey was away buying goats in the Lebanon. Nothing had changed. All that dust and people dying in the street.'

She seems to pine a little still for that dream time in India. On the staircase of her home there are photographs of the four Jaipur children, looking almost edible with their appealing eyes, a world away from the detached house near the railway station in Haywards Heath.

Other nannies and nursery governesses were content to stay with their charges for several generations. In Kotah, the English governess married an Indian doctor and became Mrs Dastoor. The Yuvaraj still remembers how 'she clucked like a mother hen leading her chicks' when Lady Willingdon, the Vicereine, came to Kotah. The Crown Prince was dressed in a white romper suit with a dark blue tie and his sister Mimi wore a pink frilly dress. Their nursery governess had taught them to curtsey and bow and on no account reply, 'Quite well, thank you' when asked, 'How do you do?'

The Yuvaraj thought he had never seen anyone quite so large as Lady Willingdon, who 'extending her big hand and, speaking in a deep booming voice', asked 'How do you do young man?' His governess breathed a sigh of relief when he bowed and replied in a most upright way, 'How are you, madam?' The children had hardly had a chance to feast their eyes on the tea trolley 'all gleaming with a silver service and fine china cups', as well as plates full of dainty little cakes, pastries, the inevitable cucumber sandwiches and Indian delicacies, before Nanny was hurrying them away at a discreet nod from the Maharani. The little boy left the drawing room and to this day, though now fifty-one, says, 'What I could not forget was the big bulk of Lady W, with greying hair . . .'

Most of the nannies and nursery governesses came home from India to end their days in cottages and flats in Shropshire and Hereford, Cumberland and the Home Counties, with boxes of photographs of their charges, captioned, 'Here we go gathering nuts in May,' or 'Princess Ruby's birthday party'. Mrs Dent was on a generous pension from the Maharajah of Bikaner, but most were not so lucky. They often lost touch, it was hard to keep up. British nannies went all over the world. Sometimes an employer would write an emotional tribute.

A granddaughter of Queen Victoria, the Grand Duchess Kirill of Russia, was at the deathbed of Nanny Marian Burgess, who had been with her for ten years. Later she described the funeral: '. . . the snow was lying thick on the ground and the coffin was taken on a sledge to a little church on the top of a steep hill by moonlight. The light of the church seemed to take the form of a cross and to be backing her on her journey.'

In England there was not the obvious emotion of the foreign employer, but the death of a nanny was just as deeply felt. Usually just a simple notice: 'Nurse Violet Gray. Friends will be very sorry to hear that her useful life has come to an end . . .'

It was as if the old family pony died and it is hard to know who would have been missed more.

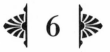

6

A Fine Collection of Women

THE TIME HAD COME for the Maharajah of Kapurthala to marry.
But there was a problem; the nineteen-year-old ruler was so fat
there was some anxiety about his ability to consummate a
marriage. Nevertheless a bride had been chosen by the royal
advisers, picked from 250 girls, all from good Rajput families.
They had to be beautiful and not more than seventeen years
old.

The beat of a drum warned the parents that the royal marriage
team was on its way to their village. Each girl was examined
and some of the courtiers took this duty to such meticulous
extremes, there were complaints about their zeal. Doctors were
on hand to do any alterations to make the girl perfect. The only
problem was the bridegroom: Jagatjit Singh weighed 19 stone.

But British ingenuity solved the fat Prince's problems. An
idea based on elephants' lovemaking was to ensure the future of
the Kapurthala dynasty. The design was inspired by a manmade
hillock of mud and stone in the forest near the palace, against
which the female elephant leant, the slope making things much
less of a slog for the heavyweight jumbo. J. O. S. Elmore, an
inventive Englishman and the chief engineer of Kapurthala,
working closely with a knowing courtesan, dreamt up a reclin-
ing bed of wood and steel.

The courtesan, the glamorous Munna Jan, did a rehearsal with His Highness which went beautifully. The royal wedding took place. Nine months after the Maharajah's wedding, Edward VII was sending him a telegram of congratulations on the birth of a son, Paramjit Singh. The courtesan got a pension for life.

Women were one of the Maharajah's two major passions in life. His other love was France. He became an ardent Francophile when French tutors took him to Europe and this impressionable, overweight boy was captivated by Paris. His sugar pink palace was modelled on Versailles. It was a scrap of Paris in the hot, flat lands of the Punjab, where he ruled over 630 square miles. He was a remarkable man. Kapurthala was only a 13-gun state, but with his tremendous personality and flair Jagatjit Singh managed to override any disadvantages.

A cultivated man, he was thought one of the best hosts in India. The palace, nestling under the snowy tips of the Himalayas, looked like a strawberry soufflé topped with vanilla ice-cream, or a vast stone and stucco town hall somewhere in Provence. The Sun King of the Punjab travelled on an elephant fanned by an acolyte holding a whisk of white hair, and yellow turbaned warriors would salute the figure on the silver howdah. 'L'état, c'est Moi' was his motto.

Guests arriving at the palace were driven through gardens and allées in the style of Le Nôtre. If they were not staying in the palace, they were in a comfortable pink villa in the grounds. Inside the palace, there was a little bit of England with Georgian furniture supplied by Waring & Gillow. It competed with ornate French furniture, ormolu and pink marble bathrooms where Highness frisked and was sprinkled with rose petals.

Some fifty rooms, including the Louis XV Salon, were elaborately decorated in gold and white rococo whirls and shells and carpeted with Aubussons. Crystal lamps in the marble recesses lit capering fat white nymphs on the ceiling.

The master used to enjoy a few childish games in the harem – lots of hide and seek. There would be great roars of delight when he spotted the tell-tale wisp of a girl's gold sari as she hid, stifling giggles, behind a tall blue column of lapis lazuli. Garlanded French courtesans in the Gobelin tapestries stared impassively back at the high jinks through parted lips. These uneducated village women, with the slenderness of girl children, must have imagined Europe full of dough-coloured ladies who wore garlands in their hair and were always followed by a troubadour or a sheep.

The Maharajah spoke excellent French, and became a courtly figure with his trim moustache. He wore a Cyclopean clip of three thousand diamonds and pearls embedded in the folds of his turban, which changed colour with the seasons, yellow for spring, pink for summer, red for weddings. He travelled to Europe constantly and represented the Princes twice at the League of Nations. He was also one of the first to travel on the trans-Siberian railway.

Such opulence and his taste for French food and furniture lured all sorts of beautiful and sophisticated women to the palace in the Punjab. Anything these Western women wanted, whether it was a little diamond necklace from Cartiers, sapphire earrings, a Fabergé egg, he never quibbled about the price. He owned the best emeralds in India. The chairs they sat on were covered in gold brocade; sheets were of Irish linen trimmed with lace; clothes were made in Paris and cared for by impeccably trained French maids. Even the butler spoke perfect French.

The Maharajah's advisers wished their master's eye would rest more with the static beauties of the Louvre, rather than on some of the 'adventuresses' he invited to Kapurthala. The trouble with these European women was, as the courtiers found, they refused to join the rejects in the zenana.

One of them was a Spanish dancer, Anita Delgrada, whom the Maharajah married in 1910. The palace in the Punjab went through a Spanish phase; the Maharani was pushed out to live quietly in a shooting lodge in the grounds called the Villa Buenvista. When the affair was at its height, Edward VII, not always a model of propriety himself, was shocked when the Maharajah and his Spaniard were given a suite next to his in

Biarritz. Anita Delgrada eventually ran off with the son of one of Kapurthala's older mistresses.

It was the summer of 1930 in Nice when Kapurthala's greedy eye spotted a stylish French girl, sinuous in an elegant pink silk pyjama suit, browsing round a boutique in the Croisette. Germaine Pellegrino was smart in every sense of the word. After a couple of decorous meetings, tea at the Carlton, Mlle Pellegrino agreed to visit the Punjab, but was coy: '*Oui Majesté, j'accepte l'invitation si Regi est d'accord.*' Reginald Ford, her American guardian, agreed that his ward should see India.

When Mlle Pellegrino arrived at the 'Elysée Palace' in Kapurthala, the French Ambassador could not have been given a better welcome. There was a full guard of honour and a band played the French national anthem.

The palace was like a French château, but much more comfortable than one of those draughty piles in the Loire. She felt completely at home. There was the English launch, the *Sutlej*, with its handsome mahogany finish and gleaming polished brass, much more fun than a cruiser on the Seine with all those peasants reeking of garlic from coarse *pâté* and rough *vin rouge*. The food was often better than anything she had tasted in France because, as the Maharajah's granddaughter explained: 'All grandfather's chefs came from the Ritz and the George V in Paris. So it was wonderful: exquisite French sauces and, of course, excellent wine. We had the best.'

But Germaine Pellegrino became bored. One evening, wearing a gold-embroidered sari with a thin, pale pink, transparent blouse cut rather low, and diamond earrings, Mlle Pellegrino lapsed into a sulk over a glass of '*bienfrappé*' champagne in the Louis XIV drawing room. The Maharajah could not bear to see her upset. Making a little moue, Mademoiselle suggested he thought of her as just '*un petit jouet*'. Totally captivated, he swore she was no plaything. She could have anything she wanted, and to prove it he summoned his advisers to tell them he had just appointed her Chief Adviser for the state of Kapurthala. Amused, she watched their faces intently. The Maharajah was so thrilled that his 'little jouet' should want to help him run the state, he immediately gave her a tiara of rubies and pearls.

Not surprisingly she found attending cabinet meetings, receiving the Viceroy and stuffy colonial officers and, worse, their wives, was not much fun. By now, Mlle Pellegrino knew enough about the Maharajah's administration, especially the Exchequer, to plead nostalgia for France. Kapurthala could deny her nothing and agreed she should go, but followed quickly afterwards.

Over cocktails at the Ritz in Paris, he proposed to Germaine. Demure, a little sad, Germaine answered softly: '*Comme c'est possible, Monsieur?* The Maharajah looked bewildered, but then heard the dreaded words '. . . *quand Regi est mon fiancé.*' Kapurthala exploded. He had met Ford, an American businessman, once or twice in Paris. This was the ultimate treachery.

Other mistresses with less instinct for self-preservation fared badly in that formidable hierarchy of women. One from Czechoslovakia, when discarded, was convinced that she was going to be assassinated. One day in Delhi she ordered the purdah car, took her little dogs with her, and all of them committed suicide by jumping from the top of the Kutab Minar, the monument celebrating the coming of Islam to India.

Behind the veneer of Western civilisation, there were grisly happenings. Women and courtiers who did not please could be murdered, by poison, or by happening to fall off a parapet . . .

Having overcome the initial sexual hurdle posed by his weight, the Maharajah remained enthusiastic about his harem almost to the end of his days, when he cut a rather sorry figure trying to dance a foxtrot at the age of seventy-four, on shaky legs and with a partner just a quarter his age who was bored stiff. By now he was lean and spruce, had a little white moustache, and was so pernickety about his appearance that he stationed servants along the white and coloured marble corridors to dust his shoes as he walked from his bedroom.

By the time he was in his fifties, he had a fine collection of women, some 300 in all. The hierarchy in the palace started at the top with Maharanis, who were listed A, B, C and D; then came the Ranis, who were listed numerically depending on their talents 1, 2, 3. In this '*crême de la dame section*', there were some 150 concubines and these were the élite.

Choosing women for Kapurthala became much easier for his team of connoisseurs. They were sophisticated men, often leaving the running of the state for this more pressing task. One complained: 'I have been to Kashmir and recently brought back two girls for His Highness. The difficulty is that you can never get over Highness's suspicion that you have used them too.' Sometimes he had a craze for oval-shaped breasts: 'like the Alfanso mango' he would say, lips growing soft at the thought; at other times a sensual whim would stress 'peach shape'.

The lowest category were the simple village girls, known simply as A1, B2, a bit like American fighter planes. If a woman was in doubt about her standing, mealtimes would give the clue. The Maharanis' food was served on gold and they had a selection of about one hundred dishes; the Ranis ate off silver and the lowest grade women were left with brass bowls. They were well treated. The concubines were glad of the security of the harem, even when they no longer appeared with a tick on the royal clipboard. When a woman had had two babies she was sterilised.

All the year round, battalions of prams with chic Parisian '*pour le bébé*' layettes were pushed round the gardens laid out with the neatness and formality of Fontainebleau, complete with decadent cherubs astride seahorses in marble fountains; a hundred gardeners just waiting for a stray leaf. There could be as little as a day between some of the baby Kapurthalas. They were cared for but never got recognition.

The Maharajah remained 'keenly interested in sexual science' until his death in 1947. Mistresses (and only the Europeans made trouble) were never allowed to intrude outside the zenana. He had ruled for sixty-nine years, and in that time his son and heir, the Yuvaraj, Paramjit Singh, conceived with such difficulty, had annoyed him by making the fatal mistake of falling in love with his English mistress.

His father, wanting to upgrade the Kapurthala dynasty, had bought a bride for his son from a good family in the Himalayas.

He sent the girl, Brinda Mathi, niece of the Rajah of Jubal, off to France to be educated. Her family were Rajputs and had barely a 1 acre of land, but were of the right caste. Her father, a chief near Simla, was paid handsomely. But he hardly recognised his daughter when ten years later she came back to India a sophisticated young Frenchwoman. She had been brought up in Paris with the publishing family Hachette; was fashionable, amusing and had tremendous dress sense.

She returned to Kapurthala to marry a man whom she found dull and insipid and she was a failure as a wife. She produced four daughters but no son.

Divorce was never accepted in India, but Brinda Mathi was desperately unhappy although anxious not to lose out on precedence. She went to see the Viceroy, and when he intervened she became wife 38B. Retired to Buenvista, a villa in the grounds, and given lots of money, she cared not 'two hoots' that the marriage was finished, but wrote a book and became a jet-setting lady.

The Yuvaraj was a mild-mannered man, who wore pinstriped suits in London. He was educated at Harrow and also the Sorbonne, and liked to spend seven months of the year in Europe. Paramjit did not have his father's flair, and even his romance with an English dancer, Miss Stella Mudge, lacked the old man's flamboyance. Curzon, that upright Viceroy, made it a law that no child of a marriage with an English wife or any Western woman could succeed to the throne in an Indian State. Knowing how susceptible the Princes from the Punjab could be, excitable and with a Pan-like capacity for pleasure but also guileless, he insisted also that none of them should go abroad without his permission. He had enough difficulty controlling these lovable, but lascivious Princes in the far-flung states of the Indian empire.

. Stella Mudge had been appearing in cabaret in a nightclub when she was spotted by the Maharajah's son in Italy. She had a chocolate-box prettiness, reddish blonde curls, big blue eyes and, according to one of the family, 'big rubbery lips' which were to crumple and pucker in disappointed old age. The family still speak about her with disdain, and cringe when they remember how she looked in a sari, but agree she had 'most beautiful legs', as you might expect from one of Cochrane's Young Ladies. Mudge, they tell you, means elephant in Hindi. 'Stella Mudge was not liked,' a Kapurthala grandson explained. 'I feel cheated that she was ever brought to the palace.'

The family thought her accent decidedly 'East London'. She was, they remembered, 'always very showy', covered in diamonds, 'even in the daytime'. The royal children quickly made up their minds that she was 'not well-born'. One of them, Kanwar Durmila Devi, is scathing. 'Stella was not at all well-spoken and very acquisitive.' Their own mother lived only three miles away from Miss Mudge but out of earshot of that high-pitched tinkly laugh. They swear that Stella insisted on a crown and that there was a coronation in 1949. It sounds like a fairytale, but without the traditional happy ending.

When the Yuvaraj brought Miss Mudge back to Kapurthala, knowing his father's weakness for European women he thought he too would be captivated by Stella's dainty feet and lively ways. But the Maharajah was appalled. Stella and the Yuvaraj had married and the old man feared she might produce a Mudgeraj, which with the Curzon ruling could mean disinheritance and disaster. So the marriage drums beat again and the experts found a simple fecund Indian girl.

The new royal marriage was fixed. But there could be no more unwilling bridegroom than the Yuvaraj, now being bullied by his father and tormented by Stella's jealousy, who felt threatened by the arrival of some 'jungly' girl. Four days before the second wedding, Miss Mudge ordered her servants to pack her bags. The lovesick Paramjit was demented. At the thought of losing his beloved Stella, and with no appetite for his expected role as stud for a new wife, he collapsed into a useful trance. Nobody could get him to stir and Stella was nowhere to be found.

The victim of palace intrigue for so long, she now handled the situation deftly, by hiding in her suite where she sulked contentedly. There was pandemonium and a Cabinet meeting

was called, presided over by a furious Maharajah while his son
and heir lay prone.

Sycophantic servants hurried along the corridors with messages on silver salvers, but only an offer of compensation rumoured to be a million rupees could bring a flicker of interest
to the English girl. The marriage could take place but Stella
insisted on one condition: the Yuvaraj would only visit his new
wife for one hour between 7 and 8 in the evening once a month
until she conceived. Astonishingly the Cabinet consented.

Miss Mudge, with a hint of tragedy, promised to revive the
comatose Yuvaraj. She approached him trilling: 'My Doggie
darling, *mon petit chou, mon bien aimé*, I love you.' At this
'Doggie' revived instantly and at Stella's bidding, agreed to the
wedding his father insisted on.

Pouting tearfully, Miss Mudge left to recover in Dehra Dun,
and to be consoled by an Indian friend who had been in love
with her for years. It is understandable that the Kapurthala
family should say that Stella Mudge was a money grabber, but
at this time she was in a precarious position with very little
security. As it happened Paramjit would remain devoted to her,
but she was not to know this.

It seemed that his father had succeeded, but not completely.
There were more hurdles for the Maharajah, as consummation
of this second marriage was constantly put off by the bridegroom. His new bride was always being bathed and scented by
some of her forty maids, who massaged erotic oils into her skin
and then swathed her in a gold and silver sari to wait for a
husband who never turned up.

It was a row with Stella Mudge – her temper rather ruining
her chocolate-box sweetness – which at last drove the Yuvaraj
to see his bride. It was hardly a moment of impetuous passion
as his valet went with him carrying his master's silk pyjamas
and dressing gown. Both seemed a little unnecessary, he could
only stay an hour.

An inhibitingly large crowd silently watched his arrival at
7 pm. Ministers, relations and singing priests all remarked on
his gloomy, hangdog expression. At 7.55 pm he re-emerged,

looking pensive and tired. He was seen again heading straight back to the arms of Stella Mudge, and they left almost immediately for Europe.

The son of that brief union is a delightful and gentle man, Maharajah Sukhjit Singh, known as Sukhie, a towering figure with his Sikh beard. His grandfather kept his promise to Guru Gobind Singh, that if the baby was a boy, in gratitude for their prayers he should be brought up as a true traditional Sikh.

Sukhie made a career in the army and was decorated during the war with Pakistan in 1972. His palace is now a police training college and he lives in the grounds by a river which the family calls the Kapurthala drain. His own life has had its share of heartache. A doting husband, after the birth of four daughters he was persuaded by his mother-in-law to have a vasectomy.

His wife, pretty and bored, became restless. As a close friend of the Maharajah's recalls bitterly: 'Poor Sukhie, one day when he was in Assam, busy defending India's frontiers, his wife turned up in Kapurthala with a huge truck and removed her possessions and jewels.'

Stella Mudge's stepson attracts affectionate salaams and hands folded in traditional 'namaste' greeting. He is lunching at his club where Indian intellectuals sit around in languid postures drinking lemon sodas or lassi. Hindus and Moslems go out of their way to shake his hand. A middle-aged white spinster, dressed in drab Indian print, grey hair shortly cropped, bulky legs in brown sandals and sand-coloured shawl, crosses the graceful lawn to ask him about the Punjab. In the aftermath of Mrs Gandhi's death, Delhi seems overrun with earnest, dedicated people who have the well-meaning bleakness of British Council workers; the men wear voluminous shorts, and smoke pipes. They stay in hostels, are immensely concerned, carry big folders and go to every ethnic evening where they may be free dhosas and tea. Brigadier Sukhie towering above the spinster shows perfect courtesy. The Sikhs he drolly refers to as 'my bearded countrymen'. The Indian Government, he thought, had been 'hacking up the wrong tree' in the handling of them.

The true Sikh wears five symbols, each beginning with the

letter K. They are a Kirpan which is a knife, a Kanga which is a comb, Kesh, uncut hair, Kaura, an iron bangle for faithfulness, and Kuch, a pair of shorts protecting their manhood. It was impossible to see where the black thread sneaks under his beard and Kesh to tie his turban.

Maharajah Sukhjit Singh, this gentle man, attractive, with a greying beard and dressed completely in brown, has an air of command and dignity. He wants to talk about the Punjab, 'forged in the crucible of adversity', and of the 'Sikh psyche of these large hearted people'.

Patrician and careful, he is almost too nice, and after the excesses of his father and grandfather, it is an irony that his own only marriage should be less than happy. He was kind about his father's love affair with Stella Mudge: 'All I can remember is that Stella was a very lively person,' he remembered, 'a redheaded pixie, an elfin woman and very vivid.' His own mother simply wasted away after his birth, dying at twenty-one of tuberculosis and loneliness. She was cremated in the Palace gardens without fuss.

The Maharajah Paramjit died in 1955 aged sixty-three. He and Miss Mudge loved each other to the end, and lived in a house at Kapurthala called Stella Cottage. They always kept their bed which was shaped like a gondola because they had met in Venice.

There was a squabble about the will. Stella claimed that two weeks before Paramjit died, he changed his will and left everything to his English-born Maharani; but not surprisingly the family disputed this deathbed change of heart. She was given a tantalising glimpse of the Kapurthala treasure under the supervision of a French judge at the eleventh hour. There was a 44-carat turban diamond surrounded by brilliants, 4 pearl necklaces, 200 gold watches, 32 chessmen in gold and coloured enamel, and jewels estimated to be worth £500,000. But the French court ruled that the jewels and the treasure belonged to the Maharajah's only son.

Stella got nothing and came back to London 'a bit blowsy from too many gins and oranges,' remarked a Kapurthala princess. In 1970 she was trying desperately to sell bits and pieces, including a piano, to make a bit of money. It was an unhappy end.

Her mother, Mrs Emily Mudge, an articulate eighty-year-old, still living humbly in her semi-detached house in Bromley, lamented, in the best tradition of Victorian melodrama, her daughter's downfall and dismal end. 'Don't let your daughter marry an Indian Prince,' she moralised, and added, 'I married a wire-walker myself.'

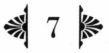

7

Learning to Sign Cheques

MAYO COLLEGE, the 'Eton of the East', has been educating Princes for over a century. The first pupil was the Maharajah of Alwar, who arrived on 23 October 1875 on a caparisoned elephant with a procession of trumpeters, bearers, camels and aides on horseback. He had 500 servants, 12 elephants and 600 horses.

His view of education was the same as the young Prince who, rebuked recently by the headmaster for not working hard enough, replied: 'Well frankly, sir, we are only coming here for learning to sign cheques.'

The first princely school was Rajkumar College in Rajkot founded in 1870. The second was Mayo, also for the education of the Princes, but with more glamour than its older equivalent in Kathiawar. Eligibility for either depended, as the Prince of Wales said when he visited Mayo in 1921, 'on nobility of birth'.

Mayo is set in the romantic shadow of the Arvallis, in Ajmer midway between Jodhpur and Jaipur. It is on the edge of the Thar desert and, with its white marble and bougainvillaea flopping frivolously over the colonnades, looks more like a palace than its sterner model, the English public school.

New boys strolling the 300 acres of grounds dotted with poinsettias and hibiscus, still admire the massive Carrara marble

statue of Lord Mayo, the school's founder. A boy in a cerise
turban reading out the inscription under the tall, heroic-looking
figure, gives a few reverent shakes of the head. Lord Mayo,
Viceroy of India for four years until his death in 1892, had
achieved his dream to start a school for 'the sons of the aristocracy'. Rudyard Kipling's father Lockwood, an art teacher in
Lahore, designed the Mayo coat of arms with Rajput warriors
in red, gold, white, green and blue, peacocks and swords.

Modern Indians think that these colleges were part of a
devious plan to create British schoolboy clones. But the maharajahs were never forced to send their sons to princely colleges.
Some kept their heirs at home with nothing more intellectually
taxing than a daily reading of Charles Kingsley's *Water Babies*.
Homely nannies were more worried about a princeling's dislike
of rice pudding and custard than his ability to recite Milton or
Dryden. Later a British guardian would keep an unruly Prince
under fairly strict control.

Mayo College had the framework of an English public school.
The boys were 'expected to behave like gentlemen at all times,
to teach their servants to be clean and respectful and to wear
English boots at football'. They had classes on flowers; recognition of a hollyhock or forget-me-not would later bring a glow
of pleasure to an English guardian's wife.

These impressionable young Princes at Mayo, used to eating
off gold and Sèvres in the nursery, would grow even more apart
from their people as they enjoyed school copies of *Punch* and
London Illustrated, played rugby football and ate English food.

These were the star Princes and the sybaritic tradition was
maintained half a century later in 1938, when young Baria,
Prince Jaideep Singh, had three cars, a French Delage and two
Chevrolets, at the age of nine.

An exception to all this luxury was the orthodox Hindu
young Maharajah of Benares. He could never sit at table with
his friends and have fun throwing chappatis, but had to eat his
food from a stool and drink sacred water from the Ganges.

There were no timorous new boys. Young Kotah arrived
with 200 servants. Most of the Princes had vast stables, special

cooks, watchmakers, tailors, barbers, watercarriers and sweepers, peons, secretaries, clerks and writers. Their accountants paid the garden coolies their 5 rupees a month and the 11 rupees for one month's supply of grass for the horses. Each Prince had his own pastel pink or cream-washed house named after his state – Bikaner, Jaipur, Kotah, Mewar – all with archways, gracious terraces and *porte-cochères* where the chauffeur could keep the Bentley or Silver Ghost pleasantly cool, a few pristine schoolbooks scattered on the cream upholstery.

Life was full of delicious distractions. The Maharajah of Jaipur was married while he was at Mayo in 1923 when he was twelve. It was hard for the boys to concentrate on their sums; they would never carry money anyhow. There were no serious expectations of exam results, so days could be spent hunting in open limousines for black buck and sand-grouse, playing polo or planning the London season at the Ritz or Claridges, rather than droning on about iambic pentameters and the Fifth Crusade. Princely teams were elegant in silk jodhpurs, playing chukkhas on the red earth of Ajmer.

'Oriental boys are more dramatic. English boys are not so free of *mauvaise haute* as the Mayo boys,' Colonel Trevor, Agent to the Governor-General, thought as he watched a school play. English houseparty charades would hold no terrors for these young maharajahs.

The school museum has a catholic collection: letters from Buckingham Palace, a double-headed coconut, a chicken with four legs, the tin holding food eaten by some Russian astronauts, two stuffed tigers handed over by the Maharajah of Kotah, the agonisingly shy Chairman of the Board of Governors, a left-handed whelk from Zanzibar, sapphires, emeralds and beryl. But the dilettante days have gone. Today Mayo specialises in computer science, medicine and business administration.

The boys get up at 5.45 am in the summer when the days are dry and hot and the monsoon has made the rocky valleys bright green. Assembly is the usual scamper after breakfast with 800 boys rushing in to hear a reading from the Koran, or, on other days, recite the Lord's Prayer. Sometimes there is sitar music by

Ravi Shankar, or one of the boys will wind the handle of the old gramophone and put on the Arnold Bax Symphony No. 1 or Tchaikovsky's 'Dance of the Sugar Plum Fairy'. And there will be a reading from Tagore or *Time* or *Newsweek*. 'I like to strike at the root of the penny, so the boys must keep their ears open,' says H. L. Dutt, the Indian headmaster.

For some of the maharajahs there was nothing to compare with a genuine English public school. Eton, Harrow, Winchester, Charterhouse and Shrewsbury were the favourites.

The young ruler-to-be of Indore, Yeshwant Rao Holkar arrived at Charterhouse in June 1923, aged fourteen. Boys mostly came from comfortable homes tinged with an insularity captured so well by Dornford Yates. Delicious, adorable girls danced to popular tunes like 'Our Love Goes out to an English Sky' at Jonah Mansell's house which was called White Ladies, and the twin Bentley coupés were trendily named Ping and Pong. Snobbishness was rife at Charterhouse. A headmaster's career was ruined because his pronunciation of 'breaown ceaow' made pupils and parents wince.

Holkar, in his Eton collar, short black coat, pepper and salt trousers, was soon known by the other boys as 'that black devil'; 'one was well advised to have no dealings with him . . .' This seems extraordinary now to a travelled generation but in the 1920s only the rich went beyond Deauville and Madeira; experience of countries like India was left to poor darling Freddy sweating it out in the colonies as ADC to a Governor, or 'HE' as he would put it in letters home to mater and pater.

The only other dark-skinned prince the schoolboys knew was at 'Greyfriars School', where Hurree Jamset Ram Singh, the Nabob of Bhanipur, joined in tormenting the Fat Owl of the Remove. Hurree knew the slang, calling out 'Hold on, old porpoise' as the hapless Billy trundled off in search of freshly made cream puffs.

To Frank Pritchard, almost a contemporary of Holkar's, Charterhouse, sitting high on a plateau above Godalming, seemed rather monastic. His first day as a 'newbug' at the school was

on a fine September afternoon sixty-six years ago. He recalls
two small boys walking aimlessly in the grounds, having sur-
vived what Max Beerbohm called the 'awful geniality' of the
housemaster. At least these 'newbugs' had each other; Holkar
had to learn on his own. Christian names were never used, a
public school habit touchingly clung to in India to this day. The
food was very strange. At the far end of the stone flagged
passages Holkar would find sausages, tinned pilchards or mince,
dished out by the butler, Frank Tice, from a small stove. But,
strangest of all, there was fagging.

Another Old Carthusian, Maurice Burn, says, 'I don't think
he ever understood fagging . . . and understandably he was not
very efficient.' Burn was the one boy who befriended Holkar
and this was because they had their weekly 'toshes' on the same
night. Soaking in the hot water, you could have long chats.

Burn remembers that Holkar never had enough money. He
even used to sell his books to Burn and with the money buy
the whipped cream walnuts which he loved at 'Crown', the
school tuck shop.

Even for the average Carthusian, weekends could be awful if
they were not seeing friends and family. On Sundays, 'dragging
their slow length along', there was chapel twice, maybe a walk
with the boys wearing 'the ridiculous billycock hats', excursions
to the Puttenham caves and, the height of excitement on a
summer's day, a warm ersatz ice-cream soda.

Games were much more important in the 1920s than they are
now but Holkar was not sporty. It was not until he came back
to the school as Maharajah that anybody realised he loved tennis.

Nobody spotted Holkar's isolation. Masters seemed remote
or crabby. He left after only five quarters, when the British
forced his father to stand down after the mysterious death of one
of his mistresses. They brought his young son back to rule as a
minor.

On his accession, aged sixteen, covered in jewels, worshipped
by his people and now owner of thirteen palaces, the young Old
Carthusian remarked, tongue in cheek, that he wished he was
a 'fag again at Charterhouse'. Three years later he returned to

lunch with the headmaster in some style: a Sunbeam Open Tourer with Foreign Office security men and a turbaned Indian chauffeur. He was to remain anti-British for the rest of his life.

When the present Nizam of Hyderabad first went to Harrow it was as a day boy. His mother, Princess Berar, insisted that he stay at the Savoy with her. So every day the Prince left the hotel with an ADC who took him on the underground to Harrow, returning in the evening to collect him. The Princess was delighted. Her son was getting a fine education; she had a chance to enjoy art galleries and read poetry in her suite.

Philip Mason, who retired from the Indian Civil Service in 1947, had become Tutor and Governor to the Princes at her request. Now at last he could go home to enjoy a Tolstoyian phase in Dorset, 'digging fields, picking up potatoes and looking at compost heaps'. 'I don't want some old colonel who would make a job of this and stay for ever,' Princess Berar had always said.

In contrast to Holkar, the Maharajah of Palitana was hugely popular at Shrewsbury. He arrived in 1913 and excelled at classics but, even more importantly, on the cricket ground. In those days of old empire if you could play games well, you could get away with almost anything. He used to skip up the windy staircase to the roof of Allington Hall each morning after breakfast to smoke his exotic hubble-bubble pipe. Boys and beaks would smile indulgently. 'Old Pally,' they would say, 'is a bit of a rum cove.'

A glamorous figure, he sent his bouncy son Shivendra to Shrewsbury in 1950, when the talents of his contemporaries, Richard Ingrams, editor of *Private Eye* and William Rushton were not only allowed to flourish but encouraged by the masters.

Nicknames have always been an important part of boys' public schools. The 'Noob' of Pataudi never liked being called 'Draccers' or 'Syd', but was happy to answer to 'Tiger', his nickname from childhood when he used to race round the 150-room palace on all fours like a tiger cub.

His father, 'Pat', another great cricketer and member of

Douglas Jardine's Bodyline team of 1932–3, handled his son's Winchester entrance form in a novel way. Ignoring all the complicated questions, he simply scrawled flamboyantly, 'My Son'. Not many parents could get away with that except perhaps the Prince of Wales.

But it was Tiger's mother, the Begum of Bhopal, who had spent years in purdah at home, never being seen by any man except her husband, who brought her son to England. 'Pat' had died in January 1952, on Tiger's eleventh birthday. As she swept round the lawns of Winchester in her sari, the masters thought the widowed Begum 'absolutely sweet'. But she insisted on two things; her son in accordance with the Moslem faith must not eat pork and he was to be treated like all other boys: 'You must beat Tiger if you want to; he can be very naughty.'

He had an ideal housemaster in Podge Brodhurst, regarded by generations of parents as 'thoroughly sound'. Humorous, compassionate, athletic and clean-cut with his fair hair, Brodhurst seems to belong to an altogether more wholesome era. His wife Meg had a soft spot for the 'Noob' and his homesickness never escaped her alert brown eyes. 'But he always had a twinkle in his eye, a lovely sort of mask which was helpful when he was found devouring a plate of forbidden fried pork sausages.'

He managed never to be caught smoking but was in trouble with one of the more irascible masters, who reported, 'I found a *Caesar* belonging to that young pup Pataudi, and judging by some of the drawings, I think he is pretty mature for his age.' He was about fourteen at the time. At home he was caught putting mud in the sandwiches at his sister's wedding in Delhi. Wedding photographs were sent to Winchester and he was anxious that Peter Jay and others in his class should not see him in his traditional Moslem finery with curled up slippers.

Religious instruction for the Noob had been a delicate issue for the school. So every Sunday Mr Kamil, 'a most delightful man, who wore a gorgeous little grey fur hat', arrived punctually at 2.15 pm from the mosque at Woking. He had the Koran under his arm for an hour on the Islamic faith in Mrs Brodhurst's sitting room.

In his third year, the Begum announced, 'Tiger will be going to Oxford,' and there was a slight intake of breath at Winchester. Brodhurst spoke to Marcus Dick, then senior tutor at Balliol, and an old Wykehamist. 'Tiger Pataudi, oh yes, the cricketer,' sniffed Marcus Dick, 'quite brainless I should think, and my dear old boy, there are thousands wanting to read History.' There must have been a guardian angel flying low that day, because Brodhurst had a brainwave and cast around for an unpopular subject. 'Oh, he would really like to read Oriental Languages.' Tiger was in. When you ask Pataudi today what he read at Oxford, he says 'Cricket'.

The present Maharajah of Jodhpur's mother, another forceful widow, worried that her son was being spoilt in the palace by a gentle English governess. His father had been killed in a plane crash at the age of twenty-eight, so 'the pampering had to stop'. In 1956 he left India for Cothill Preparatory School, which he hated: 'All those early mornings and cold baths . . .' He would spend half-term with his uncle, the Maharajah of Dhrangadhra, who had a small flat in Oxford. Here he would wail, 'They are treating me as a foreigner . . . as an Indian.'

When he went to Eton, which he enjoyed, he shrewdly adapted his English style for holidays in India. He remembered coming back to Delhi for school holidays and speedily changing his English from Etonian to sing-song. 'I did a switch in my mind on the plane. My sisters wanted to see me in my Etonian uniform, but as soon as the plane landed in Delhi, I would whisk off my jacket and be an Indian schoolboy again.'

He was very popular, 'Quite,' said one contemporary, 'the most unmalicious person you could meet.' He used to get wonderful parcels from home and would share out the luscious mangoes. He made good friends at school and at Oxford but there always had to be an apartness about him. If things got too hot or exciting, he would tactfully retreat. He could not afford a scandal.

At Oxford, the Maharajah remembers how his maid used to

shout, 'Get out of bed, Mr Singh.' On his honeymoon, he took his wife to Eton and then for a green wellies weekend in the country with old schoolfriends.

Education for girls was not taken seriously in India except by a few sophisticated princely families. The Rajmata of Jaipur remembers Glendower day school in Queensgate: 'I puzzled for weeks over a mysterious word that every girl repeated each morning at roll-call in answer to her name; I eventually discovered that it was "Here Miss Heath", the name of the headmistress.'

Later, Lady Zia Wernher, who was a friend of Ma Cooch's, suggested a finishing school, the Monkey Club, where she had just sent her own daughter Gina. The principal, welcoming the future Maharani of Jaipur with extended hand, said heartily, 'You are the first Indian Monkey we've had here.'

The Maharajah of Baroda does not approve of English public schools for boys who will spend most of their lives in India. His young nephew 'Brownie' is at prep school in England and due to go to Uppingham. 'He is thirteen years old and already he is an Englishman, a brown Englishman.' Rolling his eyes and with mock sadness the Gaekwad said, 'His parents can't understand what he is saying. Only I can understand his short, clipped, staccato sentences. When he goes home to them, he refuses to eat. I saw him in London at half-term and he ate sausages and baked beans and not long afterwards roast chicken with stuffing and came back for more.'

The argument goes on in princely families about the children's education. While there is still a sneaking regard for English public schools, there is a new mood and the fashion is to keep a boy in India and then send him to America for business studies.

The trendy public school at the moment is Doon near Dehra Dun. It has a fine reputation academically and its most famous old boy is India's Prime Minister Rajiv Gandhi. It caters for the 'new maharajahs', the industrialists, the civil servants, the bright young men who want careers in industry and science.

But Mayo is still the choice for some of the oldest princely families. Arvind Singh of Udaipur says, 'Our children, especially our sons, must have the sort of education which does not ignore their heritage. It is important for them to know who they are. Mayo will create the right atmosphere. It is really like Eton and Doon is more like Winchester.'

The fees are 8 to 10,000 rupees, about £1,000 a year, which is costly in India. Arvind Singh is full of praise for the government schools where you pay about £50 a year and sometimes get better academic results.

Rajkumar at Rajkot is now less fashionable. Dormitories are crowded wall-to-wall with mosquito-netted beds in princely houses once exclusively for the use of the Nawab of Cambay and his servants, or the Maharajah of Wankaner. It is low on funds and none of the public schools any longer has government support, a tacit indication of disapproval. The Principal, Peter Rogerson, is the last English public school headmaster left in India.

Jack Gibson ran Mayo College when it was at its peak and could not bear to leave. He retired in 1969 and was given an OBE for, as he says, 'Other Buggers' Efforts' and from India the Padma Shri. Lean, resilient, droll, with an intellectual peace, Jack has retired to a pretty house near the school. 'I bought it for a song, £1,500.' He often gets a call from the present headmaster – 'Jack, old boy, how about a beer?' He roars with laughter, 'I am staying on.'

He puts down his out-of-date copy of *The Times*, ambles onto the roof terrace which is a riot of terracotta pots filled with remarkably English flowers. Geraniums, dahlias and snapdragons nod cheerfully in the Indian sunshine, while in his garden he has rows of beetroot.

Money is a little short. 'But then I sell a little something so I have enough to pay my debts.' His servant had cooked an excellent sponge cake in a solar cooker. He hovered then disappeared behind pink doors, beaming at the cake's success. Jack, lanky, tweedy, sprawled in a wickerwork chair. He poured tea with swooping wrists from a large silver teapot.

After Partition, Mayo lost some of its Moslem pupils and

became a bit run down. He was chosen to revitalise it and became headmaster in 1954, retiring fifteen years later.

Always a bachelor, he was originally not at all drawn to India, 'I looked at the map, it was rather brown. All that one knew about it was the Black Hole of Calcutta.' He travelled out P & O first class from London round the Cape, but as he left his teeth behind, he ate scrambled eggs all the way while everyone else had lobster. It was a dreadful journey and he has hated his false teeth ever since. 'Look here, I only put them in today because you were coming.'

Jack Gibson inspired affection though he could be strict. Trips to the cinema or too much money spent in the tuck shop – often a cart outside selling coriander and tomatoes beside the chocolate bars – were the worst crimes. Drugs, hangovers and illicit sex were not problems, though one boy did have a daughter. Much more difficult was the battle against the Princes' innate languidness. 'In India they love learning but don't like thinking,' he says.

Corporal punishment is alien to the Indian schoolboy, who is temperamentally law-abiding, though Gibson says he would occasionally give a boy 'six of the best if I caught him throwing a stone into a bee's nest'.

Often a guest of the Princes' parents, Jack Gibson used to shoot with the Kotahs and the Udaipurs. He still takes an avuncular interest in the old boys and recently offered to mediate in a battle between the two sons of the late Maharana of Udaipur. 'India likes dynasties,' he says.

He is building his servant a house. 'I enjoy my life here. I don't wash up. I don't make my own bed, I don't cook. If I am absolutely desperate for money, I sell a family heirloom or send a picture to England.' He pats a piece of Chinese porcelain.

On trips to England he goes straight to Heffers bookshop in Cambridge and visits English gardens. He once raced to Sissinghurst but found it closed. Looking up he recognised a beaky face peering through a latticed window. 'Please, I have come all the way from India.' Vita Sackville-West could not resist.

He finds Britain is changing socially all the time. 'I rather like being called dearie; things are very friendly, class is almost blotted out.'

Letters beginning 'Dear Daddy' still arrive at Harold Barry's home in Cheshire from boys he taught at Aitchison College in Lahore. When he went there in 1933, he thought it more a luxury hotel than a school for the aristocracy of the Punjab. There were 36 boys; 53 cows in the dairy, polo ponies in the paddocks, herbaceous borders of dahlias and chrysanthemums and 150 green acres irrigated all the year round. When the Maharajah of Patiala swept up to the school in his Rolls-Royce, it was through an avenue of flowering jacarandas, side by side with coral trees. 'When the petals fell together on the grass, it was miraculous, white and coral.'

Patiala was a great favourite and supporter of the school which today has 2,500 boys. 'He was a lovely, wonderful father,' Barry recalled, 'a very attractive man of the world, though his private life may have been a bit dubious.'

All the Patiala boys were sent to Aitchison; the daughters went to Queen Mary's College, Lahore, a rather good progress-ive school and to educate girls at all was extraordinarily en-lightened.

Michael Charlesworth, who taught at Shrewsbury, had a spell in Pakistan as headmaster of Lawrence College in Murree, a rival to the top school, 'Chiefs' College', the vernacular for Aitchison in Lahore. He found that even dealing with the *Private Eye* team at Shrewsbury was no preparation for his Pathan pupils. 'The trouble was, everything revolved around Izzat, that sense of pride. Izzat must never be dented even on the playing fields.' There were extraordinary scenes at inter-house matches when five hundred boys fiercely yelled the school motto 'Never give in' while their Pathan masters waved their swords in the air, fiercely urging on their teams. The English masters could only mutter a restrained 'Well played!' through clenched teeth. Once there was a difference of opinion between the boys and one of the masters. As he was walking back to his study, the students followed him hissing disagreeably. Suddenly

he turned on them, pulled out a revolver, fired four shots in the
air, and said, 'I may be only vice-principal, but I am a Pathan.'

When the 17-day war between India and Pakistan broke out
in September 1965, Charlesworth found his warlike pupils
wanted to 'kill lots of Indians'. 'We just said, "Get on with
your maths", but there was a very ugly atmosphere.'

To this day the telephone will ring at Charlesworth's Shropshire home and an excited voice will say, 'Hawlaw, sir, I was
fifth form, it was very nice . . . remember me, sir?'

On his way back home, crossing the dusty Deccan plateau
and wondering what good he might have done in Pakistan,
Charlesworth's truck broke down. From nowhere, a little boy
appeared, barefooted in tattered shorts, and solemnly recited,
'O Mary, go and call the cattle home . . . Across the sands of
Dee.' It seemed to sum up everything for Charlesworth: 'There
I was slap in the middle of India, with England thousands of
miles away, and I thought, How splendid, how absurd.'

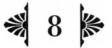

Romance Clouds Your Judgement

MARRIAGE IN INDIA is called 'arranged love'. Parents do the courting, and it is all about economics and dynasty. Love? Maybe, but that comes later. Arranged marriage is inevitable for most Indians whether they are Princes, farm workers, bourgeoisie or God's children.

It may seem outlandish and medieval, but Indians tend to smile at the Western idea of chemistry between two people. They say the success of Indian marriage lies in the fact that the couple cannot be disillusioned. For a start, they hardly know each other, and there is none of that potentially destructive narcissism of courtship. A married couple may even fall in love after a few years, quite the reverse of Western marriage when dogs and golf can become the ruling passions.

A few resist and make up their own minds about with whom they would like to spend the rest of their lives, but risk a bitter rift with their families for ever.

Some arranged marriages have been genuine successes after hesitant beginnings. The Dowager Maharani of Gwalior, now an attractive, forceful widow, remembers her first meeting with her future husband at the Taj Hotel in Bombay. Lekha Devi, as she was then, felt miserable and dowdy in a long-sleeved, close-necked 'Cossack' blouse designed by her grandmother, and stared uncomfortably out of the bay window, looking at the warships. It was not long after Dunkirk.

Jivajirao Scindia, Maharajah of Gwalior's, quick, impish smile
impressed her more than his chunky, muscular build. He was
amused by this beautiful and rather sulky girl. Her uncle and
aunt were hovering nearby, and winced when their niece told
the Maharajah that she did not like being called 'Princess' as,
frankly, she was not as royal as his family thought. Fearing
they would have to look again for another husband for this
wilful girl, they took her home.

But an hour later the telephone rang and they were invited
to lunch at the Maharajah's seaside palace in Bombay to be
followed by an afternoon's racing. The Scindias were the most
successful owners and breeders of racehorses in India, and two
of the Prince's horses, Garland and Fire Alarm, won that day.

When the racing was over the Maharajah's ADC, Captain
Vithalrao Lagad, escorted Lekha Devi away. As he handed her
into the car she thought it odd that 'he bowed low and made as
if to touch my feet with his hand before lifting it to his chest
three times'. This greeting, known as Mujira, could only be
given to the royal couple. Lekha Devi said that in that instant
she knew she would marry the Maharajah. Outspoken as
always, she protested, 'You must not do Mujira to me, Captain,'
but he bowed and said solemnly: 'I must, to our Maharani.'

The Maharajah's staff had been told the news before the girl
and her family. An hour later the telephone rang in their hotel
room. His Highness would like to marry Lekha Devi as soon
as possible. In an emotional moment, Lekha Devi's grandmother took off the diamond solitaires she had always worn
and gave them to her granddaughter.

The wedding was on 21 February 1941 at 10.31 pm, as
arranged by the astrologers. They laughed afterwards at a
photograph taken during the ceremony, saying they looked
'like a couple of untidy bundles of washing'. But it was like any
Indian royal wedding, with horsetail fans and the air heavy with
the scent of jasmine. They set off for their honeymoon aboard
the Scindia cream and gold royal train, the family crest on the
doors and looped velvet curtains inside; there were apricot silk
sofas, large beds, a cocktail bar, flowers and incense. Lekha

Born to rule: Jam Shri Vibhaji of Nawanagar in black patent Chelsea boots, with his tiny successor. The great Ranjitsinhji, India's finest cricketer, succeeded in 1906 and proved himself a good administrator when he was not abroad

OPPOSITE ABOVE: Maharajahs in the making. These eldest sons of the élite amongst Indian princes are already confident and poised as they attend George V and Queen Mary at the Delhi Durbar in 1911

OPPOSITE BELOW: An unusual view of the 1911 Durbar when Delhi became a city of tents

ABOVE: A visit from the Viceroy was always prestigious for the Ruler. When Lord Reading went to Bharatpur to inspect flood damage, he also managed to bag 1700 duck. Here the Viceroy sits apart at an elevated table while his host is below with the entourage

RIGHT: The boy Maharajah of Bharatpur at the Delhi Durbar in 1911. He was to prove a disappointment to his British advisers later when he became dedicated to sybaritic japes and forgot about the Empire

The Lord Sahib's wife, Lady Reading, in chintz
armchair keeps a steadying white-gloved hand on the
turbanned toddler Maharajah's head for this classic
photograph taken in Simla, where the garlanded
memsahibs were guests of the sophisticated
Maharajah of Bharatpur
INSET: Gracious lady sahibs enjoy a hop while their
escorts look doubtful

LEFT: The Maharajah of Alwar, known as a 'man sinister beyond belief', sits beside a monocled British adviser with a handsome tiger at their feet, its back legs delicately crossed for the photograph
BELOW: The Rolls was a status symbol as important as a British nanny. They were not always treated with reverence by their princely owners. Here the Maharana of Udaipur tries to persuade his English wife to take the wheel

LEFT: The Maharajahs were easily bored but never tired of the delights of shikar. Mir Allahdad Khan, implacable son of the Khairpur dynasty, has bagged a few elands and a couple of big cats, but seems poised for more
BELOW: The Maharajah of Bharatpur, who eventually turned conservationist, poses with guests after a particularly successful shoot

ABOVE: Barely into her teens, a beautiful Kashmiri princess, totally innocent about the meaning of marriage, marries the Maharajah of Jaisalmer, aged 22

LEFT: Only four years later, now a mother and a sophisticated Maharani of Jaisalmer, 'Dolly' – as she is affectionately known by family and friends – has the poise of a film star in this studio photograph with the Maharajah, who was the ruler of this desert kingdom where once the early caravan traders broke their journey

RIGHT: The Maharajah of Kapurthala, Jagatjit Singh, was overweight as a teenager. Advisers felt a three-wheeler was more reliable for the Crown Prince exercising in the palace grounds in 1889. British invention helped him consummate his first marriage

Devi's husband gave her pearls and rubies and diamonds, and saris of French chiffon and georgette in gold and silver and pale yellows and blues, the colours of freesias and butterflies.

But not all arranged meetings had such a happy ending. A viceregal aide recalls how he was organising a meeting between a prospective bride and the Maharajah of Kashmir at Government House. The girl, a daughter of the Maharajah of Dholpur, was to come to the ballroom by the special zenana entrance and 'I was to look after her while the ADC brought in the Maharajah. Right at the moment when His Highness came in, looking very grand, I suddenly realised I'd lost the girl. This diminutive, sweet little thing was quite overcome and felt impelled to sink onto her hands and knees and wiggle along the polished parquet towards him. I didn't know what to do, and felt rather foolish. But that was the end of it anyway; she didn't please.'

Outside the aristocracy and wealthy classes marriages in India are fixed by advertising. The boast of a respectable newspaper like the *Times of India* is that it is read by 809,000 eligible bachelors. Every Sunday, space is paid for by families of 'handsome, broadminded Maharastrian Brahmin medical doctor, aged 26, 180 cm, model, having business in cement . . . seeks extremely pretty, non-working bride'; or 'Airline executive solicits alliance for daughter, convent educated . . .' and 'Match for Marwari Agrawl boy, 24, handsome, BA English, income six figures, teetotaller . . .' There is advice for the engaged couples: 'When you are getting married you are thrilled and anxious . . .'

Everyone is keen to tell you that arranged love nearly always works. Jayvantsinhji Gohel, father-in-law of a Bikaner princess and awarded the CBE by the Queen for his valuable work in Britain, says: 'Romance clouds your judgement in the West. You all think marriage is going to be a moonlight sonata and that life will be a rainbow, but then comes disappointment.' He shakes his head mournfully.

Only the bravest would reject their parents' choice of ideal husband. The spirited Indira Gaekwad of Baroda was one of the 'modern' princesses who defied her parents by refusing to marry the boy of their choice. A great beauty who broke many hearts, she had attended a co-educational school in Baroda and a finishing school in Eastbourne. But early photographs show a hint of sadness, perhaps because she was being ardently chased by a minor canon from Chester Cathedral. He wrote to his mother constantly about glimpses of Indira's exquisite figure under the folds of her sari. He was ignored by Indira, but as he was attached to Baroda for a year, had to take plenty of cold baths.

The Barodas launched their 17-year-old daughter on the social scene when they were in London in 1911 for the Coronation of King George V, and arranged a marriage with the 34-year-old Maharajah of Gwalior. Bluff, chauvinistic Madhavrao Scindia was more interested in tigers than romance. He had been married once, but there were no children. Both families were equally wealthy, and more importantly the astrologers agreed to this ideal dynastic match.

Princess Indira went on a tremendous shopping spree in Paris, Rome and London for her trousseau. In Gwalior to this day they still use some of the bedlinen, tablecloths and napkins which she had made on French and Irish looms with her married initials I.S., Indira Scindia, intertwined and embroidered in matching silk under a crown of her own design. Such ostentatious thrift was galling for her Goanese successor.

There was a lavish party at Ranelagh by the River Thames, and it became public news that Indira would be married in the New Year and afterwards go meekly into purdah.

But for Indira it was all a nightmare. She had fallen in love with the infinitely more attractive Jitendra Singh, brother of the Maharajah of Cooch Behar. They had met in London. He was a fine shot, a good horseman, had 'the manners of an English gentleman', and was an excellent ballroom dancer. A handsome man, suave, educated in England, Jitendra was not quite up to Baroda standards in terms of wealth. However, the social Cooch Behars with a mere 13-gun salute and a paltry 1,318 acres in a hill state, considered the Barodas mere shepherds. The Barodas on the other hand thought the Cooch Behars not pukkah

Hindus, believing as they did in Brahmasanmudj, which shook
off the strict irrelevant barnacles of the faith. After Independence
in 1947, Cooch Behar became part of West Bengal with a privy
purse of twenty thousand pounds a year.

At the Delhi Durbar in 1911 the young couple became inseparable, riding out in the early mornings and dancing waltzes and
foxtrots in the evenings in the jasmine scented marquees draped
in gold and cream silk held in great swathes. Elaborate pre-
parations for the wedding were being finalised when Indira sent
Gwalior a 'Dear Madhav' letter, breaking the engagement.
Gwalior was extremely huffy and sent a telegram to Baroda
asking querulously: 'What does the Princess mean by her letter?'
It seemed clear enough, and the Barodas, just home from the
Durbar, were mortified. They had no influence over their
wayward daughter. All the wedding arches were dismantled
and the special trains cancelled.

Indira was sent to England, and went skiing in Switzerland,
but all the time she was seeing Jitendra, who sometimes disguised himself as a very old man to fool her guardians. Two
years later, in 1913, the young couple ran away and married in
a registrar's office in London, but had an Indian blessing at the
Buckingham Palace Hotel in Victoria.

The Barodas had been particularly dismayed because their
beautiful daughter was not even marrying a son who would
inherit and rule. But the ruling Maharajah of Cooch Behar,
who had been forbidden to marry an English actress, took to
the bottle to drink himself to death on champagne and succeeded
admirably. By a strange irony he died only three weeks after
the runaways' wedding, and Jitendra became Maharajah in 1913.

Eight years after the marriage, Jitendra died, leaving a 29-
year-old-widow, 'Ma Cooch', and five children, one of whom
became the celebrated Gayatri Devi – and widow of the present
Maharajah of Jaipur's father.

But very few princesses run off, and the Rajmata of Jodhpur
thinks orthodox arranged marriages are best.

Relaxing in the royal apartments with the reddish gold light
of a Jodhpur sunset mellowing the art deco, the Rajmata of

Jodhpur, a plump grandmother in a grey sari, is drinking tea.
Widowed at twenty-five, her own marriage in 1943 when she
was seventeen was traditional and brief. She is formidable but
loving. An English friend compares her to the Queen Mother
in her ability to get her own way, but saw her in musical terms
as a 'cellist rather than a violinist'.

No retiring grandmother, she seemed to thrill as she described
the early days of her marriage to a man she had never seen: 'I
had to bribe someone to get me a photograph of him.' But what
if he had looked like a gorilla? She stemmed these questions: 'It
is much more exciting when you don't see the person first;
electricity goes through your body.' For a minute, the passionate
memory of such a typical Indian marriage seemed to be turning
this granny into a young girl with a vibrant sparkle.

Her husband had not even spoken to her for the first six
months. It was extraordinarily lonely. Life in the zenana in the
nineteen forties was lacklustre compared with a more exotic
era, when Jodhpur women wore diamond-encrusted slippers
and eyebrows of diamonds looped over their ears with hooks.
Giving birth to a son meant happiness and more jewels. The
mothers, perfumed and cossetted, swished barefoot across the
warm marble floors, bracelets jingling to make their babies
laugh by dangling a string of rubies and toys of solid gold.
When the baby got bored, they rocked its gold cradle, swinging
in the breeze near the lotus shaped windows.

The young Maharani of Jodhpur had a far less glamorous
time. 'My husband would be out till ten at night, but he used
to encourage me to learn Gujerati, to have English lessons and
not be so shy.' Her days were astutely spent watching her
mother-in-law. 'I learnt a lot from her. She had come from a
village to marry when she was fourteen. If she saw my father-
in-law eyeing a woman, and if he looked at her more than
thrice, she would copy her, her clothes and her style.'

The Maharajah, a tall, flamboyant character who hated being
described as one of the richest men in the world, was an
enthusiastic magician. His English nanny had given him a box
of tricks when he was seven: 'She wanted me to have a hobby,'

he said. One of his great achievements was to become a member of the Magic Circle after a performance in front of six hundred wizards and their friends.

Their only son, the present Maharajah of Jodhpur, was born in 1948. To the Maharani, 'He looked so blue and rather Chinese, what an ugly child I thought.' That year her husband secretly married his mistress, a nineteen-year-old nurse from Scotland, Sandra McBryde. She had been working as a matron in an Indian nursing home when she met the Maharajah at a party. The Maharani, she said, welcomed her as 'second junior wife' to the palace.

Sandra took her princely husband home to meet the family. Her brother Dennis was a commercial traveller in Stoke-on-Trent. They stayed in Claridges. She wore jewelled saris, became a Hindu, and changed her name to Sundra Devi. After the Maharajah's death she went home to England and took up nursing again in the Midlands.

'It always astonishes us that Western girls ever get married,' says the irreverent Dr Karan Singh, Maharajah of Kashmir. He was just nineteen when he married a thirteen-year-old girl, Asha, granddaughter of the Prime Minister of Nepal and last of the Rana dynasty. But then Indian girls are grown up by the age of twelve or thirteen. The Maharajah of Kolhapur gave his only daughter, aged fourteen, in marriage to Tukoji Rao, Maharajah of Dewas, with strict instructions to his son-in-law: 'My father-in-law says that if she is disobedient, I am to beat her with a shoe, and that the shoe shall have nails. But I shall not do this . . . I shall send her back to Kolhapur and the Maharajah can beat her himself.'

When Dr Karan Singh and his wife were married in 1960 in Bombay, they had only met for half an hour. The bride was carried by eight servants on a silver palanquin while eight maids in vivid red saris went ahead waving auspicious white horsetail whisks. The groom waited, dressed in a light pink shirt, tight pyjamas, a brocade coat, a red turban and diamond jewellery. His father wore his emerald and diamond crown with matching sword.

The newly-weds played a game of dice with ivory pieces as part of a delightful little Nepalese ceremony and, of course, the bride won. After the wedding ceremony a black goat was lifted and swung over their heads to avert the evil eye. There was a great party with diamonds glittering and bubbles winking in gold and crystal glasses as champagne flowed till dawn.

Dr Karan Singh sensitively described how, at two in the morning, 'after we had taken off all our jewels and brocades we realised that we were, in fact, very young strangers. And thus is was that we became man and wife.' The marriage worked and Karan Singh is still hopelessly in love with his wife and writes her love poems, his romantic soul intact despite a battering in politics.

In aristocratic families marriage is still arranged in a business-like way. When both sets of parents have decided that their children are compatible, then the couple's first meeting is usually a stilted tea in the marble lobby of a large hotel. The young couple will eye each other demurely. The girl will hardly speak, and will keep her eyes on her mango juice.

The present Maharajah of Jodhpur's wife was quite put off at their first meeting. It had been engineered by his mother, who thought he was 'getting on' at twenty-five. Time he married. She happened to have found the perfect wife for him in Hemlata, daughter of Rajah Sivraten Deo Singh of Poonch, a state in the north-west which is now in Pakistan. There had been a shortlist of girls, but her son, an old Etonian, and attractive to women with his diffident charm, long eyelashes and easy grace, never took to any of them.

'Mummy,' he would complain, home from Oxford, his head full of girlfriends entertained in the discotheque he ran in England, where he wore velvet trousers and coloured shirts; 'not another of these meetings . . . looking at a girl as if she were a goat or a cow and not a human being.'

Friends in England did not help. When he went back to Oxford and told them about his mother's efforts, they were appalled. 'For God's sake, Bapji,' they pleaded, 'don't marry someone your mother or the astrologer chooses for you.' Bapji, which is a family pet name meaning son of the ruler, Gaj Singh, Maharajah of Jodhpur, was in no hurry to get married and somehow kept putting it off.

But the Rajmata, visiting a local baron's family, liked the girl. Brought up by her grandmother, Hemlata was natural, spirited and fun. The women got on, driving together in Dehra Dun.

A meeting was arranged in the government Ashoka Hotel, a vast pink palace famous for conferences. 'I know you are scheming,' the Maharajah told his mother, and went along most reluctantly. In this unromantic atmosphere – bureaucrats rushing about with folders under their arms and looking self-important – the young couple were supposed to make one of the biggest decisions of their lives.

Hoping to catch the Maharajah's eye, Princess Hemlata offered him some biscuits. 'I passed the plate to him, but without even looking up, he said "No thanks," and I thought, "How stand-offish, so aloof; I am definitely not going to marry that snobbish man."' It was a disastrous meeting for the relatives.

After the unfortunate biscuit incident Bapji went back to Jodhpur, to his chess, his golf, his music and his cars. He had taken over the running of the vast art deco palace when he was twenty-two. 'I was more or less alone in this house with all these large rooms,' he says solemnly, appearing from behind a screen with decorative Chinese birds and flowers in the royal apartments.

The private sitting room is pretty and relaxed; the coffee table is covered with glossy French and Swiss art magazines. You could be in a country house in Gloucestershire, except you are overlooking formal thirties lawns where precision is overwhelmed by a marvellously uncontrollable profusion of pink, orange and white bougainvillaea, and peacocks strut around the wickerwork chairs. He is surrounded by yapping dogs.

The Maharajah's wife is away in Jaipur, their frisky chitzu called Simba hops onto his lap. The servants hurry in and out, respectful but not obsequious. 'Your Highness wanted to know the rate for the dollar today . . .'

He has the engaging poise of the old Etonian but is not overweeningly self-confident. He tends to be a bit solemn, his BBC Radio 3 accent is pleasant without being clipped. He seemed so Western in his creamy cool twill jacket and cords that his ethnic habit of clearing his phlegm neatly into a brass pot was disconcerting.

There are friends staying from Oxford days. They tend to be bright, amusing and well connected: Hal Charteris, son of Lord Charteris of Amisfield, and publisher John Rickardson-Hatt – so discreet he is sometimes known as Reticent-Hatt, but does appear at fashionable weddings in *Tatler* and publishes unusual travel books.

Lunch in the palace is old English; first partridge with redcurrant sauce, peas and cauliflower in a heavy white sauce. The Maharajah rings a crystal bell for the second course: rice, curry, lentils; then crème caramel and delicate carrot halva. Monkeys are busy swinging about in the grounds and Simba is eating a ballpoint under the lace tablecloth.

Like many men, the Maharajah claims he had very little to do with his own marriage. He has a nice blend of dry, low key humour, 'My mother, wife and her uncle all schemed together. I had very little to do with it.'

However, one day, long after the Ashoka incident, Hemlata's uncle rang him up out of the blue. 'He is large and jovial but tends to get rather agitated. "Hemlata is to be married," he said.'

The uncle, 'a wily old character', went on: 'This poor, innocent girl. Her whole future is at stake . . . not at all happy.' The Maharajah smiles, remembering the childlike deception. 'Clearly she had to be rescued. He had trapped me.

'I put my bargain to him. I said, "Can you arrange a meeting for us without anybody there?"'

He agreed. The couple met again, this time in a little Indian Fiat car which they have kept to this day out of sentiment.

'I was very apprehensive; you have to look at physical compatibility. You start with minimum expectations but I liked Hemlata's personality. I felt she had a rich spirit. I was taken with it. Then you grow together and learn to love each other.

'We sat in the car for ages and talked it over logically. The older you get the fussier you are and that is why young marriages are encouraged; so we came to a conclusion.' They were married on 19 February 1973. Some friends in England were disappointed that Bapji conformed.

It is a lively marriage. 'Her uncle played another trick on me. He warned me: "Look out, Hemlata has a fiery temper." This was not true.'

The Maharani is no subservient Indian wife. 'Hemlata,' her husband says, 'can be a little too dignity conscious.' What attracted him most was her ability to get on with people and her sense of fun, a good foil for his own earnestness. She can be a little bit schoolgirlish; their friends have memories of a skittish Hemlata having some success wrapped up in a sheet haunting nervous guests and she loves practical jokes. On another occasion a rather randy guest who was drooling over some Indian girls he met at a party in the palace was promised a date with one of them later that evening. When he got to his suite, the beautiful creature was shy and he courteously introduced himself, coaxingly asking her name. To his mortification the girl threw off her sari revealing the gardener. From behind the curtains came the laughter of members of the Jodhpur dynasty.

As a couple, the Jodhpurs are in demand, socially fashionable. A Japanese photographer trying to get a romantic shot found them looking far too formal and solemn like a Deen Dayal ancestral court photograph. 'Maharajah, look with love at your wife,' he kept saying, 'just for a moment.' The Maharajah is amused; the results give him an untrue podginess, a little like the outdated Air India symbol of a dumpling maharajah.

There are two children, a daughter, Shivranjani, born in 1974, who wears track suits with navy piping and a gold ring in her nose and likes reading Enid Blyton, and Shivraj, the heir, a little fat Prince who has thrown away his tiffin box. At dusk they came bounding in to see their grandmother but first charmingly touched her feet – a custom in India: when it is dusk, and the lights go on, you acknowledge your elders.

They have been posing for Italian Vogue – *Bimbini*. Servants carry their tennis racquets to the courts, their soft drinks in cans, and remain to pick up the balls which go out. When the weather is cold they skate along the corridors past snarling stuffed tigers and leopards hunched in the alcoves, defensively baring their teeth.

Soon the family will move to a house on the hill outside Jodhpur. The thought of moving out of the palace sustains them all. 'I am going with them, they say they refuse to move without me,' the Rajmata says complacently.

Around the private wing of the palace at Jodhpur, whether the young Maharajah is seeing a lean, dynamic Air Force Commander – 'I've got the video for you, sir,' or an archivist from the Metropolitan Museum in New York who wants to talk about transporting a seventeenth-century tent for a Festival of India in America, you can always spot the Rajmata's shadow hovering.

She passes the time letter writing and taking her grandchildren out, and on holy days paints symbolic red feet and hands on the white marble steps to honour the gods. They are a series of rather delightful little feet, hands and swastika signs, which at first look childlike but have all been delicately done with stencils to celebrate Diwali, the festival of Light, when fireworks from every rooftop in Jodhpur splutter their sparks into the sand. She continues to guide her son.

If all this gets too much for Bapji, always courteous, restrained and mature, he is too wise to say so, but he will admit that he does slip out of the palace through a secret door; and you sense the great pleasure he gets from peeking through the slatted blue blinds to the hill where he hopes for some privacy.

9

Giddy Abandon

THEY DANCED on floors of long-seasoned Balkan oak to the music of Jack Hylton and Vincent Lopez. Geraldo and his Gauchos introduced them to the tango and the rumba, and in Deauville Monsieur Max was the master of the complicated Scissor steps. Laughing girls wearing gardenias jived with the Princes till dawn to 'Alexander's Ragtime Band' and 'Everybody's Doin' It'. They loved night clubs like Les Ambassadeurs, The Embassy and the Kit Kat and the jazz of the Californian Ramblers.

It was thought important for the young maharajahs to learn to dance well. But first the Turkey Trot, then the giddy abandon of the Charleston and the Black Bottom. Their guardians were not at all sure that this shimmying with young flappers shedding hundreds of beads from their twenties frocks was a good thing.

The Maharawal of Dungarpur had dancing lessons in Brighton. 'I remember one night, being taken by Prince Victor, he had been my father's class fellow, to a dinner party and then we all danced the foxtrot and listened to jazz at his flat in Kensington. It was easy. I loved it.' But his guardian, Mrs Benn, was not so happy about the young Prince's dancing. 'We were sitting in the Rembrandt Hotel and she turned to her husband and said, "Bob, I don't like this young man being taken to dancing school more than is absolutely necessary." Of course she was frightened I would become attracted by night clubs and caught by a pretty woman.'

Dungarpur's night clubbing was watched closely by Mrs Benn. 'She gave me a good talking to, saying severely, "You are a young man; you should not blot out your reputation in any way. We want to see you going back as a good Ruler."' The young Prince listened but to this day he can reel off the names of Englishwomen who made an impression on him as good dancers at his palace. Lady Lothian apparently was a real mover, so too was Lady Ogilvie and Lady Glancey could shake a mean leg. When the Maharawal became Ruler, he had his own State band. 'I had a Goanese bandmaster. He's a millionaire now, a first class chap.'

The Prince of Wales liked watching glamorous Tallulah Bankhead and Lady Mountbatten swooning about the dance floor with young maharajahs in silk jodhpurs. They sashayed and swirled to 'I Can't Give You Anything but Love, Baby', crooned by a favourite black singer.

The Coronation of King George V was a glorious excuse for a tremendous number of maharajahs to leave their states and come to London. A Russian orchestra played in the Savoy ballroom which had been decorated in white and gold for the Coronation 'Ball of the Century'.

It might be three in the morning when a peckish prince demanded Russian caviare, best Beluga, plovers' eggs at a guinea each, clear turtle soup made from creatures weighing over 600 lbs, frogs' legs, stuffed oysters, bird's nest soup and out-of-season strawberries at 25s. a dozen.

When the Maharajah of Rajpipla's horse, Windsor Lad, won the Derby, he simply changed his booking for dinner that night from twelve to a hundred. Often Mayfair restaurants had the mixed whiff of curry and incense. One attentive floor waiter went to India for six months as a maharajah's pampered guest.

On a whim one of the Princes ordered woodcock bécasse au fumet. It was wheeled to the table on a silver platter, served, smothered in brandy and flambéed, but then, indolently, a plump wrist waved it away. 'I'm not hungry,' he shrugged, turning to his guests, 'but I loved the show.' 'Oh your Highness, too witty,' simpered some of the women, secretly thinking how the rejected fowl could have kept them going in their South London flats for a week.

They liked to drink 1911 Montrachet, 1921 Château Latour and loved Château Yquem. It appealed to their taste for heavy, sweet puddings like their own native carrot halva; but they found Neige au Clicquot, a sorbet of cream and 1906 champagne of the widow, an elegant refresher.

Others were philanthropic. After a lunch with the King at Buckingham Palace, the Maharajah of Patiala insisted on dropping in on a Salvation Army hostel and left a handsome gift in cash to be shared amongst the residents.

The good flower shops never had enough orchids. Mimosa and carnations were shipped in daily from the Riviera for the Princes constantly fell in love. A legion of girls: telephonists, nurses, balloonists, waitresses, night club singers, chiropodists, trapeze artists, beauticians and dancers were whisked to the Ritz and Claridges, to Henley, to private boxes at Ascot, to Cartier and Asprey.

First, kisses in the backs of gold and ivory trimmed Rolls-Royces, next dozens of red roses, then lavish presents, finally proposals. Suddenly these Sandras, Jeans, Normas, Joyces and Kittys were given names like Lotus Flower, Light of the Moon or Goddess of the Sun and became Hindu princesses. Patiala liked his girlfriends to have the names of flowers, Marigold, Rose, Daisy, Violet, Hibiscus. He also liked to pierce their ears himself.

Girls who, in London, had found the Princes more exotic than they could admit, were often horribly disillusioned when they got to the Maharajah's palace and found a senior, respected Indian wife in control. Their new husbands who had seemed so sophisticated and attentive in the Kit Kat Club and Ciros now seemed dismissive, expecting them to go quietly to the women's quarters, do their puja and listen to wailing Indian music on a gold plated radio.

Their Prince would laugh and chat in Hindi or Urdu with

his native wives and mistresses and the new, fairly unsophisticated wife felt like a prisoner. Of course, there were some very successful marriages to foreigners, but these were done on a correct, formal footing, not in a London nightclub on a heady whim.

Prince Haroun, son of the Nawab of Bahawalpur, was having freshly squeezed orange juice in his hotel suite in London and reading the newspaper when he saw the equivalent of a stunning page 3 girl. But in those days it was a beauty queen, Katherine Scott, aged sixteen, and fully clothed. She had just been to the J. Arthur Rank charm school and won a screen test with Ray Milland. The Prince rushed out, ordered every rose in the florist's and proposed to this railway porter's daughter from London; they were married three weeks later at Caxton Hall. 'I didn't know he was a Prince,' she said innocently. 'Everyone knew him as Harry in Fulham.' Her father said he could not go to the wedding because he could not afford to lose a day's pay.

The Nawab of Bhopal, Mahfooz Ali Khan, was enchanted by Marjorie Mayling, a seventeen-year-old waitress. As in every good fairy story, he had to make sure that her love for him was genuine and that she was not just a gold digger. 'You won't love me any the less because I am poor, will you, Moti Pearl?' he wheedled. When she got to Bhopal and saw his ice-cream palace and vast array of servants, she burst into tears. But eventually she left India, happy to give up everything and go back to work. No longer Princess Haseena, but nor was she still a 'two cod and chips, love'; the waitress had new poise.

Telephonists had to cope with calls and whimsical messages at all hours. A prince's 20-page cable gave detailed instructions as to what his favourite wife should be wearing to greet him on his return from Europe.

The maharajahs came to the best jewellers in London, Paris, Rome and Geneva. Asprey of Bond Street, which began in 1781 as an ironmonger's in the lavender fields of Mitcham in Surrey, by the middle of Edward VII's reign, offered gold, diamonds and the most famous fitted dressing-cases in the world. Suites of ivory inlaid furniture, made by Sir John Betjeman's father in the 1920s, were ordered by the Indian Princes

The Poet Laureate was never drawn to the family business but appreciated its artistic traditions. In 'Summoned by Bells', he captured the world

> Of shining showrooms full of secret drawers
> And Maharajahs' dressing cases.

Cigar smoke circling opulently, the maharajahs would stroll in after lunch with their wives or current girl friends in expansive mood. They never wanted anything less than 18-carat gold. Those were the days of horse-drawn traffic; broughams, phaetons and dog-carts, all with footmen, drew up outside Asprey's imposing front with its handsome windows. Before lunch young Guards officers would call in wearing their long black frock coats, escorting actresses from the Gaiety, Daly's and other theatres. Any sybaritic whim could be indulged, and Asprey kept open until well after six so that customers could call in on their way to a party in order to buy gifts.

A Bahawalpur Prince, terribly Anglophile, smoked a pipe, wore tweed and ordered dozens of onyx and lapis lazuli desk sets as handy gifts. Another Maharajah was a hypochondriac who ordered a crocodile skin case with twelve of the smallest possible glass jars and pillboxes, each with an 18-carat gold lid. Ladies' dressing cases in brass-inlaid Bengal wood were fitted with crystal jars, glove stretchers, secret drawers for jewels and gold coins, even folding candle-branches.

When you walk into Asprey today Sloane Rangers behind the counters in their stand-up stripey collars wait for five o'clock to strike. Huge gold camels, Kuwaiti pearling dhows in silver gilt, 18-carat gold palm trees with leaves of green gold and garnets as fruit standing on rose quartz, all come as rather a shock. But the top jewellers must be adaptable. Now it is the princes of the Middle East, in the next decade their market might be Pago Pago.

One Maharajah came in and asked Lewis Insole, a young

jewellery salesman, if he could have a diamond bracelet made up like an eternity ring. Flights of fancy whisked Mr Insole and the bracelet out to India and he was dreaming he might even become acting deputy to the third assistant on his return. In a languid desultory way the Maharajah pointed a jewelled finger at one of the designs, worth about £1,000 in 1930. 'That will do.' 'Thank you, Your Highness,' Mr Insole said, 'we will get on with it at once.' 'It!' growled the Maharajah. 'It? Don't be ridiculous, man, I want twelve of these bracelets.'

Teak trunks for five of the wives of the Maharajah of Patiala were simple enough, each one lined in blue velvet fitted with solid silver wash-bowls, soap dishes, hand-basins, and tooth-brush holders. The bottles for pouring hot water had tiger head spouts and the 'goesunders', the coyly named chamber pots, in one-eighth inch silver.

The maharajahs had an eye for whatever was in fashion. They loved art deco design, then known as 'moderne' or 'Jazz Modern'. The palace at Jodhpur has suites with cocktail cabinets, 1930s angular walnut veneered dining tables and chairs, pristine and glossy, hardly used. One almost expects Fred Astaire and Ginger Rogers to come prancing into this lavish Hollywood setting.

Sotheby's held a sale in Monte Carlo which did justice to the Maharajah of Indore's hardly used moderne furniture. His great aluminium bed fetched most. Designed by Louis Sognot and Charlotte Alix, it was bought by a Frenchman for £58,333, four times its estimated price. Yves St Laurent bought a pair of lamp stands designed by Muthesius and four tubular chrome chairs by Luckardt. Amused and intrigued, the bidders had never seen such perfect examples of the Jazz Modern style.

Indore, who loved America and two of whose wives came from the United States, shunned the taste of his fellow Princes who, urged on by Residents, furnished their palaces like grand English country homes. Instead in 1930 he commissioned the German architect Eckart Muthesius to furnish his palace and design it in completely Modernist style. Some of the most avant garde designers of the day such as Le Corbusier, Eileen Gray and Emile Jacques Ruhlmann were commissioned. The results were novel. Le Corbusier came up with a tubular chaise-longue covered with leopard skin, while Ruhlmann created a splendid macassar, ebony and chrome desk for the Maharajah in the shape of a fan. Indore's son Richard Holkar, who designs jewellery, has inherited the same sense of style and flair for good modern paintings and furniture in the 1980s.

There has always been a constant trafficking to India of young men in pin-striped suits. Polished, articulate and with sharp watchful eyes they know how to conduct themselves well in the palaces and represent the great dealers like Sotheby's, Christie's and Spink. They may have a History of Art degree, have specialised in the Mogul period, or be experts on Indian miniatures. Their lament is the lack of knowledge Princes have on their *objets d'arts*. Had the Indians conquered Britain, would memsahibs have learnt to do the Indian dance with eyes rolling and would there have been true appreciation in stately homes of the little elephant god Ganesh, eating with fingers and speaking Hindi?

One Indian dealer used cunningly to ride his bicycle to a nearby palace and the Maharajah, feeling sorry for him, heaped *objets d'arts* into his basket including a little Fabergé. The dealer changed into a smart suit and took a 'hopping flight' to Bombay and then on to Amsterdam to sell it. Nor is it unknown for Indian gentlemen with sturdy, unobtrusive suitcases to gather in Geneva for lucrative and secret transactions with dealers from South Africa, Britain and France.

The fate of some of the Baroda jewels has been as intriguing and inconclusive as the Royal Family's wistful enquiries about the haul of jewellery in the hands of the late Duchess of Windsor. It is an irony that two women who shared the admiration of a prince as well as a sensuous love of jewellery should end their days in darkened sick rooms far from their homes in America and India.

The present Maharajah of Baroda's father married a stunningly beautiful woman, Sita Devi, as his second wife. Devi and the Gaekwad threw superb parties; he would wear the pearls and his wife the diamonds and a silver sarong. When asked about the fate of the family jewels her stepson just gives a philosophical shrug. Sita Devi used to invite guests to touch the 30-carat sapphire on her finger for luck before a race at Ascot.

Some of the Princes had no idea how much jewellery they possessed and did not keep inventories. Then they became upset when there was no record. The Maharajah of Nabha, Sir Pratap Singh, sued the Crown jewellers, Garrard, for alleged detention of eleven parcels of jewels including 175 diamonds, 203 rubies, 11 pearls, 256 emeralds and 19 suites of emerald, ruby, diamond and pearl necklaces, bracelets and earrings. John Davis of Garrard said the matter was settled. 'No need to bring that up,' he countered briskly. 'Indeed one of our staff went out to stay at the palace.'

In 1978 the great excitement was to be the sale of the Nizam's jewels. For Harry Winston of New York, Greek shipping tycoon Stavros Niarchos and the boys from Bond Street it was a rare chance to include on their shopping lists trays of rubies and emeralds, an emerald encrusted box owned by the last Tsar, a seven-strand pearl necklace with ornate diamond clasps, 370 pearls, sword hilts and turban aigrettes but not the Jacob diamond. The sale was expected to raise about £11 million for the thirty-nine beneficiaries of the Jewellery Trust, of which the Nizam was one. They were all to be bitterly disappointed when Mrs Gandhi's government imposed a last minute export ban.

The Princes are apprehensive now of the authorities in India who can swoop on their palaces without warning. Anything over a hundred years old is an antique and cannot leave India. The Maharajah of Mysore's household had trouble exporting an ivory screen which he wanted to sell, so it was made into a cumbersome modern bed and shipped off.

The Maharajah of Bilaspur wanted to sell his silver gilt throne through Spink. Their man in Delhi was appalled when he was taken to see this elaborate chair, with its own incense burners, locked up in a dirty garage whose door had to be broken down. The throne arrived in small pieces and had to be put together again before it was sold to a coin dealer.

In one palace, sixty Kashmir shawls were wrapped up with naphtha mothballs between them. They had not been looked at for forty years and fell apart; the stench was awful. Only one was vaguely intact but it had been used as a napkin and was streaked with mutton fat.

A sad figure today, one Maharajah comes wandering into the rarified atmosphere of the St James's salerooms. He examines the stone gods from Kandy, the tapestries and miniatures. He talks to one of the deceptively baby-faced young men alert to a bargain as a hunter on point. The Maharajah produces from his pocket a miniature and a small ivory piece and there is a brisk but superficially elegant chat about reserve prices. Then the Maharajah asks if he may borrow £200. It is fearfully difficult for anyone in India to get cash out of the country; many Princes have Swiss bank accounts and all are immensely discreet. They swear you to secrecy about where they are staying in London.

Their tailors in Savile Row and St James's would post orders to India: 'Boy, take this to the post office; it will cost 12/6.' The messenger would send off one waistcoat with fancy back, one Shetland beaver collar overcoat and a new sea otter fur collar to the Maharajah of Patiala's orders in the summer of 1921. His two Harris tweed suits and four pairs of socks and garters costing £53 were picked up by a servant in London; they were hardly needed in the heat of the Punjab. The Maharajah of Baroda's fancy striped flannel short lounge suit with silk linings was the height of fashion in 1900. This cost £6 18s 6d and five years later his check tropical angora suit cost two shillings less. In 1933 his tailor was proud to make him a first quality blue satin GCSI mantle – when he was given the Grand Cross of the Star of India.

Eric Lobb sits in the bow-fronted, St James's first floor office of the cobbler's shop started by his grandfather. It has burgundy brocade wallpaper and aristocratic brogues with shoe trees in them beside his desk. The shelves below are still piled high with maroon shoeboxes and craftsmen in white aprons work on fine leather riding-boots for pop singers who want to take up hunting.

These days the names on the boxed orders tend to be European. D'Abo and Baron Von Barknow, rather than Patiala and Dungarpur. There are framed cheques from 'HM's Private Bill Account' for a modest £21.50 and one on Earl Spencer's House Account signed by his wife Raine.

In 1939 as a young man fresh from Cambridge, Eric Lobb was sent with Charlie, the old fitter, to call on the Maharajah of Nawanager who was staying at the Savoy for the War Council. 'He had ordered some polo boots and tennis shoes. A hand-made pair of shoes in 1939 cost seven guineas and a good suit fourteen.'

Charlie and young Mr Lobb presented themselves at his suite at 11 o'clock in the morning. 'His Highness came wandering out into the corridor, still in his dressing gown, and I remember he had an enormous stomach and no teeth. But in came a little boy with a silver salver and on it were the upper dentures. Then in came another little black boy with the lower dentures on a silver tray. We produced his monogrammed velvet slippers and again servants individually held each one to the royal foot.'

Manicurists, tailors and cutters, jewellers, art dealers and gunsmiths trooped in and out of Mayfair apartments and hotels with princely orders beyond belief.

Famous gentlemen's hairdressers in Mayfair like Trumpers and Norton were most distressed when they discovered what had become of one costly order of exclusive hair oil. The Maharajah said that his valet found it very effective on his riding boots.

❧ 10 ❧

Laughing Maximum

TWO SMALL HANDS shoot out from under a white tablecloth to take monogrammed glasses of orange squash from a brass tray; the bearer bows. The royal grandchildren, and the Maharao of Kotah, are watching *Hum Log,* a weekly series about an Indian family rather like *Coronation Street.* Food is served in front of the television set. His Highness the Maharao, Kotah's seventeenth and last ruler, loves television. He likes the huge set switched on in the palace dining room in the early evening and watches until the final news bulletin around eleven.

Silver-haired, slight and painfully shy, it is hard to imagine him shooting all those stuffed tigers lined up in the palace corridors, prone in evocative, sepia photographs or as growling busts in the billiard room.

Kotah was unique for its river hunts. Queen Mary was taken by the famous barge along the river Chambal where crocodiles yawned on the rocks of the river banks and tiger, panther and bear scurried in and out of the jungly gorges in the cliffs. Nowadays Maharao Bhim Singh would rather see the bared teeth of the women in *Hum Log* and savour a glimpse of life below marble stairs. The twins, his daughter Mimi's eight-year-old children, are 'Highness's pets'.

Hum Log is a story about a lower middle-class Indian family. The young couple live with his parents; father is hardly ever seen, but there is a querulous mother, a Delhi Hilda Ogden but without the same warmth, who blames her daughter-in-law for everything. Her dim, inept son has been to the Middle East. Not only has he been unable to get a job in Saudi Arabia, but he has also been duped out of 10,000 rupees, the family savings. The son, now home again in Old Delhi, can only shake his head foolishly while his mother screams at his young wife. The power of the Indian mother-in-law is not exaggerated.

Her Highness Princess Mimi keeps up a cheerful commentary on the goings-on of this hard-pressed Indian family in *Hum Log*, which means 'Us'. 'Sometimes,' she says, 'it is so comical we are laughing maximum.' There is a strong possibility that *Hum Log* may be coming to Britain, and India may buy *Coronation Street*, uniting lovers of curry, chips and tea.

The Maharani, a statuesque woman who lives in a separate wing of the palace, has fluttered in to join her husband for dinner and for *Hum Log*. A Bikaner princess, she was engaged to him when he was seven. The Bikaners and Kotahs were friends and keen on the marriage, which took place when she was fourteen. Her husband ruled over the sixth largest state in Rajasthan, with almost six thousand acres and a 17-gun salute.

She is modern and outspoken, blaming a lack of knowledge about sex for some of the fearfully unhappy marriages in India. Coming from a sophisticated background, she found purdah difficult, but being 'a bit of a tomboy', used to skip off to tiger-shoots with her husband and hide in the machan.

They seem more like old friends now than husband and wife. The Maharani is much more social, being seen at parties given by another gay granny, Gayatri Devi, in Jaipur.

The twins come up for air. The mother in *Hum Log* is not being at all nice. Conversation stops, and all eyes are on the screen as she is seen hurling her daughter-in-law out of the house, to roam the bazaars . . . and who knows what will become of her . . . until the next episode. It is news time.

There are no full-time newscasters on Indian television. Often it is read by civil servants who just fill in for a few bulletins. They wear any old thing, short-sleeved shirts, old cardigans, and certainly no makeup, then scuttle back to the Ministry.

There never seems to be anyone on the studio floor saying 'sorry love, but you're going to strobe in that white shirt'. However, the Prime Minister, Rajiv Gandhi, himself an elegant dresser, has ordered the television presenters to smarten up. Viewers are hoping this does not mean that Salma Sultan will have to remove the rose from her hair.

News from Britain looked grim. The miners' strike was on, their leader, Arthur Scargill looked hostile, his eyes more resentful than usual. In India, land of fatalism and poverty, long-drawn-out strikes are yet to come. Against the intoxicating backdrop of Rajasthan, blue skies over the Kotah deer park, the purple of the bougainvillaea spilling onto the palace terrace, England in winter seems as grey as an eastern European capital. Delegates in mock British Warms bustled self-importantly into Coal Board talks. Miners' wives were seen hurrying to supermarkets as if brussels sprouts had just arrived from Helsinki.

The news has reminded 'Highness' of Europe and he recalls the sweetness of violin music at a concert. His voice is extraordinarily quiet but everyone listens respectfully to what he has to say. After the tomato soup, fish and spinach arrive the twins suck their thumbs and disappear under the table again in case they are sent to bed.

A film is next, but Hindi movies are unlikely to shock eight-year-olds. Violence is allowed, but it might be a one-legged stuntman carrying two children along a tightrope over a motorway while the baddie shakes one end of the rope. Sex is usually symbolised by monsoon rain, or, in moments of heightened excitement, a girl might put her arms around a chair or a tree, even a radio. Rumour of a glimpse of thigh sends hordes of young men scurrying to the cinema. Goodness has to triumph. The Indian wife scores over her rival, a sexy 'Westernised' girl in a glittering bikini doing an old-fashioned samba. Distinguished, responsible Indian film makers Ritwik Ghatak and Satyajit Ray must abide by the censor's strict ruling. Meanwhile melodramatic kitsch thrives and the studios keep pumping out 'collective fantasy' for a hungry audience of millions.

The servants are patrolling the table like mosquitoes, never glancing at the screen. The butler, who is also Major Domo, is a swooping figure in a military beret. He bends low to hear His Highness. It is praise for the pudding, a light and subtle halva made from green gram and pure sugarcane juice.

In some palaces there is a feeling that everything is crumbling, including the staff, but not in Kotah. Guests are met at the station by an ADC, the court physician, the major domo or his deputy, and Amer, an adorable old retainer with a snowy white beard who does not know how old he is: 'We go by horoscopes, but I am coming to work for Highness in 1928.' He says he is sixty-eight or seventy-two, a good age for a villager in India. Like many old people in the villages he is scared of tape recorders. There is a superstition that if your voice is recorded, it may be the last time it is ever heard.

The Maharao lives in a yellow-grey stone newish palace, called Umed Bhawan. It is a bit like a Midlands town hall or railway station. Designed by Swinton Jacob at the turn of the century, it is comfortable; the guests' suites lead onto a terrace and the family drawing room is Edwardian.

The servants are almost too attentive, wanting to sew buttons on, take buttons off, 'make bed', 'run bath', 'do dhobie'; you race to keep up with them. A bearer is asked to hold a mirror for a second. He is dumbfounded: I look lak that!' It is the first time he has ever seen himself. It is touching he is so endearingly surprised.

At 5 pm, the main ADC, a superior, silver-haired person, appears. 'His Highness says "please to join him for evening drive."' The twins are tearing about on their bicycles, chased by highly strung, pampered pedigree dogs.

A blue Ford van draws up in front of the palace. The Maharao gets in, takes the wheel, the ADC and bodyguard jump in the back. He drives through the palace grounds, once planted with lime and mangoes but now military cantonments.

'Just here, once you could see a panther or a bear.' His Highness leans forward, a flash of gold in the dark as he rests his wrist with its mint-thin watch on the steering wheel. He

seems mesmerised by Kotah, now India's fastest growing indus-
trial city. The fluorescent light has come to Kotah and almost
every hut is selling tyres.

He knew what would happen to his city. Forty years ago he
was flying low in a single-engine plane with his twelve-year-old
son over the Chambal river gorges looking for possible sites
for hydro dams. Now there are four; not even the Maharao
could prevent the main Thermal Power Station being built close
to the city on the windward side.

In the middle of the ugly development, the gold-tipped,
fluted domes of the eighteenth-century ancestral palace rise up
triumphantly gleaming above the high factory chimneys. The
Jersey cream filigrée balconies sit sublimely dignified above the
flowery archway with a carved elephant and mahout on either
side. Their trunks are almost touching, and behind them a
princely wedding procession unfolds in delicate green and sepia
murals. Haunting, royal 'shehnai' music is played on a wind
instrument which once welcomed Kotah rulers returning to the
airy elegance of the palace after a battle with marauding Moguls.
Once this palace held 15,000 servants and royal aides, now
about a dozen people look after the museum with its celebrated
Rajput miniatures, inlaid mirror work, ivory and ebony carvings and frescos.

The traffic hoots unmercifully. Indians do not park, they
drive and stop. His Highness always stops and turns back by
the High Life tailor's and a shack selling nothing but blue plastic
washing up bowls.

Near the palace it is rural again, figures gathering round dried
cowpat fires; and the air smells of incense, honey and dried tea.
Farm labourers huddle on the bullock cart, luminous figures in
white, smoke curling up from the bidi cigarettes on a leisurely
journey home. Home to a cowpat, and a charpoy.

'As far as we know he is an elderly man with white hair and
a walking stick. I have seen him myself because he was murdered
in the first floor bedroom which is now my suite.' Honey, the
Yuvrani of Kotah, is swinging on a hammock, reading Leon

Uris's *The Third Reich* and talking in a matter of fact way about the ghost of a British major who haunts her. Her husband is son and heir to Kotah, Yuvaraj Brijraj Singh. He is not only divorced, but married a second time. 'I chose my wife myself,' he says gleefully, aware of how unusual this is in India even amongst sophisticated Princes.

He spotted his second wife, Uttara Devi, a Cooch Behar princess, when he was sitting on his bench in the Lok Sabha, the Parliament. She had come to the visitors' gallery to hear her aunt, the stunning Maharani of Jaipur, leader of the Opposition Swatantara Party, make a speech. The Yuvaraj, normally an enthusiastic MP, heard very little of it and afterwards raced to be introduced to her niece.

The Kotah family kept quiet about the Major. They felt he might jeopardise the marriage of their son who had fallen head over heels in love. But even a ghost could not stop this romance.

'Luckily our families agreed, and even more important, our horoscopes were right. But my husband had said "Whatever, I am marrying her."' The Yuvrani smiled. You sense her pleasure still at this unconventional love match and her escape from 'arranged love'. The wedding was in 1963, a year after they met.

The ghost has a delightful place to haunt. The Yuvaraj and his wife live in a nineteenth-century palace, Brijraj Bhawan, which was once the British Residency. It is a big, white-pillared colonial-style house with wickerwork chairs on the verandahs and green lawns, set high above the river Chambal. When the chintzy hammock swings forward, and squinting through the bougainvillaea, the half-finished bridge suspended above the river looks like modern art, and women seem to be doing their washing dangerously near the dozing crocodiles.

Talk of ghosts seems foolish in such a pretty English-style country garden, where cornflowers and petunias cluster round the white marble nymphs. Roses and herbaceous borders cover the spot where in 1857 the two leaders of the rebels who murdered Major Charles Burton in the Residency were hanged.

The ghost of Major Burton has never rested. The trouble is

he never goes off duty. He wanders round the palace, and if he catches a servant asleep gives him a quick slap on the cheek. He is the only restless soul around on summer afternoons when it can be like a furnace in Kotah. 'Ah,' says the Yuvaraj, who is as flamboyant and outgoing as his father is introspective, 'the old Major has never appeared to me. We Indians have a belief that there are three types of humans – and the type Deva Yoni are never bothered by spirits, so I guess I belong to that group. But you know he is a benign ghost.' In India ghosts are accepted as a part of life although susceptible guests at Brijraj have complained of distinctly 'discomforting and oppressive feelings'. Queen Mary, however, seemed unperturbed by Major Burton's presence. Another more recent guest was France's President Giscard d'Estaing. He wanted to shoot bear.

The Yuvrani, a bright, lively woman, opened the door into her bedroom, which is pink and full of flowers. 'Now this is where Major Burton was killed . . .' The idea does not make her in the least nervous. It is a lovely room in a house of European comfort. Jade lamps are used, and not chipped or covered in dust; paintings of flowers are mixed with Kotah ancestors; there are lots of trendy cushions scattered on beds; deep windowsills where their nineteen-year-old daughter curls up to study Russian. Her room is blue-sprigged, very Liberty. Meissen and Sèvres sit on highly polished mahogany furniture, and the Yuvaraj's Panama hats and slippers are delightfully battered.

Their only son, Bhanwar Ijyaraj Singh, is twenty-one and doing computer science in America. 'I worried at first,' his mother smiles. 'We have only one son, and we didn't want him to lose touch with India. We have so much to give him. But we needn't have worried, he loves Kotah and comes straight here from America, not bothering to stay in Delhi.' This surprises the Yuvrani, who in delicious understatement, explains: 'There is not a lot of social life in Kotah.' They are a close family and like nothing better than supper on a tray in the Yuvaraj's study, an enticing jumble of books to the ceiling, paintings, binoculars, cameras, music.

'A quiet evening for us is no problem, we are a family who love books.' In his personal library there are 6,000, '. . . on everything: sex, religion, quite a few of them have been read by me,' the Yuvaraj says, tongue in cheek. In many princely libraries there are beautifully bound books in deep red, blue and green morocco leather, their fine pages trimmed with gold. Princes love to tell you how many books they own, but they often look too pristine to have been enjoyed. Unlike himself, the Yuvaraj's children have never known the other, princely India, and now must struggle for their own careers and 'kismet'. His own kismet will be inheriting his father's palace, Umed Bhawan, which he will turn into a hotel. It would be ideal. But they will go on living in their present home, with the Major.

Time to leave Kotah, and at the station, waiting for the Frontier Mail to Delhi, the palace staff line up on the platform for farewells. Old Amer poses for a last picture. A man is combing the track for stones with something which looks like a giant egg whisk. A white goat waits contentedly on the platform beside a baby with hair standing up in perpendicular spikes. The mother has a glittery comb in her hennaed hair.

A warm day; there are pillows for the back; the railway inspector comes in and wants to put the heating on. 'Please lock door,' he urges, 'dacoits, dangerous, desperate men who kill and rob.' He leaves. The door of the air-conditioned, first class carriage creaks open; the train has not even left the platform. Giggling like schoolchildren, the palace staff push the septuagenarian forward, 'Madam,' the Major Domo says, 'he is ready for London.' The old man, wearing his best orange turban, is like a teddy being pulled and pushed by boisterous children. He enjoys the joke, he has never been anywhere except the palace and the station. Some dacoit.

11

Sardine Sandwiches and Pink Gin

'HIGHNESS IS WAITING FOR YOU.' It was Lt-Colonel Fatesinghrao, Gaekwad of Baroda, bearded, eyes half raised in quizzical amusement at surprise that he should personally be at Ahmadabad Airport with its signs saying 'Prohibition of Liquor and Intoxicants like Opium'. He had just flown in from Bombay, 250 miles away, and the chauffeur was ordered into the back seat of the Fiat so that the Gaekwad, wearing driving gloves and looking rather splendid, could take the wheel for the drive to the palace.

The polished, navy sporty Italian car overtook cheerful lorries painted blue with pink flowers and signs saying, 'Please Pass, OK.' There were green fertile villages, fields of cotton near the Sabarmati river, donkeys pulling carts full of purple shiny aubergines, an unlikely pink teashop and a murky Vadodara (Baroda) soda fountain.

He was everyone's idea of a Maharajah: 'Highness' to his staff, 'Fateh' to his family, 'Jackie' to western friends, Mr Gaekwad or Mr Fatesingh in India, the military title is of the romantic cavalry regiment, the Baroda Lancers. Gaekwad means protector of cows rather than herdsman, a sacred role in India. Family emblem is the elephant, symbol of strength, on an orange crest.

Baroda was one of the big five Princes for whom the Raj fired a 21-gun salute; the state measured 8,135 square miles.

The present Maharajah is fifty-six, one of the richest men in the world, a widower, conservationist, industrialist and author; loves pretty women, reading Chamberlin's Entymological Dictionary, cooking and intrigue.

He chooses a picnic stop under a cool banyan tree for sardine sandwiches and pink gin. It is by a riverbank where buffaloes are having a swim and baboons hop about irritating the goats with their curly fantails. The Gaekwad is proud of his heritage; 'not the trappings, but it helps to know who our forefathers were and that they enjoyed power uninterrupted.' He is directly descended from a remarkable great-grandfather, thirteen-year-old Sayaji Rao, son of a peasant farmer.

The old Gaekwad of Baroda was deposed in 1870 by the British, who alleged that he had tried to put poison in the Resident's grapefruit juice. A successor had to be found. Three illiterate village boys were brought to the palace, and as in fairy stories and legends, the fairy queen asked them three questions. Actually, it was the Dowager Maharani of Baroda, the shrewd widow of the deposed ruler's father. When asked why he thought he had been brought to Baroda, the eldest boy said, 'To see the sights.' The youngest said he had no idea really. But the third, replied: 'To rule Baroda.' This boy from a village two hundred miles away would bring Baroda out of the Middle Ages, his enlightened rule lasting for sixty-two years until his death in 1939.

In the care of an English tutor he was quite quickly reading Jeremy Bentham and Plato in the Greek, but preferred the adventures of the Mad Hatter in *Alice in Wonderland*, which he had translated into Marathi. He later suffered from dreadful headaches and felt his brain was always racing, so he slept badly. He was a kind man with twinkling, humorous eyes who insisted on education for the poor. He disliked the cruelty of the caste system, and cared for the Untouchables. He was against purdah and tried to introduce a form of separation for unhappily married women. The Baroda children used to tease their mother about having a husband who was so keen on divorce. They remember her trying to remain 'dignified and huffy, but soon overcome by that wonderful silent laugh, her face contorted, her body shaking like a jelly, and not a sound out of her'.

She disliked purdah too, and was a fine shot, once bringing down two herons without moving from the table where she was enjoying an al fresco lunch. The solid gold cannon, weighing 280 lbs each, gleamed during their reign, and the royal couple were carried through the streets in a solid silver and gold coach drawn by white bullocks.

As an old man, the Gaekwad had little time or need for British advisers. He had great fun sending a telegram to a departing Viceroy: 'God speed. May India never see the like of you again.' He was frequently followed by Scotland Yard because he met Indians in Paris on his way to Gstaad and St Moritz, giving them money to campaign for Independence.

The present Gaekwad is still seen by the people as the much loved heir. They worry about his health, and remember his first speech. 'I was seven. I said: "I hereby declare open the Baroda Civil airport." Friends tell me I haven't stopped talking since.'

The chauffeur puts away the picnic hamper, sure-footed camels with bells, looking like disaffected dowagers at saletime in Harrods, pad snootily past the open boot; boys drive bullocks under the shade of the mango trees, their horns painted pink and blue as a mark of ownership; an old man with a white moustache in a stunning shocking-pink turban, lies sleeping as for dead in the shade of a broken down car.

Only the women are working in this high heat; girls in orange, green or yellow saris, delicate and straight-backed, are in the cotton fields, sorting the cardamom seeds. Others are working on the roads, where these slight creatures can be seen splitting huge boulders.

Baroda, and the car swings through the elaborate palace gates where fires are ritually lit at night by the chowdikars. The gardens are overgrown now, the massive bronze bull in the centre of bleached grass, clumps of bougainvillaea and old rose beds surrounded by spindly orange and mango groves. The cricket ground is still cared for but the tennis courts are neglected.

It is a handsome Indo-Saracenic palace, with Mogul domes and a Carrara marble entrance. It is called 'Laxmi Vilas' which aptly means a residence of wealth. Built in 1907, it is a living palace and belongs to the Maharajah. The Gaekwad's Australian friends write 'Laxmi Villas' on the envelope, giving this Arabian Nights palace a comic, homely touch. It is three times the size of Buckingham Palace, the kitchen two miles from the dining room. At one time, the Gaekwad used a scooter to speed from the bedroom to his meals.

The servants are waiting. 'Aha,' Highness smiles as he spots his personal valet, one of four, standing on the steps, 'the Professor is here.' He looks rather elegant with his gold ring and dashing yellow silk hat, the colour being the clue to seniority. The Professor is the one to step forward; hands clasped he gives a neck bow.

Once the corridors would have been lined with impressive house guards in white breeches and dark royal blue jackets, standing to attention. The 600 servants dwindled to 300, and today the Gaekwad has a staff of 150 who are devoted to him. 'I don't need so many servants,' he says, 'but I must look after these people.' He has set up a trust fund 'to save them from a cruel fate should anything happen to me'. It is still one of the best-run palaces in India.

Not long ago there was a cleaner, mechanic and chauffeur for each car. For some reason, perhaps just because it was chic, the Fiats all had Italian chauffeurs. Today the Gaekwad has a fleet of twenty runabouts and trusty old Ambassadors, India's national car. He also drives a black Bentley.

In common with many of the Princes the Maharajah has a relative on the staff: this is especially wise because, though astute, they are not usually self-seeking. C. K. Gaekwad, Staff Officer to His Highness, has a mournful profile, is guarded but polite.

Dusk comes quickly in Gujarat; the air was still warm when the Venetian chandeliers first lit the gilded ceilings, the soft sages and Tuscan golden beiges of the Italian marble in the entrance hall. A carved, trumpeting elephant symbolically guards the Maharajah's apartments, and he goes slowly up the ornamental staircase past mosaics of peacocks and exotic birds. He is surrounded by a press of servants who scurry around excitedly because 'Highness is home.' His visits are all-too rare. The older ones remember Fatesingh as a little boy.

'As a child I would run through the corridors and talk to the servants about the Mahatma, and for ten years I drank only goat's milk,' he recalls.

Today the servants are affectionate though respectful, for he has an unassailable dignity and dislikes sycophancy. His Baroda social secretary and political secretary both take dictation before dinner: 'It travels with me round the world.' The Professor pours Highness a pink gin.

There is a strange secretive stillness in the corridors. The guest wing seems a good mile walk. It has its own minaret and huge palm trees swish and whisper their secrets in courtyards of pale marble where goddesses hold lamps in graceful poses by bubbling fountains. Victorian lamps light paintings of sad-faced, pretty maharanis and mahogany cupboards are full of delicate Venetian glass, Dresden bonbon dishes, a turquoise tortoise by Wedgwood. There are coy Western nudes, a huge picture of a mortified tiger, and a Lalique vase is a crouching Venus.

The style is still there with the crystal chaise-longues and ivory chairs where vicereines rested, pale skins softened by Tiffany iridescence, and ticked an embossed card marked 'elephant, car or horse' for the morning. The mother-of-pearl tables and Chippendale escritoires are not just for decoration, they are polished and used. The carpet woven in pearls and diamonds has gone but there are some Persian ones left for the cheeky squirrels playing in the Palace.

Tea is being served from a huge silver teapot and the tray is covered with a Belfast white linen cloth trimmed with lace. Thin tomato sandwiches are served, biscuits clutter a Sèvres plate with its delicate green border around a centre of pale pink and red roses. Oranges and papaya are presented on stately dark blue and gold Limoges china with the Baroda elephant crest.

There is a call from London and three servants line up to take you to the telephone, using the lift though it is only one floor away. Dust flies up from the cushioned seat. Two more servants are holding the phone. 'Haw-law, London, haw-law' – the line is quite dead. Perhaps a telex? The palace code is Fate-in.

Servants softly moving about in white and orange turbans are so quiet that the sound of running bath water makes you start. There is almost too much attention; it is like being a doll they cannot wait to call in the morning, give her tea, wash her clothes and put her in the sunshine on a mahogany chair. At night they cover her bed with mosquito netting draped from an ornate hook, then lie crouched outside the door throughout the night as the blades of the fan whirr from the embossed ceiling.

The palace locksmith magically finds a way of opening an over-stuffed Western suitcase, and the royal electrician gets the power back on when heated hair-rollers fuse part of the palace. There is a comforting glow again from the thirties marble bedside lamp with its satin shade.

The menu on a gold-embossed card is brought on a silver tray with a note from the Gaekwad: aperitifs in the Blue Drawing Room at 7. There are different reception rooms for guests, depending on rank. This is a pretty, feminine room, with its green and pink velvet chairs and a painting called The Music Lesson. Swallows fly in and out, hiding in the chandeliers.

Courteous, with large expressive eyes and greying at the temples, there is still a leisurely elegance about the Gaekwad's movements. When he was a young man the sculptress Alfreda Brilliant thought him an Indian Apollo, 'such a magnificent body'. Now, overweight and worn by illness, he is watchful, weary, cautious, but his mood is relaxed and there is many a kindly wink and roar of laughter at some piece of news: 'Aha.' Or being asked a favour, 'Yes, yes,' as if it were nothing.

His mood in Baroda is different: responsible, serious, none of the flamboyance of the parties in Sydney and Delhi, the fun of being pursued by beautiful Austrian diplomats bringing orchids from Kathmandu.

To guests who are inclined to go into raptures about the palace the Gaekwad says with irony, 'What inheritance, I say? It all belongs to the people. They still come to me with their problems. "My wife has run away." What can I do? They want help with land deals, marriages, it's amazing. They appeal to me, "If you can't do it, nobody can." Yet I should be worried if the people didn't come.'

Dinner with the family, and the Gaekwad's mother and one of his five sisters, who teaches at the University, chivvy him about his health. 'I am okay; no gins and tonics, but no lectures either, please.' It had been a bad year with shingles in the autumn, but he put himself in the hands of a group of young doctors at the Middlesex in London who tried out a new cure and it worked: 'I willingly agreed to be their first human guinea pig.'

The Maharani, a gentle, contained woman, mutters, 'It worries us old people you falling ill so often.' But her son laughs, 'What is all this; you are only fourteen years older than I am.' He has just undergone an endoscopy. 'In India they don't knock you out. They argue that they can't tell if they are hurting you with an anaesthetic.'

After dinner there is a film show of the legendary Baroda performing parrots who do all sorts of tricks with cameras and bows and arrows. They ride bicycles, walk tightropes, drive little silver cars; there is even a dramatic scene where one of the birds is run over by a car with a feathered driver at the wheel. A parrot doctor rushes in and examines the victim who is carried off by parrot stretcher bearers. Their finale, a salute fired from a dinky silver cannon, brings tears to the eyes.

In the small hours there is still a lighted window in the Gaekwad's wing of the Palace where his library overlooks the lawns originally laid out by Mr Goldring from Kew. Tonight he will not be reading his beloved Macaulay but will spend much of the night, as he has others, signing degrees by hand. 'My average is 250 an hour, four a minute.' He is Chancellor of the University of Baroda where there are 25,000 students, but fortunately they do not all graduate at once. Some fail, but

5,000 will get certificates signed by the Gaekwad, who has just been given his own academic laurel: 'I am a doctor now.' He seems very pleased. 'A doctor of literature.' He may read a few pages of the dictionary before he goes to sleep. He is a fusspot about language, says he never reads it without learning something new. It certainly influences his speech, 'Etym. dub.' he will say about some questionable character – etymology dubious.

The next day he presides at the University and then there is cricket in the afternoon. Under a striped canopy languid socialites gossip. 'Saw Ayesha at Ascot,' and 'Are you going to the Melbourne Cup?' But the Gaekwad has no time for idle chatter now and watches the game on the perfect ground intently. Cricket drones on until servants spread pink damask cloths on the wickerwork tables for tea in floral bone china cups.

In one courtyard of the Laxmi Vilas Palace, snuggling under a palm is a family of tortoises. Before dinner the Gaekwad visits these Palace favourites. Hunter turned conservationist, Jackie Baroda is very attached to this little group; he likes their style. 'As soon as the creature is born, its eyes are open and it immediately has to start fending for itself. There is total parental detachment.' It sounded like the upbringing of Indian and English aristocrats.

'Precisely,' says His Highness.

❧ 12 ❧

Weddings Spell Hope

INDIAN WEDDINGS are like a child's fairy story; never mind the lack of love, nor the importance of dowry. For five magical days it is a celebration. The bride must bring a handsome dowry and in princely families this once included hundreds of maids, for the bridegroom's pleasure.

In poor families, girls may be harassed by their mothers-in-law for 'not bringing enough presents' like a television or a refrigerator to the marital home. In Bangladesh in one year, 80 per cent of suicides were by brides, sometimes pushed accidentally close to a frying pan by their mothers-in-law so that their saris would catch fire.

The verdict on 'bride burning' is always suicide. To try and prevent these tragedies engendered by poverty, communal marriage has been introduced in Kerala, where recently 175 couples from poor families were all married at once. The only gifts were brass bowls from the state.

But weddings spell hope and more children. In the poorest, dry, parched villages, canopied pavilions in patchworks of vivid reds, blues and yellows dotted with silver mirrors go up over a stage with strings of fairy lights. It is a distraction from poverty.

Whether the couple come from a city slum or a palace, the groom arrives in gold brocade on a white horse with gold strands falling from a crown in white and gold. He is surrounded by musicians; girls in stunning jewels, earrings and necklaces of rubies and emeralds dance provocatively around him, skirts whirling and flashing jewelled reds, yellow and deep blue, studded with gold and mirrored dots. The bells on the ankle bracelets chime in with the flutes and tablas; coins are strewn along the groom's path and grinning boys carry trays of heavy coconut sweets on their heads.

The doll-like bride, smothered in garlands of marigolds, wearing diamonds in her ears and nose, emeralds and rubies on her toes, will be waiting at her parents' house, scented and demure. She listens as the singing and dancing gets nearer.

The groom is formally accepted when sugar is placed on the bride's tongue and she is given a brocade shawl by his family to cover her hair during the marriage ceremony. The bridal couple stay in a sort of trance on a dais. The guests eat themselves silly, and there is a smell of freshly boiling rice. Brass pots are filled with water.

The bride has a mark of red sandalwood paste on her forehead where her hair is parted, to symbolise a straight virtuous path as a wife; earrings heavy in diamonds and gold remind her not to listen to gossip; a heavy necklace keeps her head bowed in humility; a jewelled ring in the nose, for some reason, is a curb on extravagance; ankle bracelets mean best foot forward in marriage. Instead of the Western wedding ring, the bride is given bangles which she wears up to her elbow.

On the third day, the couple are anointed. In the bridegroom's case it is all rather lighthearted as married women, with lots of giggling, cover his head, knees and feet with turmeric, rubbing it in with a mango leaf for good luck. The bride has less fun as five matrons of her husband's family rub the clingy yellowy spice into her skin. They are really doing a hawk-like check on her body, which must be perfect.

The couple spend at least three days enduring several stages of the ceremony before they are finally married. The Maharajah of Jaipur – the glossy Jai – got very impatient during the elaborate ceremony for his third marriage to Gayatri Devi, telling the holy man, 'Get on with it.' The Ruler of Mysore found it an awful bore. His wedding meant missing a polo match, and wistfully he confided during a break in the ceremony, 'I am getting no exercise, except a bit of skipping which I do on the roof of the palace.'

The astrologers play a dictatorial role. If they say it is auspicious for a couple to be married on a certain date at five in the morning, one dare not go against them. And no matter how sophisticated a young couple or how travelled outside India, they obey the stars.

For foreigners like Sally Holkar, the decorative American wife of the Ruler of Indore's son Richard, the whole ceremony was extraordinary. Headlines in American newspapers had screamed: 'Average American girl marries Indian prince.' They had met at Stanford University where they were studying political science and fell in love.

Richard was twenty-one and Sally, with her gentle manner, and ingénue earnestness, nineteen. 'We had known each other for a year and a half, what with my ardent pursuit and Sally's rejection,' Richard said drily. 'Marriage was inevitable.' They wanted a wedding in India, fixed a date and sent out invitations to friends around the world. They had been married first in a registrar's office in Dallas, Sally's home town.

But to their consternation, the priests and astrologers in Indore would not hear of their marrying in August. It was not auspicious. Richard got a cable in America saying 'No, absolutely not.' Telexes cancelling the wedding were frantically sent. It was a bit bewildering for Sally, coming from a rich oil town where the only possible reason for a cancellation might be not enough room at the airport that day for the guests' private Lear jets. But she dutifully went along with the new date suggested by the astrologers.

There was a five-day party, then, Sally remembers ruefully: 'I had to go through a two-day purification ceremony sitting by a cow dung fire in a white sari for hours and hours, watching it burn.'

Sally, who speaks in a slight sing-song Hindi voice, is very much a softly-spoken Indian wife. She has a great admiration for Indian women which is not patronising. 'I want to instil into my daughter Sabrina some of the femininity of Indian women.'

A jet-setting couple, they moved round the world for several years, bought a house in Grasse and renovated it themselves. When it was time to have children, they decided to go back to India. Richard and Sally laugh when people are surprised by their choice. 'But we felt this was the place for family values.'

Curiously they chose Bombay, that very commercial city, centre of the Indian film industry. A city where the holy man in his saffron robes keeps well out of the way; even the beggars are professional, maiming their children to make the most impact as squeamish Western tourists sweep into skyscraper hotels overlooking the city's handsome crescented bay.

'My father thought India was no place to live.' Richard Holkar says the late Maharajah was anti-British, but was also disenchanted with his own country after Independence. 'He married three times, two of his wives were American. They lived in Connecticut – but he came home for large doses of Kashmir.'

Richard Holkar, who is amusing and sophisticated, picks his son up and shows him how to smoke a cigar. 'He must be the only blond Yuvaraj in India,' he says.

Sally does not wear the sari but sticks to trendy Western clothes. She has varnished toenails, but wears very few rings or bracelets, although her husband designs jewellery. 'I am making bread and butter as a designer,' he says. She has the languid air of social women in India, a cultivated reluctance to be excited, with much running of hands through manes of hair. She has recently had a bad bout of hepatitis. An excellent cook, Sally Holkar has published a book called *Cooking for Maharajahs* containing lots of recipes with slyly mischievous titles.

. She describes her first meeting with her cook in India soon after she married. 'His name was Dulji and he looked like Mahatma Gandhi. I call him "maharajah" which means great ruler.' Together, Dulji, his sacred thread looped over his ear and round his toe to ward off evil spirits, and the girl from

Dallas in designer jeans concocted provocative Indian–American dishes.

There is wit and innuendo about some of the recipes, not so much the Camel Hump Kebabs as How to Separate the Boys from the Mince, and Cobra Cooler, not for mother-in-law. Instead she gets Eldest Daughter-In-Law's Dinner. The book was a glossy success, being bought by their princely friends the Gwaliors and Udaipurs.

Sally was a bit disappointed at first when some of her dishes received no comment. Not even an enigmatic 'mmh, this is interesting'. But she quickly learnt to wait, like other eastern wives, for the sound of a belch, the highest compliment.

She reads Hindi and American stories to the children. Had she stayed in Dallas, she might be on her second or third divorce by now, she thought, and wondering whether to have a purple or yellow Cadillac.

13

Not a Sob Story

'I AM,' said the Maharajah of Kashmir, 'the Tony Benn of India.' Poet and politician, he is fifty-four, ascetic, but unlike Anthony Wedgwood Benn does not have staring eyes or smoke a pipe. He seems in no hurry to overthrow the government, sitting contentedly in his flowery Delhi garden, throwing biscuits on the grass for his black and gold labradors.

The darling of the intellectuals and the aesthetes is wearing bi-focals, the traditional Kashmiri hat which is like a stewardess's cap, and a brown close cloth suit. He likes to be known as Dr Karan Singh: 'Any moron can be a Maharajah,' he says, 'but not every moron can be a doctor.' He is a doctor of philosophy, who writes abstruse papers: 'I am very into Hinduism,' and attends esoteric spiritual summits.

Karan Singh is gregarious and charming, with a wicked wit, the very opposite of his father, a withdrawn man of paralysing shyness and remoteness. Sir Hari Singh, Maharajah of Kashmir and Jammu, sadly became best known for being the victim of a blackmail case in 1919.

The 'Mr A case' had all the ingredients of a twenties play. Main character was the wealthy 24-year-old Indian Prince, with hooded eyes, large nose, owner of an aeroplane finished in silver, two dozen polo ponies and pearls as big as gull's eggs. He was in Europe for a first visit.

Enter, in Act I, the villain, the caddish Captain Charles

Arthur. He had met the Prince during sick leave in Kashmir after a spell in Mesopotamia. Against all good advice from the British Resident in Kashmir, he becomes ADC to Sir Hari, the heir apparent.

The scene shifts to London where the Prince and his Indian secretary are at the Viceroy Ball in the Albert Hall. In the box next to their own is a beguiling, pouty, full-bosomed woman dressed as a grasshopper. Mrs Maudie Robinson, wife of a bankrupt bookmaker, having chosen the optional fancy dress, did not have to work very hard to capture the Prince.

In Act II, the couple are in bed together in a Paris hotel called the Hotel St James and Albany, off the rue de Rivoli. It is Boxing Day morning. The peace is shattered by a loud banging on the door. Mrs Robinson gets out of bed, wiggles across the carpet and opens the door. A man with a fake black moustache leaps in, points to the bed and, with the grimness of a cuckolded husband, says, 'Now I've got you.'

The Indian Prince was described in court by even his own counsel as 'a poor, shivering, abject wretch'. He immediately consulted his ADC, supposed to be a trusted adviser in times of trouble. The heir to the throne could not afford a scandal. The ADC advised that his only hope was to write a couple of cheques for £150,000. which he would see went to the right people. One cheque was eventually stopped by Sir Hari's lawyers but the other was divided between the blackmailers, who, of course, fell out.

In the final Act, the scene is a courtroom in the year 1924 in London and Lord Justice Darling is about to hear the 'Mr A case'. The Prince's real advisers manage to keep his name out of the newspapers, but this only whets the journalists' appetites. In the dock is Mrs Gertrude Robinson (courts always like full names) although she is known by her friends as Maudie. She says she has a home in Chapel Street, Belgravia. She simpered to the judge that her dream had always been to go to the East, where she would be the Prince's mistress, because 'some of these people can give a little more happiness than white ones'.

There was some discussion also about a little engraved silver box with a razor in it. The Prince had asked Mrs Robinson to shave all her body hair, because that was the custom in Kashmir and Jammu, and she had agreed.

Closing scene, Mrs Robinson in tears; one of the villains is sent to jail. The British rally heroically round the Prince, embarrassed that such a thing should happen.

On 23 September 1925, Hari Singh succeeded his uncle. There were gallant attempts to make his coronation memorable but unfortunately the Mr A case had a much more vivid appeal than the new Ruler's plans for education and employment for his people. The sad fact is that he was not really a womaniser and was a rather solitary figure. He had married a simple girl and Karan Singh was their only child. He was born on the 9 March 1931 in suite 318–19–20, the entire third floor of the Hotel Martinez in Cannes, in a room filled with flowers and overlooking the Mediterranean. The Maharani, a poor village girl, was just twenty-one.

When the baby heir, who weighed 9 lbs, was six weeks old the family sailed to India on the P & O steamship *Kaiser-i-Hind*. Karan Singh grew up in Kashmir in the white palace the size of Versailles, its domes reflected in the Dal Lake amongst the floating gardens and pretty houseboats. The palace is surrounded by blue hills topped with snow, looking down over valleys of bright green paddy fields, sheets of brilliant yellow mustard and carpets of dwarf irises on the lake. There was tea on the lawn near the huge Chenar trees with deep purple irises in clumps beneath; they even grow on the roofs of the tall, dark brown wooden Hansel and Gretel houses which look as if they might topple into the water.

He has a dim memory of playing with diamonds as a child. A Hindu boy he was educated by Irish nuns and studiously gazed at technicolored pictures of the Virgin Mary and Jesus and thought them lovely and unusual. In 1942, he was sent to the Doon School in Dehra Dun. He was so upset at the thought of leaving Kashmir that he fainted into the arms of one of his mother's ladies-in-waiting.

Karan Singh was miserable at Doon, hated the coarse blue

blankets and damp blue sheets. But rather as Gordonstoun has been good for the Queen's sons, he thinks Doon prepared him for the shock of no longer being a pampered prince and being catapulted into a competitive world as plain Dr Singh.

He was never good at games, but could hold a croquet mallet and enjoyed biffing his opponent's ball into the beds of dahlias, delphiniums and hollyhocks surrounding the lawns of the British Residency; and he did captain the school chess team.

He was growing up in the turbulent climate of India's adolescence on the eve of freedom. Nehru as a Kashmiri Brahmin was a hero to the young Karan Singh.

He vividly remembers Pathan tribesmen invading Kashmir in 1947, egged on by Pakistan. The electricity was cut off at the palace and as each border town was taken his father would wince inwardly, 'as if something had died in him'. There were tears in his eyes as he muttered, 'We have lost Kashmir.'

The Maharajah appealed to India. V. P. Menon flew to Kashmir and Sir Hari Singh signed the Instrument of Accession with the Indian Union. Indian troops then moved into Kashmir repelling the Pathans and the Maharajah decamped to Bombay where he died at the age of sixty-five.

Nehru, who was a father figure to Karan Singh, intervened so that the boy could be appointed Regent of Jammu and Kashmir at the age of eighteen. But he never had any power and went into politics in 1967 to become the youngest Cabinet Minister ever at the age of thirty-six, cynically aware of the effect of 'being a real live maharajah' in the travel industry when he was Minister for Tourism.

There are two sons, one in America, another in college in India, a married daughter and a thoroughly modern, Nepalese wife teaching philosophy in a woman's college.

Karan Singh is one of the few really intellectual maharajahs. He is a kind, compassionate and humorous man but has always been impatient with fellow Princes who moan and long to live in the past again. He compares them with the Romanovs and admits to having a preference for European royal families,

finding them more stimulating. Like some academics, he becomes impatient with those less gifted and nostalgic for a feudal
past.

The fate of the Princes, he says, should not break any hearts.
It is true there have been stories of hardship and a lot faced
psychological problems. 'But theirs is not a sob story,' he points
out with a tired smile. 'It does not evoke a well of sympathy.'
Brown eyes bright with the question, he asks, 'Does it matter
what you had in your palace? "Oh my Lalique," the Princes
say, but there are starving millions in India; you must get things
in perspective.' He criticises them as foolish, inflexible and
pompous and for believing in bonds and promises made by the
Raj. He also happens to think that the British left India one of
the ablest civil services, rigid and colonial, but impressive.

When Mrs Gandhi decided to do away with the Princes'
privileges in the early seventies he was the only Maharajah who
volunteered to give up his privy purse. He says the title meant
nothing to him but admits he has a social umbilical cord with
Kashmir and goes back for six weeks every year.

Another Prince, the Rajah Lalit Sen of Suket, a Ruler with
delightfully white teeth, took the same line. The irony was that
the richer the Princes, the more petulant. Their behaviour has
eroded all credibility. Suket did not give up his princely acres
in the Himalayas, growing rice, wheat, apples and peaches. But
he too felt that the princely privileges had never been earned.
He was in parliament and an MP for sixteen years. It was he
who was instrumental in bringing the Princes and Mrs Gandhi
together, fixing sulky meetings at the Imperial Hotel. He believes it could have been much worse for the Princes and nobody
would have shed a tear.

By contrast the Maharajah of Gwalior is breezy and dynamic,
with all the confidence of a newly appointed minister in his
friend Rajiv Gandhi's reborn Congress Party. He is an abrasive
young man wearing the traditional white khadi and soft tweed
waistcoat seated at his desk in South Block of the Parliament
Building.

It is a large, gloomy office and he sits under a picture of Rajiv, who has appointed him Minister of State for Railways. In India, trains carry 10 million people a day; this is as tough as being Secretary of State for Northern Ireland. People rarely ring up to say the trains are running well or that they have noticed less violence in Belfast.

At seven in the evening there are still crowds of men waiting patiently in the corridor outside the Minister's office. Time means nothing. Some have been there for hours, sitting on white carved chairs: devious schemers and petitioners. Young men who look rather like the Minister, not the usual shuffling babus, wander in and out with folders of that peculiarly utilitarian buff paper you get in Indian offices.

It is clear the Minister is busy, but as he rocks back in his chair, you can sense also his euphoria at being in power. He cultivates a high-flying modern image, with scant regard for a royal past. He insists that his fifteen-year-old son, Jyotiiaditya, will be known simply as 'Mr Scindia, citizen of India.'

'These titles are an invention of the British, the very words His Highness are totally foreign to Indians; there is no Hindi translation. This British influence is not something our generation accepts very easily.'

When Mrs Gandhi was assassinated by her Sikh bodyguards, Madhavrao Scindia, ambitious aristocrat that he is, gave up a safe seat and campaigned vigorously in Gwalior in the December elections with his heart set on obtaining a seat in Rajiv's Cabinet.

On the campaign, he cleverly travelled in a bullock cart under withering welcome arches of dried bougainvillaea, and he skilfully played on the old feudal ties. Here in the villages of his ancestors he was happy enough when the people called him 'Highness', and 'Maharajah' while at the same time his 'son of the soil', and 'we are where we are through blood, sweat, tears and toil' approach went down very well. 'Unlike some princely families,' he says, 'we do not pretend to be descended from the sun or the moon.' Here there is a curling half smile. 'We are not aristocratic, we are farmers, peasant stock.'

His build is stocky, and agrarian. He is attractive to the crowd, with his large, dark eyes, and whether he is stepping out

of a private plane or a rickshaw, he has that cheeky ebullience.
Standing in a one-cow village, he stretched out his arms: 'Ah,
this is where I shot my first tiger.' Like the Maharajah of Baroda
he has been converted into an enthusiastic conservationist.
'Hunting once was an interest, not any longer, and polo is too
princely for me.'

In the shadow of the medieval fort, he lists what he has done
for his state, which is about the size of Portugal. Well, he
brought a television relay centre to the city, got the Taj Express
to stop there and also persuaded the Indian Air Force to base
their Mirage 2000 fighters at Gwalior and fly over the Jain
temples. This quiet religious sect who wear masks over their
mouths for fear of hurting any living thing in the atmosphere
do not find that their lives have changed. These achievements
might not be attractive in Dorset or the Cotswolds, but in rural
India, they get the votes.

He plays the prince with the common touch. 'Do you remember what you used to call my grandfather?' he asks a venerable
voter in the crowd with a white beard and a bicycle. 'Annadata,'
the old one answers. It sounds like an instruction for a computer
but it means – 'breadgiver': a perfect touch, the combination of
Prince and man of the people.

'Sure, the title is a great asset in an election,' he says. 'It
connects me with my ancestors and that generates a lot of
goodwill. It is very easy to be progressive, condemn it and say
it is a burden. It is my heritage of which I am very proud.'

This young man, known simply as the Scindia, comes from
a wealthy, princely family, one of the five meriting a 21-gun
salute. His mother, the 66-year-old Rajmata, is in politics too,
but in the opposition. Once a friend of Nehru's and an asset to
the Congress Party, the Dowager Maharani of Gwalior became
disillusioned and crossed the floor, much annoying Mrs Gandhi
in the process. She has not wavered since and is an industrious
party worker. Along with the Rajmata of Jaipur, another beautiful and determined granny in the politics of opposition, she
went to jail in the 1975–77 Emergency and has been unrepentant
ever since. It is all extremely embarrassing for her son, the

Maharajah, whom she calls Bhaiya, though he too once belonged to the Jana Sangh party which stands for Hindu absolu-
tism and conservatism, and was an outspoken critic of Congress.
In the last elections, in her white widow's sari and with her
distinctive madonna-like calm, she campaigned fiercely against
him but lost.

Mother and son have been locked in one of those bitter Indian
family feuds which leaves even their own advisers gasping. A
friend described it as 'a rather sordid struggle'.

Meanwhile the nineteenth-century Jai Vilas family palace in
central India, a riot of Tuscan and Palladian architecture, is
locked and desolate. There is dust on the gold leaf and in the
folds of the looped brocade curtains stitched with gold thread
in the white marble Durbar hall. But nothing can stop the
Viennese crystal chandeliers 'sparkling like myriad diamonds'.
Each of these neo-Belgravia colossal chandeliers has 248 candles;
only one other in the world is a rival, the chandelier in the Tsar's
Winter Palace in Leningrad. Twelve elephants were hoisted onto
the roof to make sure it could stand the weight. But the delicate
green ceiling with ornate scrollwork stood the test and the
chandeliers glitter against the delphinium blue walls.

The little silver train is still. Once it was the best known
model train in the world, delighting viceroys as it wended its
way on silver rails round the table. It was electric, and trundled
along to each guest holding nuts, fruit, wine, port and brandy.
It was ingeniously stopped by lifting the decanter off the last
two silver wagons. Viceregal visitors found it all rather comical:
'a pantomime palace . . . with its glass banisters . . . but very
comfortable'.

In the dining room there were silver fountains on corner
tables and an electrically illuminated rock garden. If there was the
slightest movement of a guest's head, the glittering swing of a
tiara, a crescent of servants in white tunics and crimson turbans
circled the visitor in an instant. Then with a speedy, but graceful
gesture which said 'I am here to be commanded', they swept
the ground with their hands and touched their foreheads. This
still happens in many palaces; in Jaipur, servants kiss Maharajah

Bubbles' toes, though other more liberal Princes disapprove.

The Rajmata's father-in-law, Sir Madhavrao Scindia, was a flamboyant and energetic Ruler. He had a mischievous sense of humour and liked to see his ministers act as beaters on a tiger-shoot, or work in jungle clearings in Gwalior's enervating heat. He dressed up as a rickshaw driver to see if the security at the palace was really watertight.

On his way to London he became ill at Marseilles with diabetic carbuncles. He was rushed to Paris where they operated but he died and all the clocks were stopped in Gwalior on that day, 5 June 1925. He was just fifty, and was cremated in Hindu style in the gloomy boskiness of the Père Lachaise cemetery in Paris near the tombs of Chopin and Rossini.

His son 'George', the present Maharajah's father, was nine, but ruled from 1936, dying in 1961 in Bombay aged forty-five on a night when there had been a fierce thunderstorm and frightening monsoon rain. His 41-year-old widow became the Rajmata – the Queen Mother, Vijayaraje Scindia. Her life would be ascetic from now on, devoted to her children and to politics.

Her son Bhaiya was sixteen when he set fire to his father's sandalwood pyre. It is always the tradition for the son to start the cremation. The following spring he left for England. Already he was showing signs of a bouncy, pushy personality.

He was expected at Winchester in the New Year but his arrival was delayed by the astrologers who felt the day fixed for his journey was not auspicious. And he found the whole environment of an English public school distinctly strange; he left after only five terms. He already had five A levels from the Scindia public school in Gwalior and went up to read politics, philosophy and economics at New College, Oxford.

Gwalior was astute enough to become alarmed when, in 1966, he was described as 'Oxford's richest undergraduate, owner of three palaces, fifty cars, with an annual income in India of nearly £100,000.' To offset the playboy image, he smartly disappeared into a simple cottage in Oxford to study, saying, 'People automatically seem to equate an Indian prince with a *dolce vita* existence . . . I am working very hard and I am deeply conscious of my obligations to my people.'

That same year, he married a lively and decorative eighteen-year-old, the chocolate box Princess Rajyalaxmi. Like many Nepalese girls, she was not only pretty but also rather bright and had been hoping to go to Cambridge. And she is still one of his main distractions, the other is music. He has a daughter, Chitrangada, now eighteen, but like many of the Indian princes does not think her education important.

'Daughters are lovely things, lovely to cuddle and always favourites with their fathers. She will get married,' he said.

Although Mrs Gandhi was amongst the 2,000 guests at the wedding, when she declared the Emergency of 1975 she clapped the groom's mother, the Rajmata of Gwalior, into Tihar jail, where she became prisoner No. 2265.

Her 'crime sheet' showed that she was imprisoned for smuggling foreign currency. But, the Rajmata says, 'My offence was opposing the ruling party.' As her jailers pushed her along the filthy corridors where flies and mosquitoes hovered over a hole in the ground which was the lavatory, past 'swarms of unkempt women, some with suckling infants stuck to their bodies like limpets,' she saw the Rajmata of Jaipur at the entrance to the condemned prisoners' section.

These two beautiful ex-Maharanis greeted each other with a bow just as if they were meeting at polo. 'Whatever made you come here? This is a horrible place!' Gayatri Devi whispered, slightly distrait and not realising how incongruous it sounded.

There was a little unconscious rivalry. Afterwards the Rajmata of Jaipur said, 'I didn't put weight on in jail, but I think the Rajmata did.' Both women are stoic in their refusal to talk much about the experience. The atrocities and suppression of free speech in a country which thrives on politics will never be forgotten. They were locked in their cells all day; when they ate they had to ward off the flies with one hand and the stench was almost unbearable after a lifetime in silken sheets.

Mrs Gandhi could do nothing worse. Putting two of the

Queen's ladies-in-waiting, the Duchess of Grafton and Lady Susan Hussey, in Holloway might be an equivalent. But Tihar was like the Bastille. Although the Western world was appalled to think of the two maharanis in such conditions, in India their plight was scarcely recognised except by those few who moved in high social or political circles; and they were mostly keeping their heads down throughout this turbulent time.

The Rajmata was bitterly disappointed by what she described as Bhaiya's first 'brief and jittery' excursion into politics, and he dismayed his mother further when he was lured back on the eve of the 1980 elections. There was an acrimonious exchange but the Scindia was resolute. 'As far as I am concerned this is the parting of the ways for us,' he told his mother. She failed to understand that for him it had to be the Congress Party if he was ever to be in power. Opposition parties in India have always been a joke, as if a transatlantic salesman chose to travel by Puss Moth each week instead of Concorde.

Their relationship has been sour ever since. 'The palace is not really important to me,' he says. 'I won't say it is a burden, but it just doesn't fit in with my way of thinking.' He and his mother did a deal over Jai Vilas because they could not agree about its future. The Rajmata bought it. There was a brief reunion when he was in hospital with a broken leg, and also, the Rajmata says, a police raid on her house in Gwalior while she was at her son's bedside. The Maharajah's agent seized a number of antiques, she claimed, and suggested that they had been stolen.

Nor were matters helped when Bal Angre, the Rajmata's closest adviser, was first arrested and then had his home vandalised. The house belonged to the family and on this occasion two chained Rottweiler guard dogs were shot and an elderly maid was evicted at gunpoint with her four-year-old granddaughter. Government authorities had to take over and have now put their own seals on the property but a nasty taste was left by the unexplained incident.

Friends of the family think that the Maharajah's wife, who can be awkward and meddlesome, could still help heal the rift between mother and son. But she does nothing. London friends talk affectionately of the Rajmata as Mrs Gwalior: 'a stately, intelligent, amusing lady; old fashioned and quite lively'. They took her to see a film in Chelsea and were worried because it was 'rather juicy'. But Mrs G. fell asleep. 'She would not have been shocked; purdah humour is very broad.'

Two of her daughters have caused her considerable anguish; the eldest married the Maharajah of Tripura in one of the most stylish weddings seen in Bombay since the war. But she was more unhappy than anyone knew and her mother still agonises over her death. 'She used to take sleeping pills and went to sleep after a party and never woke up.' She grieves and accepts the possibility of a deliberate overdose.

Her third daughter, Vasu, has been alone since her husband the Maharajah of Dholpur left her with a baby son about a year after the marriage in 1972. 'When an arranged marriage breaks up,' her mother said, 'the arranger never escapes a sense of guilt.'

A devout Hindu, she prays a great deal, lighting her oil lamps and thinking not unkindly about the prospects of her political enemy, Rajiv Gandhi. 'It will be a difficult battle,' she says. 'It needs guts.' About Independence back in 1947 she is more outspoken. 'The Princes were finished off,' she says, 'a class wiped out; so many different eggs broken to make a common hash called bureaucracy.'

Rajiv Gandhi has been Prime Minister for nearly two years. People were moved by his striking composure at his mother's cremation when he stood, like a soldier, in ethnic white with the high collar made distinctive by his grandfather. Around him was a continuous dizzying circle of crouched figures with petrol tins of ghee, adding more to the flames. Sometimes there was a quick, very rare shutdown of the eyelashes. This was the only hint of emotion. It could have been the smoke. The sky in Delhi which had been grey that day got dark and as he drove back to his mother's house everyone sensed an apartness.

'Rajiv shifting from Mummy's house,' said the government driver sweeping through Lutyens Victory Arch where the

names of World War I and II soldiers like Atkins and Brown
are engraved in the stone above the imperial flame.

The Prime Minister has a smiley mouth, a penchant for
soft leather slip-on shoes and he drives a red jeep. He likes
photography and classical music and has just moved into a
white pillared house of his own with rattan blinds, red and blue
Persian rugs and furniture in good taste, chosen perhaps by
his Italian wife Sonia. He is going a little bit grey above the
ears. Gone is the pudgy airline pilot fond of 'telly' and not
interested in politics. He listens a lot, does not go in for high-
flown rhetoric. He says in that quiet voice which compels you
to listen that he will streamline the bureaucracy.

He has been to Moscow and also to Washington, shaking off
the old Congress Party's antipathy to the New World. In
Washington, he stood before Congress, the world's youngest
Prime Minister, and stirred Republican and Democratic hearts
with the emotive words of the assassinated Civil Rights leader
Martin Luther King: 'I have a dream.'

He believes that the essence of India is her deep spirituality.
To criticise this gentle idealism is like saying that Mother Teresa,
of Calcutta, is motivated by worldly ambition.

14

Everything Which Moved
or Flew

A TUFT OF MARMALADE FUR, a white whisker, the twitch of an
ear. A steady eye is watching coolly from behind tall, yellow
grass. The spotted deer begin their nervous bleating, the alarm
call for the jungle. A feather of blue scurries into the scrub
squawking, peacock and porcupine are favourite appetisers for
tigers. The grey, silky, hanuman monkeys are skittish; they
have seen a striped tail from the top branches of the sparse
trees.

'Digar, Digar,' the mahout hisses. He gives the elephant a
good crack with a metal goad on its forehead with its painted
pink heart. 'His skull is so thick, more than 20 cm, it is
like a tickle.' Certainly the creature seems not to mind, and
moves forward gently. It has been gracefully picking its
way through dried-up river beds since dawn, whimpering when
it saw a crocodile and making a noise like a cistern as it im-
patiently whisked off huge fig tree branches and enjoyed the
milky juice. The jungle is moistly twinkling with a fresh minty
smell of lemon.

A young tiger saunters out; he pads along the sandy path.
Suddenly he yawns, gives a light skip, like a puppy, and is
gone. One of India's protected – there are about 3,500 left – he
is in a good mood; the rangers can tell he has just eaten.
Binoculars and a telephoto lens capture him flopping down
contentedly to sleep with his paws in the air.

'Guardsmen', little brown-black birds with flashes of red, are on duty. Had it been the year 1900, the jungle would have been filled with the excited shouts of the British officer Richard Meinertzhagen, as he fell upon his first tiger with a cry: 'Aha, my pretty puss,' dragged it into the open, and 'danced with delight'.

There was the inevitable photograph, of the pale sahib in his high-domed topee, right foot resting nonchalantly on the tiger's back as if single handed he had wrested it to the ground. The tiger looked as if it was asleep, its head arranged tastefully on its paws, a symbol of imperial conquest.

The Indian Princes and their British guests were dedicated hunters; that thrilling moment before a kill never failed to excite when monkeys were leaping, peacocks shrieking, deer shrinking and tigers swanking. But they were more restrained than some French aristocrats, Prince Wagram for one, who just had to kill something, in and out of season. His son said that could include 'partridges on their nests' and, if he could find nothing else, 'dogs and sometimes beaters'. Bagging a poacher was even better sport, leaving them 'quietly buried where they fell'.

Sport was an abiding passion for the British, hunting and polo for the upper classes, a bit of football for the lower orders. It was thought an important way of 'sweating the sex' out of the other ranks.

'Come and stay with us in India and we will arrange for you to shoot tigers from the back of elephants or elephants from the back of tigers,' Lord Curzon offered a friend in England as an alternative to boring old fox-hunting.

The Princes were clever hosts and artfully used special tape measures to give a flattering estimate of the tiger's size, never less than 10 foot for the Viceroy. Tiger skins, panther, crocodile were all shipped home by P & O steamer. The dead elephant's feet held umbrellas; tusks were used for gongs and the penis made a stalwart golf bag.

At first light, a tiger-shikar party moved off by elephant, into the jungle with hundreds of beaters and villagers playing flutes and drums, beating tom-toms. This was not ceremonial but a rhythmic movement to encircle the tiger and drive him to where the hunters were waiting. The atmosphere became tense and nobody spoke. The beaters moved rhythmically in decreasing circles. Dr Mohan Kautaria was once astonished, watching the sea of dark bodies, half-naked, coming nearer, beating the belt of trees.

'What did I spot in that sea of dark bodies but an absolutely white native. I turned to the Maharajah, but he said "shush". Then he winked and leant across: "That is the son of the Reverend so-and-so," he whispered, "our missionary."' There was another unfortunate incident when a tiger ate an accountant, Mr Thomas Henry Butler from Jubbulpore. He should have been secure in the machan, a little wooden hut in the trees and above the bait, a quivering deer or a water buffalo tied between stakes.

As the tiger came near, beautiful maharanis in jodhpurs took aim. As a courtesy, someone – the Vicereine or the Commander-in-Chief's wife Lady Chetwode – would be offered first shot. They may have looked frail with their porcelain skins and appealing in their becoming jungle skirts made by the dhurzie, but they would lie for hours on their stomachs resilient and elated.

Lady Audrey Morris vividly remembers a tiger-shoot with the Maharajah of Dholpur and her aunt, Lady Chetwode: 'We crept along very quietly and lay in wait. A lovely, huge black bear waddled up the opposite hill, two minutes later an immense tiger cantered by not more than ten yards from us. Aunt Star had first shot but missed it and it got clean away . . . An ADC shot it. It gave a mighty roar but did not fall, then volleys of shots followed and the animal rolled over as if dead . . . two minutes later it rose again and roared; another shot was fired, still it wasn't dead, they have most tremendous vitality. It rolled down the hill a little, Beryl put the last bullet in it.'

This tiger which seemed to live after it was dead was a beauty, 9 foot 7 strung out on a pole, as the bearers carried him away with twelve bullet holes.

The Maharajah of Gwalior was a dedicated and daring hunter. The summer palace at Shivpuri was about ninety miles from Gwalior. There the family had a tiger preserve and a hunting lodge called George Castle after the King.

They liked to watch their two dozen tigers 'gambolling like kittens', or a tigress with her 'yellow puff-ball' cubs. But sometimes the Maharajah had 'an irrepressible desire to shoot an animal of unmatched magnificence'. Seeing an enormous male tiger crunching some buffalo bones, he whispered in his wife's ear that he was going to kill it. His gun-bearer handed him his big rifle and he killed the tiger with one shot. The Maharani proudly described how swiftly the tiger fell: 'death seemed to pass in a single tremor along the spine and down to the tip of the tail, which twitched just once and fell still. By 1965 Gwalior had shot 1,400 tigers.

There were stylish hunters like the utterly fearless Maharawal of Dungarpur. 'Ah, I have felt a tiger's breath on my face, and when there were no roads near my palace, I used to ride out about fifteen or sixteen miles, shoot a tiger, come back and have breakfast.' The Maharajah of Bharatpur shot his first tiger when he was eight years old. The Rajah Kalinaraian of Dacca used to appear at a shoot on his elephant, stripped to the waist with a little white muslin round his forehead while a servant in the howdah held up an umbrella.

Ayesha of Jaipur, who looked so slight she could hardly be imagined holding a rifle, is now a conservationist, but before her conversion, she managed to bag twenty-seven tigers on the road to Damascus.

The Maharajah of Cooch Behar bagged 365 tigers, 438 buffaloes, 207 rhinoceroses and 311 leopards. Lord Glendevon remembered sitting on an elephant with 'Cooch' on a tiger hunt: 'The villagers had put up little archways made of palms "Welcome to our Maharajah" but he was sound asleep. They had gone to such trouble I had to shake him to wake him up. He drank too much but I liked him awfully.'

The Maharajah of Rewa was perhaps the most cavalier. He would relax in the machan and read, relying on his monkey on a lead to alert him to a tiger. The monkey would give a discreet cough and the Maharajah would reach for his gun; in seconds it would all be over.

'They shot everything which moved or flew,' Lady Birdwood was wry; for her the great pleasure was the ten days spent in the jungle in luxury. The Princes' idea of roughing it was a string of carpeted tents and for days beforehand heavy deal cases full of Fortnum & Mason delicacies were brought by bullock cart to the shikar. There was always excellent champagne and hock, beer, soda, and ginger beer, seltzer, brandy and liqueurs. The cook would ingeniously create excellent menus in a mud kitchen.

The residential tents had brick floors and fireplaces and were furnished like an English country house; there were dressing rooms, al fresco drawing rooms with Persian rugs on the floors and walls and dining rooms for banquets lit by fairy lights. Artificial roses were brought from Paris; the dew on the petals was expensive scent. The tent corridors connected.

Lady Audrey Morris never slept easily in her tent and was terrified of spiders as big as plates, or worse, panthers. But the pine needles in the forest pinched their pads and kept them away. She was not awfully pleased when her cousin Penelope Chetwode, who later married the poet Sir John Betjeman, fearlessly insisted on keeping her gazelle Rupmati tied to her bed: 'pretty good bait I should think'. Rupmati came to an end when 'It got so full of itself, it did a somersault and turned over and broke its back.'

It was hardly rugged, as Rolls-Royces and Daimlers bumped gently along jungle paths. The Crown Prince of Bharatpur said that when the Prince of Wales visited in 1921, 'there was a silver-bodied Rolls-Royce with a thatched roof which had the honour on this special occasion of picking up the dung from his horse.'

Not surprisingly, the Maharawal of Dungarpur, on a shoot in Scotland in 1921, found it was heather and hardship and rather damp. He only got four grouse. 'The weather was too awful, the rain came sweeping down. Then we were asked to gather together under some tree on some moor and given green hot tea.' He made it sound extremely unattractive.

When the Princes went fishing in Ireland or Scotland they never actually held the rod themselves but sat in their tents, reading, having drinks. When a salmon was on the line, a servant rushed in, 'Highness, Sahib, fish has come.'

Whatever the sport, it was done in style: floodlit tiger hunts, duck shoots by Rolls-Royce, best guns – Purdys – and plus-fours and jackets with poacher pockets and tweedy deer stalkers. The one exception was hunting, which the British had brought to India. It could have been Gloucestershire, with kedgeree for breakfast, huntsmen in pink coats and white breeches and a pack of hounds longing to be off. But it was Ooty, a hill-station in South India in the blue hills of the Nilgiris and proud to be the last British hunt east of Suez.

Women reading *Tatler* or *Country Life* and swopping gossip. 'Oh, do look, there's Bingle, isn't he a perfectly Woosterish ADC?' then jumping out of the chintzy chairs into the saddle to give chase across India's ochre plains. Instead of jumping fences in squashy, muddy valleys and farmlands, there was a dry heat and a jackal rather than a fox. Mostly it was fairly bleak and dusty, but suddenly you would come across a valley full of exotic wildflowers.

There were steeplechases by moonlight, out with the Bobbery Pack in Bombay before breakfast, and hunting picnics: 'such rounds of beef, hampers of beer . . . for tiffin'.

'When a person is knocked down and kicked by a horse, ridden as one rides when hunting, ie, furiously, rendered unconscious and bleeding, is it Army etiquette to ride away? And is it Army etiquette to subsequently express no regret for the occurrence?' asked a furious Mrs Violet Trewby in a letter to Sir Philip Chetwode, Commander-in-Chief, New Delhi, on 13 February 1934. A staff officer advised the C-in-C that 'this matter should be put before HE, who is par excellence the paragon in India of the haute école and a chevalier (ie horseman) sans peur et sans rapproche (with the average Infantry Adjutant, bien entendu). Forgive my Hindustani.'

It was all a joke, but the flavour of the letters kept by her father were treasured by Lady Betjeman. They capture the bullish high spirits of young army officers bouncing round India.

'The treatment meted out to Violet Trewby is – to my mind – typical of that pernicious doctrine, the cavalry spirit (95 per cent alcohol), which rides so badly shod over all the ordinary decencies and quiet dignities of normal pedal life. I feel sure that His Excellency – if he ever sees the complainant's letter – will agree that sometimes the voice that breathes o'er Weedon smells in the nostrils of many right-thinking women.' Sir Philip Chetwode chuckled at the mention of Weedon, the Cavalry Equitation School set in the famous Quorn country.

The maharajahs brought polo to England; it was the sport of kings, dangerous and fast. It was played in Constantinople and in Isfahan there are two stone pillars in the Piazza for goals. The Crusaders never took to it, but the Chinese did. It is centuries old and was played in the East long before the Christians thought of hockey and netball. Poets wrote about it and artists captured its style and speed of medieval jousting. Tamerlane encouraged his household to play with the sliced off heads of the enemy.

It was the Maharajah of Jaipur, a brilliant player, who glamorised polo in this country. It has always attracted lithe young Argentinians, and beautiful girls standing up in jeeps in dark glasses as the Queen or the Princess of Wales presents cups to the winning teams lined up in sexy T-shirts and white jodhpurs. It is a game for the rich; you will not find many plumbers or roadsweepers galloping about Midhurst or Windsor Great Park. The cost of a changan – a polo stick – and a good pony alone is for millionaires.

Jaipur always prayed to the goddess Durga before any polo match, standing head bowed in front of his pony, and rival teams began to long for a deity of their own with ten mythical hands. In the 1933 season the Maharajah's apparently inexperienced team, which was almost unknown in England, ran away with every major tournament. The triumphant little group, which included Raja Hanut Singh, his brother Rao Raja Abhey Singh and Prithi Singh of Baria, with handicaps averaging seven or eight, won the Ranelagh Open, the Ranelagh Challenge, the Hurlingham Champion Cup, the Roehampton Open and finally the prized King's Coronation Cup. The Jaipur team also won the Indian Polo Association Championship Cup each year from 1933 to 1939.

The year 1933 was one of the most thrilling of Jaipur's life as he mixed polo with visits to his fourteen-year-old girlfriend, Gayatri Devi, still at school in England. But although they had fallen in love, it had to be a remote courtship and they were able to see each other very rarely.

The Jaipur polo ponies were mainly Australian thoroughbreds though there were a few Indian marwari breed with curly ears. To see them crossing Barnes Bridge, led by turbaned grooms, marked the start of the summer season, Henley, Wimbledon, Ascot and Sandown. The Maharani of Jaipur was so entranced by the racing at Epsom she simply did not notice when her pearl necklace snapped; they just floated through her sari, she told the insurance men. One or two pearls were found but the others were trampled in the mud.

The season was over when the Maharajah's ponies were pushed into wagons at the Royal Albert Docks by grinning syces, watched by an imperturbable railway official with his hands on his hips as they gave a white pony, called Snowdrop, a present for baby Bubbles, a last push.

'Ah, God created all this.' The Maharajah of Bikaner is in his hunting lodge, with large drawing rooms, heavy, comfortable mahogany furniture, brass lamps and staircases covered in Frank Gillet hunting sketches: 'A Kill with Mr Jorrocks', and another, 'An Unpremeditated Fall', all very Leicestershire; and bedrooms with four-poster brass beds in pretty rooms overlooking the lake. His father, Maharajah Ganga Singh, was a very selective shot, 'only good tigers', and his Bikaner imperial sand-grouse shoot was legendary.

At 6.15 am the Rolls-Royces moved off; the Viceroy was

given a nip of liqueur brandy before settling down to a morning in the Imperial butts. A granddaughter of the Maharajah of Kapurthala remembers, with a shudder, the frantic screeching of the birds: 'It was awful, the poor creatures went berserk because the water was shut off several days beforehand so the air was black with them. As a young girl, when I was a debutante it was a very fashionable shoot, but I dreaded it, absolutely hated it.'

The sand grouse, who had come to Gajner Lake to drink, would rise in a frenzied cloud. Only the worst shot could miss and for hours you could hear the guns going. It was a poor morning if there was not a bag of 4,000.

In the courtyard at the back, Dr Karni Singh wistfully pointed at the special markings: 'Ah, this is where the day's bag would be laid out, woodcock, golden pheasant, mallard, pintail, teal, widgeon and the red crested shoveller.' If the Commander-in-Chief or the Viceroy were not good shots, beaters gathered every bird shot by the party and put them in a flattering pile beside the imperial butts.

The Maharajah of Dholpur's palace was in a hilly, pretty part of Rajasthan and rather romantic: stone, set in a moat, with verandahs overlooking deer parks, aviaries and secret walled gardens.

In the cool of the evening, he would drive his guests in Rolls-Royces and Chryslers through jungle to a natural lake about twenty miles away. Villagers seethed round the royal car, hanging on, trying to touch the Maharajah for luck, salaaming to the ground, shouting, 'Maharajah, maharajah!'

At the lake, the guns were handed out; flocks of cormorants sat silently on every tree, and peacocks did their Max Wall walks along the marshy banks. The crocodiles obligingly bobbed up within sight of the royal motor launch, opening and shutting their jaws. At the end of the evening as the party drove back in the moonlight to late dinner at the palace, two or three crocodiles would have been killed or at least wounded.

'The Rajah's taste is too terribly Victorian for words, so out of keeping with his divine clothes,' murmured the viceregal guests garlanded in jasmine. In April they left for Delhi, to be surprised by its delightfully green avenues of trees mixed with the brilliant scarlet of Flame of the Forest flowers. Their host, 'the little maharajah', standing gravely on the steps of the palace with his attendants, watched them go and grieved when the Mountbattens left India for ever.

The Maharajah of Jaipur went by special royal train with a telephone in each carriage to his royal hunting lodge in Rajasthan where Prince Philip shot a tiger in 1961. Nowadays, a train leaves Delhi at 8.20 am. Breakfast is hot buttery toast and samosas, onions and tomatoes, with tea in a terracotta cup. The train reaches the local station shortly after 4 o'clock, and a holy man in a salmon-coloured wraparound smiles at the British anxiety about the thin horse which will take them to the reserve.

This is a tiger sanctuary of a unique kind, with its lakes and Mogul fort. Guards protect the tigers, keeping watch at the porticoed gate with its friendly faced marble bulls. The evening sky is iridescent gold over the high terracotta cliffs, and the light falls on the gaudy orange and blue shrine to Ganesh the elephant god.

The Royal Lodge seems suspended still in pure thirties style, butterscotch walls and cream-coloured pillars, old wireless sets, leopardskin sofas where the royal couple waited as the guns and elephants were brought round.

The elephants were brought specially from Jaipur; padding the hundred miles usually took at least two weeks each way. At the end of the day, everyone gathered in a rather bad taste American cocktail bar, and it still has posters of wartime girls in shorts and naval caps pining for their sweethearts: 'My heart is on a destroyer and fighting for all his worth. So my signal is no to sugarbeam, for I've got the salt of the earth.'

For some reason, they felt the need for dreadful looking ornamental tigers. 'Look, madam, Paris of plaster tigers,' the servants used to say proudly, as they took topees, binoculars and safari jackets from the exhausted hunters who next morning would hunt the real thing. One of the Maharajah's aides, Colonel Kesri Singh, amused the Queen by wearing a red velvet

ABOVE: Festive turbans for prize-giving at Mayo College, one of India's leading public schools which looks like another of Rajasthan's creamy palaces

LEFT: Jack Gibson, much-loved last English headmaster at Mayo College. Now retired, he says he is 'hanging on' and cannot tear himself away from the school. He lives nearby, sustained by out of date copies of *The Times* sent by the British High Commission in Delhi

RIGHT: Education and impeccable English have always been the hallmark of the leading princely houses in India. The Maharajah of Baroda enjoys re-reading the classics and never tires of the dictionary

BELOW: There is a timeless quality about the palaces even when they have been turned into hotels. The Maharajah of Jaipur has converted the Rambagh Palace where guests sit on white wickerwork chairs drinking Darjeeling tea served by turbanned bearers

RIGHT: A mirrored salon of late 19th-century Belgian crystal furniture is just one of the features of the delicate beauty of the palace by the lake in Udaipur

LEFT: The princes' trains were luxuriously fitted with mahogany, rosewood, four-poster beds, dancing girls and cocktail cabinets. The Maharajah of Jodhpur's train has been converted now to join other princely carriages to carry tourists through Rajasthan in the Palace on Wheels

RIGHT: The Maharajah of Jaipur exudes wealth but tries not to be ostentatious. Each day he wears a bangle of rubies, diamonds, emeralds or sapphires depending on his horoscope

ABOVE: Once the centre for the great caravan traders as they crossed the Great Indian Desert, Jaisalmer has not long been opened up to the world. Overrun by goats and with more camels than cars, the town's streets are lined by almost perfect *havelis* – sandstone town houses – built by wealthy visiting merchants

LEFT: Jaisalmer is romantic, wild and hauntingly medieval. The royal palace, perched high above the arid kingdom in the Thar Desert, has intriguing filigree purdah screens. Life is not easy for widows in India – even for Maharanis. 'Dolly', the lonely widow of the Maharajah of Jaisalmer, tries to cope alone with tax problems and a run-down palace

RIGHT: Richard Holkar, son of the Maharajah of Indore, is married to an American girl and says proudly that their son must be the only blond Yuvaraj – or Crown Prince – in India. His father was married three times, twice to American women, and was forced to abdicate when guns were drawn in Bombay in jealous scenes over a mistress who tried to flee Indore

ABOVE: The Maharajah of Jodhpur, educated at Eton, found it hard to agree to a wife – a daughter of the Raja of Poonch – chosen for him by his mother. But when he heard she was going to marry someone else, he arranged a secret meeting, proposed, and they married in 1973. They are seen here at another princely wedding

ABOVE: Urbane, equally at ease in London or Delhi, the Maharajah of Jodhpur runs his palace as a hotel, entertaining a steady flow of Old Etonians but deeply committed to his heritage

A stately, caparisoned royal elephant with a purple, trimmed, ornate palanquin carrying the portly Maharajah of Mysore to be revered by his people at a durbar

ABOVE: Last of the old order, the Maharawal of
Dungarpur remembers the great days; though
in his seventies, he is still an enthusiastic
big-game hunter

BELOW: The anglophile Yuvaraj of Bharatpur,
who loves Harris tweed and cords, is battling
gamely to save his father's palace. He has just
won back a few overgrown acres from the
Indian government and is growing homely
vegetables in the royal grounds

BOTTOM: Olympic shot and effective politician
for many years, the Maharajah of Bikaner is
mournful about the future of palaces in India.
Here he looks over the lake at the Gajner
shooting-lodge, 20 miles from Bikaner where
the Raj gathered for legendary imperial sand-
grouse shoots

ABOVE: The Maharao of Kotah is philosophical about the changes in princely India. His favourite time of the day is sunset when he goes for a drive or sits in the cool of the colonnaded marble corridor. The walls are lined with photographs of staggering game trophies; the Maharao was a great hunter and used to sneak his wife out of purdah to be with him in the machan

RIGHT: An old retainer at the palace at Kotah takes a moment off in a shaded part of the palace designed by Sir Swinton Jacob, and rests under a Rajput archway. The old man has no idea how old he is but says he has worked for 'Highness' for at least sixty years

BELOW: The Maharajah of Benares is a god to his people, and wherever he goes a servant carries a silver umbrella over his head

smoking jacket which he told her had been made from Queen Victoria's curtains.

This whole forest is now part of Project Tiger which began in 1971. It is run by a swashbuckling conservationist called Fateh Singh Rathore who has a large RAF style handlebar moustache. He calls himself a 'simple forester' but is of princely stock himself. He sleeps out at night on the verandah of the pavilion built by the Maharajah and recently entertained the Prime Minister Rajiv Gandhi at the sanctuary.

Even golf had its ritual. When the Nawab of Jaora was playing a game of golf, a bodyguard walked in front of him with a rifle, a British golf professional, 'very expensively paid', alongside the Nawab himself and a couple of caddies carried golf bags. Next came a valet carrying a small suitcase, followed by a butler with a large hamper and, behind, another sentry with a rifle on his shoulder. A Rolls-Royce drove the Nawab from tee to tee.

When they got to the green, the man with the small suitcase advanced, opened it, the royal shirt was removed and a fresh shirt put on. The hamper was opened . . . the two sentries stood to attention, the pro lay full length on the green on his tummy directing the Nawab to get the ball into the hole.

The Nawab invited another golfer, Colonel Carroll-Leahy, to drive back with him. When the Colonel looked back through the smoked rear window of the Rolls-Royce, he saw a line of four men with brushes. 'They were sweeping the green, well, actually, it was brownish sand really and they were all chained together at the ankle.'

❦ 15 ❧

A Doubtful Inheritance

A FIRE OF SESAME TWIGS is crackling by the palace gates at Bharatpur; a white crane soars into an orange pink sky lit by a single star and the Crown Prince is shouting at a couple of villagers who are trespassing in his lemon groves. They are mutely insolent. The Yuvaraj is twenty-five but already has an air of authority, head down, a mop of dark hair, one minute vulnerable, the next cynical: 'Ah, we redundant Rulers.' He stops bellowing, throws his goat's hair shawl flamboyantly over his shoulder and clumps away in his wooden Scholl sandals. He is helpless and the two men know it. Eventually, they shuffle off.

The incident at the gates would never have happened in his grandfather Maharajah Kishan Singh's time. He ruled this small state in Rajasthan, just 1,982 square miles, with flamboyance. It was of no importance and yet he could not keep kings, viceroys or Princes away. They all flocked to Bharatpur.

It was not its closeness to the Taj Mahal or the deserted sixteenth-century city of Fatehpur Sikri which attracted them, or interest in the Jat Maharajah descended from the moon. It was the promise of fabulous slaughter at the Bharatpur imperial duck shoot held on the marshy acres by the Ghana Jeel lake. It was social death to miss this chic cold weather sporting fixture at which the future Edward VIII bagged 2,221 duck in one day. Today it is a bird sanctuary.

The Maharajah, who was eleven when he went to London for the funeral of Edward VII in 1910, never forgot the military ceremonial. He spent a fortune on peacock pageantry, cavalry regiments and winter and summer palaces. There were at least three hundred servants. The uniform of those on duty in the dining room was yellow turban, long green coat with crest and diamond buttons which lit up between courses. Bodyguards ate from silver personal dishes and guests sat on pure gold chairs. Jeeps, lorries and at least fifteen Rolls-Royces stood by in the palace stables.

'Bring my gun,' the Yuvaraj calls to his man. 'I'll get us a partridge'. But it is too dark to shoot. 'I'll get a duck for lunch tomorrow.' An ADC brings his army greatcoat. 'Ah, those half-mad Rulers,' the Yuvaraj says in a good humour again, imagining the conversation between the disgruntled intruders.

The lodgekeeper's wife, a pretty woman, smiles at the Yuvaraj. She looks about fifteen and cannot cope alone with guarding these back gates. Returning to her children again, she squats down by her gleaming brass pots and feeds them hot parathas, fried, one by one, in ghee on a fire. Sympathetically, she offers one to her landlord. 'Yummy,' says the Yuvaraj, relaxing and putting his feet on her dining room table which is a log in some yellow grass.

It is like a scene from one of Chekhov's novels. The disintegrating estate, nobody left, just a few elderly loyal retainers, a couple of women servants and a valet. But the Revolution has been and gone and there is no Slav gloom or inertia. The hero is buoyant. He has a catholic collection of friends which shrewdly include the local Collector and police inspector.

Shouting hello at a tiny, elderly man in a battered car, 'That's the General, he drives the local taxi,' he sets off in his own 'biscuit box on wheels', an old Ambassador car, to see a farm worker and his wife who are being harassed by the money-lender. For his age, the Yuvaraj is exceptionally caring and responsible. 'I rather love going into the villages, all that dust,' he says, making light of the work he does settling their problems – over land, marriage and petty jealousies.

But he hankers terribly for his past and has just won back 100 acres around the palace from the Indian Government. At six in the morning and at dusk the Yuvaraj is out with his dog, inspecting his homely vegetable patch struggling near the palace in sandy soil which looks a bit like the flatlands of East Anglia. 'Oh I love all this, this is my heritage . . . why did Mrs Gandhi want to take it away?' You are swept along by his enthusiasm. Bells in the small white family temple start chiming, the cymbals tinkle as the Yuvaraj pounds along. A parakeet lights on a pile of drying mustard, doves are circling the mango trees and it is not at all like Norfolk.

'Look at my peas, potatoes, carrots and cabbage. I shoot the main course for lunch and dinner, so all we need from the village is salt.' He is trying to be self-sufficient; older Princes smile at his infectious optimism.

It is time for a chilled gimlet with an olive at his hunting lodge in the palace grounds. 'I prefer a chota pink gin but we can't get the bitters.' He chases away a peacock, which is picking at sesame seed. 'Our national bird, but it is a pest.' His mother, a gentle woman with a sweet, round face is staying but everyone is sworn to secrecy, the Maharajah must not know. She is a Mysore princess, his second wife.

His first wife was fourteen when they married. There were five daughters but no son. They parted, both grieved and the Maharani, who felt she had been a failure as a wife, died soon afterwards. To secure an heir, the Maharajah married a second time and a son, Jyoti, the present Yuvaraj, was born. But it was never a love match and his mother went back to her family. The Maharajah was furious, forbidding her to come back to Bharatpur.

Family say it is brave of the Yuvaraj to have his mother staying only yards from the Golbagh palace where his father lives like a recluse.

Maharajah Brijendra Singh, who was sent to Bryanston rather than Eton or Harrow as his father 'did not want him to become a snob', succeeded in 1939. He was a dedicated Anglophile, a stocky man with a moustache and mournful sense of humour.

Once he lived on partridge livers on toast and Napoleon brandy. He wore gloves because marigold petals in the garlands were too rough on his skin and he liked to design some of his own clothes.

When he went round the world in 1959, he carried a thousand Havana cigars. Now he enjoys whisky sundowners and tape-recorded Western music in an excellent library with a tigerskin carpet and 50,000 books. As ruler he walked barefoot at the head of a religious procession at full moon followed by 100,000 people and in the evening gave a dinner party for English friends. He encouraged his pet tigers and cheetahs to come into the drawing room and lick butter off his palms and frighten the memsahibs.

Coming from this Anglophile background, the Yuvaraj knows England well and buys his guernseys and trenchcoats in Knightsbridge. He was dismayed by the venom of a man who came up to him at Marble Arch and hissed in his face, 'Bloody nigger.' But he was much more hurt by the indifference of old friends of his father's from Raj days who seemed too busy to see him.

Father and son are close. But the irony was that there should have been such heartbreak to produce an heir. De-recognition of the Princes in 1972 broke the Maharajah. There had been a privy purse of £37,500 a year, but Bharatpur was already a poor state. There were awful stories of jewellery and antiques being sent for valuation to Delhi, but nobody thought to ask for a receipt. The dealers in Connaught Place just said, 'What jewels?' Now sixty-six, the Maharajah leaves everything to his son. It is a doubtful inheritance, but in the palace, his son is fired by the eighteenth-century gold-plated fish and birds: symbols his proud ancestors carried into war.

'Come, look at this lovely lunch. You must have our partridge tomorrow, but today it is roast dove cooked in white wine, yoghurt and honey, with whole onions. And then, yummy, we are having lemon tart soufflés.' His mother smiles at the excitement. It is excellent cooking, a hint of Mrs Beeton – but light. The same chef has been cooking for the family for forty years. Many of the older servants who left in 1972 when there was no money to pay them, are filtering back because they want to help the young man.

A few even remember his grandfather, Maharajah Kishan Singh, who bankrupted Bharatpur. He died of tuberculosis when he was only twenty-eight. To his grandson he was a hero, 'a madcap'.

'Grandfather could be very mischievous. Once an English fellow complained that the soup was tasteless. Well, next night he was given what looked like the other guests' tomato soup, but his was almost neat chilli juice. I tell you, next day, the fellow was sitting on blocks of ice. Our grandmother only ate breast of button quail served on Wedgwood and drank wine from crested Belgian crystal. Oh, those wonderful days.'

In the evening there is a vast log fire in a whitewashed room of the lodge. The Yuvaraj appears wearing the traditional white khadi, armed with a bottle of Black Label . . . His manager Digvijaya Singh, who has a photographic memory and can recite telephone numbers, brings out old photograph albums. 'Oh lovely, oh what great days, such style . . . look at the Silver Rolls.' There were photographs of viceroys, of strings of cars going to the Lake, Lord Linlithgow, the Shah of Persia with his childless wife Soraya looking a bit sullen in her well-cut slacks. But she shot three tigers all the same. The Shah's ADC shot a tiger cub – by accident, but was forgiven and married a Bharatpur princess. He also helped to make special arrangements for the Shah to make love to Soraya in the Taj Mahal by moonlight in the hope that she might become pregnant.

'Ah the Shah, poor man, we are a hundred times better off than him. At least we don't have to leave our houses in a motor launch.' The Yuvaraj is sad again remembering the Iranian ruler's flight from Iran before the arrival of the Ayatollah. Then he cheers up, laughing as he spots a photo of one Ruler in immaculate co-respondent shoes shaking hands with another in turban and brocade. 'Somehow today one just feels out of place in those wonderful clothes. Oh, I really don't see why we have to finish everything off.' His tortoiseshell glasses are misting up as his mood swoops from high emotion to depression. 'People say to me, "How can you live alone in a place like this?" But I love it.'

'Come, let's go for a picnic to Fatehpur Sikri.' A string of open jeeps roar out in bright moonlight from the palace just before midnight. 'Ah, don't you love the way these gates swing open? What fun.' The sentries on the main gate are muffled in grey army blankets and salute.

But the Mad Hatter mood can change. All too suddenly there is a harsh turn of events and a swift brutality at a place called Deeg. A few hours away from Bharatpur, this is where the family had their summer palace. Cool and beautiful, it was their escape when the rains came. Each piece of red sandstone for this eighteenth-century Monsoon Palace had been numbered and brought from the Red Fort in Delhi by bullock cart. Once it was surrounded by Mogul gardens, guava orchards and fountains illuminated at night by oil lamps. The present Maharajah and his brother used to watch the turtles and there was an African cheetah, called Pompeii, which frolicked in the lake. Little princesses' jewelled fingers traced imaginary lotus flowers on the pure white marble swing and, at the top of the palace, their father's guests were entertained in the 'naughty' Kama Sutra room with its erotica.

The Maharajah's bed was 12 feet by 18 feet of solid silver and his bath was sunken marble. Screens of split reeds were sprinkled with water to cool the hot desert winds.

His brother, Man Singh, an Independent politician, was popular in Deeg. He drove about the town campaigning in the 1985 elections in the old jeep he bought from the British Army. He got irritated when his banners were torn down by supporters of a campaigning Congress minister. As Man Singh's election campaigns were often 'unusual and colourful', nobody took much notice and thought it a bit of fun when he rammed the visiting politician's helicopter and forced the pilot to jump for his life.

The next day, the Independent candidate drove through the streets again, folding his hands in the traditional greeting of 'namaste' and smiling at his many supporters. As he got out of his jeep, he was surrounded by police who shot him dead on the spot.

The Maharajah made one of his rare public appearances at his brother's cremation which was held near the palace. The crowd went wild, angrily setting fire to police jeeps. There was a tribute in the *New Statesman* newspaper in Delhi to 'Mr Man Singh' which solemnly talked about his 'election campaigns . . . with armed men and minstrels', a quirky combination.

'Most members of the Bharatpur ruling family,' it went on 'are known for quick temper and bizarre actions,' but it added, 'it has to be said, they retain the affection of a considerable section of the people.'

A few weeks after that friendly lunch of dove and then lemon tart, the Yuvaraj's mother died at his hunting lodge near the palace. A loyal son, his grief would have been tinged with regret at having deceived his father in inviting her to stay.

From the top of the palace, where the blue and yellow standard flies, the Maharajah can see the lake and the birds as they gracefully flutter down each season to sanctuary after their flight from Afghanistan or Siberia. He became a conservationist in the 1940s. Lord Linlithgow's record bag of 4,273 in 1938 still brings a twinge of shame.

It is dawn in Keolada Ghana, which is the Indian name for the sanctuary, and there is a still blue mist on the water. Royal guests huddle in grey blankets in the palace Land-Rover as the chauffeur tentatively snakes along the narrow paths by the lake. Only the Maharajah's family, their friends and the Collector are allowed the privilege of driving through; everyone else wanders about on foot or is on the lake in small wooden boats. Geese are quacking defensively, a purple heron skims over the green paddy fields and a Dalmatian pelican looks earnestly at the top of an acacia tree.

The only four-legged creatures allowed in the sanctuary are the blue bull, the nilgai and the delicate-footed sambhar. A python unfolds from his lair and slithers through the marigolds to deceive in the sun against a stone. A rose-ringed Siberian crane flaps up from a clump of ivory pink water lilies. It seems indecent to talk about duck for lunch, in the presence of blue-winged teal, adjutant storks and white Siberian cranes with red beaks, winging innocently round the lake. But the Yuvaraj chuckles, half-serious, half-joking. He has all the robust attitudes to hunting of the son of any squirearchical family.

A visitor is shocked by the noise from the Land-Rover; he tells the Yuvaraj off. 'But you are scaring the birds far more with your red trousers.' The Yuvaraj mutters, 'Bloody fellow, with his guttural sounds.' To the tourist, he was just a cheeky young man in a Harris tweed jacket and far too bouncy. Who did he think he was, a maharajah or something?

◀ 16 ▶

Bubbling with Sensuality

MARRIED LIFE IN INDIA begins with sexual innocence. The Maharajah of Travancore's wife was only ten when she married. Her husband lived in a different palace but came to see her each evening for one hour exactly. Forbidden to consummate the marriage until she was fourteen, they played hopscotch, sat on swings together and occasionally he would read his bride a fairy story. They enjoyed *Little Red Riding Hood*. 'We used to have great fun,' the Maharani recalls. For the little girl it was a very happy time; she had a playmate who had to be nice to her even if she was being tiresome.

The bride must be a virgin, and often her husband is inexperienced. A recent study showed that for 50 per cent of newlywed husbands, sexual expertise was from pornography; prostitutes taught another 30 per cent, and the remaining 20 per cent either studied the erotic temples or got on with their yoga. India has an undercurrent of deprived sexuality.

Until the 1920s, carefully selected dancing girls taught teenage Princes the art of love-making. They were the 'nautch girls' and, like the geishas in Japan, dedicated to the art of pleasing. They also danced and sang. The British tried to get rid of this custom and hoped that the young Princes would obtain more satisfaction on the playing fields of Mayo and Rajkumar, or a good day's hunting the jackal. But they were unsuccessful. It still goes on to this day although an English guest at a royal wedding in Jaisalmer did not find the 'nautch' girls very appealing as potential 'consolatrices'.

When a marriage was arranged between the Maharajah of Jaisalmer and the Maharajah of Kashmir's sister-in-law 'Dolly', she was not yet thirteen, physically a woman but mentally very much a child. These two sisters from Kathmandu are known for their beauty and personality. Lady Pamela Hicks remembered that whenever her father was in Delhi, there was always great excitement if the Kashmirs were coming to dinner. Lord Mountbatten made sure that the pretty Nepalese Maharani sat near him.

Dolly, with her sensitive, bitter-sweet face, ivory-blossom skin and fragility, was perhaps less fortunate than her younger sister when she married her desert prince. Jaisalmer, known as 'not a bad old cove', was twenty-two. He did not change his lifestyle just because he had a young wife. He was an educated man, but 'liked to sing, drink and dance'.

The palace, which has great charm for tourists, is set high over the desert sandstone, with archways and courtyards unchanged since the days of the caravan traders on their way between China and Afghanistan.

The Maharani, fine and slim, has a dry humour and a delicate way of understating things. She was glad to marry, she said, because she was bored at home. Her father was Commander-in-Chief of the Nepalese Gurkha Army and her mother was very strict. But she was still a child and knew nothing about sex. Marriage in Jaisalmer, she hoped, with a touchingly child-like belief, would mean lots of hide and seek, games and cinema shows because there was nothing like that in Nepal.

Leaving Kathmandu for her wedding, her maid volunteered: 'If you go to bed with a man you will have a baby. But do not be frightened.' That was all she was told about the facts of life. 'We knew nothing about sex; of course I did not understand. I said to her, "Why should I be frightened in the night? If there is a noise or a ghost, my husband will be with me. I am not going to have a baby for three years."'

Today she is the mother of four daughters and two sons, but

those early days were extremely fraught. The corridors in the bridal suite of the dusty sandstone palace rang with her cries for three nights as her husband came to her bedroom: 'They could hear me all over the palace.' Old servants shook their heads. The young bridegroom grew jealous and suspicious and imagined that she loved somebody else. It never occurred to him that his wife was still a child. Eventually, after five nights, the marriage was consummated.

Pregnant with her first child, the Maharani had no idea that she was expecting. She tore round the palace, sliding along the corridors and playing even more hide and seek. Her father-in-law, then the Ruler, took her to Bombay. He asked her what she would like as a treat and smiled gently when his appealingly innocent daughter-in-law asked if they could go to the Hanging Gardens. 'I wanted to go on the swings.'

Still nobody in the palace realised that she was pregnant, so she lost the baby. Then everyone thought she was running a temperature and had chicken pox, but this second baby was lost too. The nearest doctor was in Jodhpur, and even a Rolls could not bring help in less than eight hours. And it had to be a woman doctor.

An ovarian cyst caused terrible pain. The Rajamata says: 'It made me want to cry out loud, but I knew that a lady should never shout,' and remembers being so unhappy and wretched. Old women at the palace tried to massage the backache and pulled her legs vigorously. There were no anaesthetics in those days and the memory of the agony of that cyst remains clear. But when she became pregnant a third time Dolly was ordered to bed for seven months and the first of her six children was born.

Her husband, she says, was 'A good character even with the drink.' She loved him and bore with the 'nautch' girls at every Indian wedding or big party. When he died of brain cancer in 1981, she was forty-eight, still a beautiful woman and now an unworldly widow.

Like many of the princesses in purdah who were supposed to hide their faces to the world, she had managed to get out and about; these adventurous ladies would go hunting with their husbands or drive out of the palace in cars hung with grey curtains against the eyes of men.

An innate elegance of spirit and charm protects her, but she has been catapulted into facing problems which her husband found too much. With a pile of old diaries and reference books on her lap to help her with her tax, she is trying to run the palace while her son is still at school. In addition to acting as Regent, she seems to be surrounded by family intrigue worthy of some of Shakespeare's more malevolent characters. Admired by the other Princes, she is very isolated. Protection is a couple of very large Alsatians and some devoted Nepalese retainers.

An old servant in a beige waistcoat with a noisy walking stick hobbles up the blue washed stairs and leads the way into the gaudy sitting room with red curtains and Chinese vases. An inquisitive sister-in-law behind a curtain does not pull back in time as the Maharani greets her guests.

For a woman who has lived such a lonely life, she is informed and witty and enjoyed meeting one of the space programme astronauts recently. As a widow the Rajmata should not wear make-up. But she cannot resist a little kohl on her eyes and endearingly wondered if it is still possible to get Ponds vanishing cream. Most of her children are married. They hardly ever come to Jaisalmer because hunting has been banned and her sons-in-law get bored, so she visits them in Delhi, and asks a little wistfully: 'Is that where you are going now?'

The driver appears and introduces himself: 'My name,' he says with some pride, 'is Matthew. I'm a Jacobite from Kerala.' He starts up the Range-Rover; it is the ideal way to get round Jaisalmer. The Alsatians do not stop prowling until the Rajmata has gone in from the shaky palace balcony.

Expectations of male fidelity in marriage were low. Husbands married many times and princely wives did not expect companionship. If the marriage was unhappy, well, life was a question of endurance and stamina anyway. The zenana was where the princely wives and mistresses lived in some style. To the West, it is almost impossible to imagine that it was not seething with bitter rivalry and jealousy. But the approach to sex and marriage is more philosophical in India.

India is a country bubbling with sensuality: the colours, the beauty of the people, in the early morning mist uncoiling supple bodies from dusty hemp or rush matting like figures in a ballet; even the old men have a grace, with their purple turbans and white moustaches; the straight backs of the women, their poise, walking beautifully with swift, fine steps; bangles on their ankles; kohl round their flirty eyes; hours spent massaging oil into their hair and bodies.

Inside a zenana a prince could forget that another world existed beyond his kingdom. Once his principal wife had given him a male heir to the throne, she was retired. He then collected the prettiest women he could lay his hands on and had them guarded by brawny eunuchs.

The concubines spent their days combing their hair, swaying to sitar music, plucking their eyebrows with a piece of thread, still a more effective way than tweezing or wax, massaging their bodies with sandalwood oil and waiting for a summons to the royal apartments.

They would put flowers in their hair and walk in the harem gardens, coyly sniffing the roses like figures in a Persian miniature, and wait for the ruler to stroll amongst them, sometimes with a form card. He would tickle them under the chin and tweak their cheeks. Those not summoned that night would pretend to be *désolée*, others with their hair down did not expect to be chosen anyway, for this was the symbol that they were currently 'untouchable' – 'off games' as memsahibs in the twenties put it delicately, each month.

For Indian wives, the idea that a woman might have any option was European. Divorce, only possible in the West, seemed to offer the enchantment of freedom and permanent adolescence. Happiness in a Western marriage seemed fragile. One infidelity and the whole marriage was threatened. Western women were thought dangerously promiscuous But once she was married to an Indian prince, and if the dynastic wife had produced an heir, a foreigner was treated with bemused courtesy and as rather an eccentric addition to the harem.

The zenana was like a convent dedicated to sex. There was a relationship between the wives, like sisters. The modern equivalent is the Mormon religion. There was a childlike gaiety, the laughter of women together. In the exaggerated sexuality of a purdah culture, it was also a shared cocoon against the outside world and emotional vulnerability. There was the same girlish laughter of the cloisters, where consummation itself is not the goal. The strongly sexual carvings at the erotic temples at Khajuraho are of suggestion and subtle enchantment, and the whole culture in India is of desire rather than of being lost in the ultimate pleasure.

Sexual jealousy, that demon wrecker of tranquillity, was aroused in the zenana not so much amongst the dynastic wives but amongst the concubines. The wives had their status: First Her Highness, Second Her Highness, and were not competitive. A few skittish maharanis may have had affairs, but these were handled with discretion because their husbands had the power of life and death.

A sophisticated ruler like the Maharajah of Rajpipla, one of the richest men in the world, did not subject his elegant English wife Ella Atherton to life in purdah. They lived in a 27-roomed house in Berkshire, with their two children, Princess Premila, now a model, and Prince Rajsingh of Rajpipla.

The Western women who were not prepared for purdah culture were naïve girls like Marcella Mendle, who caught the eye of the Sultan of Johore when she was selling Red Cross flags in the Strand. He married her three weeks later. For her purdah meant that any outing, usually to the temple, entailed being wrapped in a sheet, or pushed on a curtained board with wheels like a mobile wardrobe, or sweltering underneath a brocade umbrella with openings for the eyes. Even the rickshaws were draped. In Udaipur the Maharani's superbly preserved old Chevrolet still has its curtains, though she hardly ever leaves the palace; women guests are driven to dinner in it. On the other hand, for sophisticated women like Gayatri Devi,

who travelled as a girl to Europe with her beautiful and wayward
mother 'Ma Cooch', purdah came as a dreadful shock. 'Ma' had
not prepared her daughter for the ordeal of sitting meekly in the
women's quarters as a newlywed, heavily veiled, while she was
inspected by the other women, ostensibly dropping a present
in her lap but actually making personal remarks about her as if
she was not there.

With their superficially gratifying titles of First Her Highness
and Second Her Highness, Jaipur's other wives had their own
kitchens, ladies-in-waiting, servants and gardens in the zenana.
The voluptuous Third Her Highness was in her husband's
newly decorated suite; they had breakfast together, maybe a
swim; but for the rest of the day he was busy and she had to
endure long stretches of loneliness and oppressive formality.

She found the other women treated her politely but as if she
were a Westerner. She pleaded with them to speak English with
her and call her Ayesha. They merely smiled deferentially,
ignored her request, and went on treating her with respect. This
simpering politeness must have been harder to bear than intrigue
or bitchiness. She spoke very little Hindi and her Bengali was
poetic as her teacher had been India's Nobel Prizewinning poet,
Rabindranath Tagore, imposing in a saffron robe and long
white beard.

It seems ultra-sophisticated, but the Maharani claims that she
and her husband's second wife became good friends. The second
wife, a Jodhpur princess, and niece of the great cricketer Ranjit
Singh, had been engaged to the Maharajah of Jaipur since she
was five. She was three years older than Ayesha and had been
very much in love with her husband, 'Jai'. Now at twenty-four
she faced a dismal life in the zenana without even the hope of a
flirtation. Friends remember her as warm and generous.

But she was a purdah girl and believed in it unquestioningly.
When she was first married, the doctor had to diagnose an
illness from a corridor outside her room. From the Maharajah's
point of view, this seclusion from men meant that his wife,
inhibited by her rigid upbringing, could not act as his hostess.
She was deeply hurt when her husband wanted to marry again.

Jai rather insensitively threw a party to celebrate and cheer her up.

In the old days the Maharanis were delicately covered by their saris once outside the palace. For Moslem women nowadays their sinister, beaky, plastic burkhas can make them look like angry blackbirds strolling round London with their bulky minders.

Purdah was not without humour. The Nawab of Palanpur, when visiting a Moslem state, was told that the women, though in purdah, wanted to see him. He had expected a few palanquins carrying fluttering creatures behind Dacca muslin blinds, but instead was suddenly faced with an enormous carpet with holes in it advancing inexorably towards him; there were eyes at all these holes . . . 'We didn't know where to look. Then after ten minutes or so the carpet went back . . .'

For some of the princesses, there was an abrupt and unwelcome release from purdah when their husbands died. It is extraordinary how well women like the Nawab of Pataudi's mother and the Rajmata of Jodhpur suddenly adapted. Their prime ministers had to communicate with them from behind a screen, but that was no deterrent to a decision. Sir Terence Keys, a civil servant advising the widowed mother of the Maharajah of Gwalior when he was a minor, often found himself arguing fiercely with a bamboo curtain lined with dark-blue muslin.

In spite of their demure exterior, the maharanis managed to follow field trials on elephants; shoot tiger and then, looking as if yoghurt would not melt in their mouths, go back to the zenana sitting in gilded howdahs, leaning back against cushions, the more daring of them peeping at men through the ornate but stifling curtains. Indian women may still be walking behind their husbands and have a timorous frailty, but only the Westerner is misled.

17

A Seat of Gold

'NEVER PAY ANY VISITS to foreign embassies,' was Lady Salisbury's view when her husband was Prime Minister, and certainly not to 'those of the South American Republics – or any of the other people who live up trees . . .'

Even in 1900 this restricted vision of the Empire was shared by many of the establishment. Lord Knutsford, the Colonial Office Secretary, known as Peter Woggy, was a slight figure of fun, in charge of all those 'wogs'. Even in the early thirties King George V was still fuelling his deep distrust of foreign countries: 'Abroad is awful,' he told a courtier. 'I know because I've been there.'

The Empire was such a thoroughly middle-class affair that Lady Maud Cecil felt that it had little to offer. 'The best class of English don't come out to the colonies and those that do are apt to be bounders.' But India was different. India was attractive to the aristocracy, who were the viceroys, and to the middle classes who did all the work. It attracted high principled Victorians, perhaps a little priggish but conscientious. They wore warm suits with waistcoats, collars and ties, heavy shoes and socks, and always put on a dinner jacket even for stew in a tent alone in the jungle.

There were patrician, dedicated, aesthetic, zealous administrators who loved India, ignored the mosquitoes, the lethargy, the heat and the dysentry, and almost forgot they were English.

Men like Sir Robert Ogilvie, in India for thirty-seven years and guiding the rulers of Jaipur and Udaipur, who wore the khadi, ate with his fingers when he went to see his old friend the Maharajah of Bikaner, spoke Hindi and liked to listen to the sitar in the desert.

When the Maharajah of Gwalior died the family chose Sir Humphrey Trevelyan, 'a man of extraordinary charm and understanding', as a mentor for the teenage heir. There were brave men like Sir Percival Griffiths, who deliberately asked for Midnapore District where three of his predecessors had been murdered. As a young District Officer, Sir Penderel Moon hated India at first '. . . this fearful grind of working through the hot weather with no relief, no let up, pouring with perspiration, trying cases of petty theft – the missing maize stalks, or a stolen cock.' But there was sometimes a tribute. 'May you ever sit on a seat of gold,' one old lady said when he put the headman in the village on trial for the murder of her son.

In the summer when the sun came up his servants would pick up the diminutive sleeping Sir Penderel and carry him, bed and all, out to the verandah. In May his bearer would find him the most luscious mangoes from the bazaar. Anglo-Indian society was narrow, middle class and unintellectual, but Sir Penderel tried to teach his clerks that rules existed to be broken.

When British rule was at its peak in India it was administered by 'the heaven born', the Indian Civil Service, which included the Indian Army as an integral part of its structure. The Viceroy, usually an aristocrat, was at the top, the direct link with the British Crown and himself represented within the States by the Residents. The District Magistrates acted for the Indian Government.

The ICS attracted young men of good family and, more importantly, good education. They became known as Competition Wallahs because it was difficult to pass the exam to get into the service. They wrote to each other in classical Greek, were just and incorruptible. They were the Collectors, the magistrates, in charge of law and order, and welfare. They have left India a superb administrative legacy.

The Indian Political Service was a subtle division within the ICS. It was rather like the diplomatic corps, with polished young men chosen to look after the Princely States and the frontiers. The Politicals sometimes looked down on the hardworking ICS as social inferiors; but they could in turn be regarded as professionally inferior by some of their able counterparts: men as young as twenty-two controlling a district of one million people as a hardworking Magistrate. For the Princes the prestige of having a senior 'political' was a mark of importance, and each 21-gun Prince had an urbane and imperturbable Resident of his own.

These Residents were in the mould of the old fashioned diplomat. They wooed the Princes, steering them away from hedonistic excesses, and tried to get them to behave more like English gentlemen. 'Those impeccable British Residents taught them all the wrong things,' Ramesh Tharpur, a leonine, anti-establishment pundit, reflects cynically. The Princes thought of them as friends or benign tutors.

As a young man in India, Philip Mason was invited to join the élite Political Service. He was given this advice by the Bishop of Oxford's son, Raymond Stobbs, then Resident in Rawnpore: 'You will find it is a toss-up whether you are sent to the Frontier, where you will be doing a man's job, very fine. But the danger is you may be sent to the Princely States.' There, Mason explains with deprecating humour, 'I would be doing nothing more than a poodle-faking job, spending a great deal of time being obsequious . . . counting exactly how many steps you would take when you meet the Rajah . . . all this stuff . . . it would be a waste of anyone's life.' Poodle-faking was a soft, easy existence.

However, there were bonuses. The Residents lived in considerable style, the excuse being the need to keep up with the Princes, and a Residency could be a real prize. A member of the Indian Political Service, Sir David Barr, was so keen to get the Residency in Hyderabad he telegraphed Curzon in Simla with a line from Psalm 132, verse 1: 'Lord, remember David,' but astutely omitted the remainder of the verse, 'and all his afflictions.'

The view of the Army and the Politicals that the clever Civils were socially inferior was perfectly expressed by a visiting General from the Brigade of Guards: 'I cannot help thinking that these people who go into dinner ahead of me,' he muttered at Government House in Ootacamund, 'are the wretched people who put up little bungalows round my place in Hampshire.' Even the servants would refer to someone in the ICS as 'second-class sahib'. A peer's wife also found that there were 'so many dull little people. If you were a lady that was enough to be at the top in the seating plan, but you had to put up with these drab nurses, doctors, engineers, rather a lot of gloomy little men.'

Apart from the Resident, in every State there was a captain or a major. He may not have enjoyed much success in his regiment, but now had the unexpected distinction of being able to guide the Ruler on defence and foreign affairs while enjoying His Highness's hospitality.

There was also a certain amount of tongue-in-cheek élitism, a snobbish rivalry, each Resident pretending that his Maharajah was extremely well-born and descended from a long line of kings. They would never admit that, because of the Hindu law of lapse when there was no heir, their Prince was a village boy, elevated from poverty.

Yet hand in hand with this self-enhancing aura, they secretly regarded many of the Rulers with contempt. 'The attitude to the Princes was one minute sucking up to them, and the next treating them like servants,' commented a viceregal aide. Highness's hospitality could be abused. 'I remember some of the ADCs thinking it would be a hoot to take us on a tiger-shoot, but Jaipur said no. This was a hospitality he reserved for the viceroys.' 'What sort of social order had the Raj devised in which its proconsuls could invite themselves to shoot tigers, accept all the hospitality that the host was capable of offering, and treat him as some sort of social inferior?' the Rajmata of Gwalior asked bitterly.

The British liked a stereotyped prince such as Sir Pratap Singh from Jodhpur, who came away from seeing Queen Victoria with tears running down his cheeks: 'I never see Queen Sahib again.' The clever Princes like Patiala, Bhopal and Bikaner were thought 'slippery chaps'. But they really knew nothing about the petty snobbery of the middle classes, the memsahib, the army officer's grass widow, the administrator's wife, who they might meet only in Simla or Ooty.

India brought out the best and the worst in the Raj. They were dedicated but saw themselves as superior saviours of an engaging people with a religion which made them fatalistic and biddable; India's middle class Raj pitied those who had the misfortune not to be British. They were cruelly identified in Kipling's *Plain Tales from the Hills* and later by Paul Scott in *The Raj Quartet*: visions of a memsahib lolling on a sofa, dropping a handkerchief and calling 'Boy'. Into the bungalow, with its gate-leg table and chintzy furniture, would pad a little old man, bent double, skinny, no teeth, stooping to pick up the handkerchief, going out backwards to sit on the verandah. 'Mistress please to call again.' Never reading, sending chits and having 'chirps', toying with greying chocolates in a silver filigree dish, nostalgic for England – 'one even longed for a fog'.

But M. M. Kaye, author of *The Far Pavilions*, recently watched *The Jewel in the Crown* on television and was shocked. The daughter of Sir Cecil Kaye and wife of General Goff Hamilton, she lived in India for many years. 'I used to say to Goff, "Were we really as awful as that?" I liked Paul Scott very much, he was my agent, but the trouble with Paul was that he was not in the right regiment – he did not know the right people.'

India was far more attractive than many other steaming corners of the empire. It offered palaces and Princes, good hunting, an ancient culture and an intriguing spirituality. The viceroy was always well born and the Bentincks, the Cannings, the Dufferins, the Lyttons, the Curzons, lived in graceful and envied splendour. After the capital moved from Calcutta to Delhi in 1911 they occupied a palace designed by Edwin Lutyens to compare with Versailles, complete with dairies, bakeries, game-larders, wine-cellars, coal-cellars, linen rooms, confectioner's pantries and special kitchens for pastry cooks. It had more room for house parties than Windsor Castle and employed 6,000 servants, including a dog man.

Lord Glendevon was a young man in his twenties when his father Lord Linlithgow was Viceroy from 1936 to 1943. 'The servants were absolutely sweet; we got on awfully well with them.' He thought it extraordinary that you never heard them in the house, they all had bare feet. They slept outside guests' doors 'like bales of living white muslin'.

Reassurance for the Princes that the Viceroy was a direct link with the Crown came with the splendour of his Durbar which was almost as impressive as meeting their King at Buckingham Palace. There was the clank of scabbards on the polished floor of the Marble Hall with its white pillars as, with the precision of a Spanish pavan, the Ruler in heavy ornate brocade advanced towards the crimson carpet in the Throne Room and his Viceroy. In the old days Princes would offer jewels and the Viceroy would give them rosewater and pan, sticky leaves wrapped in gold and silver paper. The meeting would last about fifteen minutes.

The simpler maharajahs took a long time to realise that bribes would not work. They did try, jewels in the bottom of baskets of fruit, vast sums of money in photograph albums, but as Giles Eyre, once an ADC, recalled, 'On gifts, there were three f's which you could accept: fruit, flowers and I can't remember the other.'

The Viceroy, upright and incorruptible, would not be blinded to the iniquities of a Princely State. But if there was a genuine princely plea for some favour he would put the case to London. No matter how sympathetic the Viceroy was to a particular prince, in the end he always had to bow to the India Office. There intellectually agile civil servants and India hands dissected his reports. The Princes, who saw the Viceroy as their strength and stay, were sometimes puzzled by his lack of real power.

The relationship veered between dotty japes, splendid tiger-shoots and good administration, imbueing English values and

a warm, robust and humorous friendship. It helped to foster
the idea of a continuing love affair between England and India
which was broken off rather abruptly in 1947.

Big game hunters, European princelings and maharajahs were
all entertained and some guests were great fun. One German
Prince liked to slide down the curving banisters in Government
House, Lahore. But not all the viceroys were merely socialites.
Lord Curzon, seen as a cold man, cared enormously about India
itself. He was outraged that he should be replaced by Lord
Minto in 1905, whom he thought an intellectual lightweight, his
only qualification being a 'gentleman, merely good at jumping
hedges in the shires'. As a result Curzon received him in his
smoking jacket and slippers.

Lord Minto, in his endearing way, may have appealed more
to the Indians. Once, when he was presiding at an important
meeting, while civil servants and engineers were droning on
about irrigation, he dozed off. Undeterred, the debate went
on. But at the moment when the Viceroy's final word was
needed, he came to with a start: 'No, my dear. I think we won't
take the little dog for a walk.'

Viceregal life was not all embossed invitations, marble halls
and being fanned by a yak's tail. Lady 'Clemency' Canning,
one of the more compassionate vicereines, felt sorry for the
punkah-wallahs, and was horrified when her shoes turned 'furry
with mildew in a day during monsoon rain'. Breakfast in that
heat for small-waisted memsahibs was fish, meat, pineapple,
eggs, chocolate and mango fool.

You never knew whether you were going to find a jackal
scurrying along a corridor on some sinister business, a peacock
behind a marble pillar, a fly in the champagne or a monkey at
the piano. In the twenties it was accepted that a monkey called Bobby should join princely guests at dinner. He would open
out his napkin, always used it after drinking, but tended to clasp
his glass with both hands. He poured wine and liked to clink
glasses, which was frowned upon. Sometimes he would scribble
all over despatches. He had a proper bed, used a handkerchief,
but in the end got a fearful chill. He put his arms around his

master's neck, and taking his hand he fell back against the pillows and died.

Much depended upon the vicereines. There was relief if a Ruler spoke good English. Sitting in their high-necked afternoon dresses, they were prepared to be shocked. There were awful stories about the wolfish Shah of Persia, blowing his nose on the Duke of Montrose's curtains when he stayed with him in 1879, and worse, for on being introduced by Lord Salisbury to Lady Burdett-Coutts at Hatfield, he peered closely at the elderly philanthropist and exclaimed 'Quelle horreur!' The sight of the Defender of the Islamic Faith recoiling instead of embarking on an elegant chaise-longue tête-à-tête as his host had intended, quite put Lord Salisbury off his venison.

When the Maharajah of Jaipur called, however, one vicereine was both surprised and delighted: 'His manners were quite as beautiful as my own and he made his exit most gracefully. He wore a pink moiré frock-coat, white satin waistcoat, diamond and emerald necklace, and a turban made of silk cord.'

The Princes may have found one or two great lady sahibs rather earnest and a bore, but they did not often merit Lytton Strachey's cruel description of 'fetid white wife of a Governor'. And the Princes warmed to the more vivid and flamboyant vicereines, several of whom exhibited an aristocratic indifference to the conventions which so bedevilled the memsahibs. 'Would you like me to pick you a bunch of flowers?' Lady Hailey, wife of the scholarly Governor of the United Provinces would ask. The Maharajah, knowing the Englishwoman's love of flowers, would be charmed. Reaching for her rifle on the verandah, she would airily shoot the heads off the cotton grass, just leaving the stalks: 'there', and withdraw again to her red and gold Chinese sitting room. Lady Reading gave amusing parties, hitched up her skirts to dance with the Prince of Wales, and persuaded the Viceroy, the Governor of the Punjab and the Commander-in-Chief to slide down the chute together one moonlit evening in Simla when the gardens had been turned into an old English fair, with an Aunt Sally, Punch and Judy show and baked potato stalls.

Lady Willingdon, a spirited vicereine, was not popular with the English. They thought her 'frightful'. They sniggered about her passion for lilac: even the carpets had to be purple instead of red for ceremonial occasions, and lavatory paper was mauve. Three cases among the 103 crates of Willingdon luggage contained mauve Bronco for the Vicereine. Her ADC wore lilac ties and shoes and 'Mauve qui peut' quickly became the password. The Rajmata of Jaipur remembered as a little girl the galling experience of having a bouquet she was presenting to the Vicereine turned away. 'No dear, I don't think these can be for me,' Lady Willingdon told her, refusing the red roses. A terrible gaffe. She 'fluttered about like a hen . . .' but her worst crime was imposing her flowery style on Viceroy's house in Delhi, described sniffily as 'wild duck falling into Dorothy Perkins roses'. Lutyens was furious. The sister of a well-known peer hated most 'the way she put common-looking vases on the mantelpiece. But she was common.'

They liked Lord Willingdon, 'a grand old boy' with 'sound ideas', the men said. The wives thought him 'a sweetie'. He was 'divine in pale grey hat, pale grey coat, and he gazed into your eyes . . . then you saw him doing the same with the next woman . . .'

Lady Willingdon may have been dismissed by the Raj as 'second rate' but the people she was meant to impress, the maharajahs, adored her: 'she was a terrific woman.' The Maharawal of Dungarpur has signed photographs of Lady Willingdon, looking darkly pretty, staring out from a lacklustre silver frame in the gaunt, vast, teak dining room. 'Lady Willingdon was a great ambassador for the UK. She was a complete lady and she was a great Englishwoman.'

In the early days the vicereines brought English servants with them, but in the end coped resolutely with local talent. One viceregal butler proudly dictated a dinner party menu to one of the babus: Almond Soup became Amen Soup, the 'Secan Cose' was Paregras, Klear Sace (for Asparagus and Clear Sauce); the savoury, Spiced Quail, became Espises Quil under Savri, and pudding Chakelet Krim Ice. The babu added his own view of

the hot plum pudding: Hort Plampteen Nice. Even the most
meticulous hostess did not know when to expect the violent
tummy upset, when cramps hovered like an electric storm,
prompting the architect Lutyens to comfort the sufferer with a
jolly 'I'll build you a New Belhi.'

After dinner Hindu Princes who had avoided consommé and
the main course for fear of eating any part of the cow, leant
back in their chairs, jewelled hands turning the stem of crystal
claret glasses, and sang ditties from Harkies Hymn Book. These
were not religious hymnals but beautifully bound little booklets
of old songs. Singsongs are not an Indian custom, but brocade
shoulder to shoulder they joined in Gilbert the Filbert, turbans
swaying in harmony, another merry verse about 'The Knut of
the Strand' and 'I'm tickled to death, I'm tickled to death, I'm
free'. Then lustily they sang in praise of the Roast Beef of Old
England and their Coal Black Mammy. 'When there was a
viceregal ball or banquet we used to get roaring tight,' says the
Maharawal of Dungarpur, who gave parties and dances for the
viceroys at his palace on the lake.

Amongst the viceregal set the Maharajah of Kapurthala was
known as 'Old Coppertale', and thought 'quite fun, but a randy
old man'. His granddaughter says they called him Gollywog
and Darkie. Kapurthala was sophisticated and spoke fluent
French; surely rowdy singsongs would seem very *formidable* to
him. One of his old tricks at a *moment critique* was to take out
one of his beautiful cigarette boxes and put it on the table. 'Oh
Your Highness, what a beautiful box,' all the ladies would
squeak, and he would say, in a very lordly way, 'Do show it
to everybody.' A servant in velvet knickerbockers would carry
the pretty box around, but this one had a false lid and a
pornographic picture, which made all the women turn pink
while Kapurthala sat back, immobile.

A garden party, a sapphire sky, tea in china cups from Thomas
Goode, lettuce and cucumber sandwiches, curry puffs, iced
sponge cakes known as 'melting moments', fairy cakes and
politeness, 'Oh, Your Highness,' the Vicereine, gracious,
attentive, 'How frightfully interesting.' The band playing 'Rule

Britannia' and 'Maid of the Mountains', desultory chat: 'but
Bobby and Bunty never miss Ascot.' . . . 'I know the Barodas
are going to Deauville.' Princely toes in soft white kid on
English green lawns banked with hydrangeas and ferns, the
scent of jasmine, mauve orchids and shocking pink rhododendrons by mossy rockeries. The inviting swimming pool where
later the family and friends would dive in, shrieking and still
wearing their topees.

Outside these elegant surroundings were India's people,
seething millions, sleeping and dying on the pavements; on
rickshaws and on bicycles, skidding to avoid cows; ramshackle
tongas with skinny ponies clattering along, crammed with
families underneath the pram hood; handcarts tipping over; a
crush of bodies and the ever-present smell of jasmine, bidis and
urine.

When the second Lord Clive was Governor of Madras he felt
that something had to be done so he ordered the noisy huts in
the alley behind his Residence to be cleared away and the people
compensated. Everything in India smelt, he said, except the
roses.

⚜ 18 ⚜

How're Yer Doing, Jah?

THE OLD NIZAM of Hyderabad may have been called the Shadow of God but they had another name for him in the bazaars. Parents were terrified when the wizened old potentate drove into town in his favourite, and decrepit, 1934 grey Model T Ford.

Every Friday he would visit the family mosque in the park called Baag-e-Aam, surrounded by fifty sychophantic courtiers all wearing the same beige suits and ruby red fezes. But if the Nizam spotted a beautiful young girl on his way to mourn at his mother's tomb, she would be whisked off to the palace harem and grieving parents were helpless.

In Hyderabad today palace retainers tell how the Nizam, who died in 1967 aged eighty, was an enlightened philanthropist, poet and philosopher. He built dams, schools and hospitals; they tacitly defy the visitor to ask about the Nizam's almost biblical excesses in meanness and sexual gluttony.

The last great survivor of a Mogul dynasty, rulers since 1712, he was an incongruous figure, reminding one British Resident of 'a snuffly clerk too old to be sacked'. He was born in 1886 and came to the throne in 1911, to rule over 16 million people in a state the size of Italy. These 82,698 square miles in the dusty Deccan constituted for the British the most important, 21-gun state in all India.

As a young man, he was a great dandy and wildly good-looking, especially in one of his four brocade jackets encrusted with rubies, diamonds and pearls. Yet even in those early days, many of his suits came from Burtons, the Fifty Shilling Tailors, at a time when he had an estimated £100 million in gold bullion and silver, and £400 million in jewels. His annual income, during Hyderabad's heyday in the 1930s, was said to be £2 million.

After Independence, his treasure was sequestered by the State and his income was now only £312,000. Although his privy purse was tax free, the Indian Government introduced taxes on wealth, gifts and expenditure, with the result that his fortune gradually diminished in value.

He had over 11,000 servants; 38 dusted the chandeliers; others did nothing except grind walnuts. Yet it was said that he sold one of his father's women for 30 rupees; that he wore the same greasy fez for thirty years; and that he kept his white suit on in the bath, steaming it up to save laundry bills. An ADC once suggested that he should have a new shawl, but the Nizam replied: 'My budget is only 18 rupees and a good one would cost 20 rupees.'

The Nizam was immensely courteous, had very bright eyes and funny little jagged teeth, stained deep red from chewing betel nuts. He liked to see his concubines' children on his birthday. One year he ordered the garland round the neck of Son No. 30 to be taken to the bazaar after the party and sold for half price.

For the first fifteen years of his reign, he liked to drink Moët & Chandon and invalid port. His champagne tended to be fusty – but that was because it was stored just under the roof in the blistering heat. He had his own army and whisky distillery, had been educated by an English tutor and loved dancing to tunes like 'I'm Forever Blowing Bubbles' and 'Whispering', played by foreign jazz bands.

In the days of glory, an ancient Rolls-Royce with a cocktail bar in the back would collect the guest at 4 o'clock for tea. The road was always cleared by police blowing whistles. When the Rolls arrived at the palace, guests would walk up a hundred steps and through a double line of people in court dress, very neat and wearing wide belts. In the middle of this fussy scene with bearers in yellow silk turbans, would be this little old man, his mind miles away, mulling over an opium-inspired poem in Persian.

He took absolutely no notice of his booted and spurred ADCs, who kept hissing, 'His Exalted Highness, His Exalted Highness' like a flock of geese. Tea would be served with homemade biscuits and elaborate courtesy. In the tense atmosphere, the guest dared not smoke, dared not speak, while shoes squeaked alarmingly across the parquet floor. It was even considered rude to cross one's legs in front of the Exalted One. At special banquets he used to be the only person entitled to speak.

Sometimes, after tea he would take his visitor round the palace to inspect priceless jade next to Victorian clocks, in rooms lit by sparkling Bohemian crystal chandeliers. He used a very old walking stick to point out the most odd treasures. 'See this bell pull of tooled leather? Very rare. What would it cost?' It seemed incongruous alongside the Ming vases and Dresden.

In Hyderabad on a visit, Lord Linlithgow leant down and jovially suggested to the Nizam that as his walking stick was broken in several places and tied with string, he should present him with a new one next time he was visiting. This pleased the Nizam. He thought it a great compliment – because his thriftiness had been noticed.

But personal remarks could go amiss; one vicereine, noticing the state of the old Nizam's jacket, one of those long coats with a high collar, said: 'Your Exalted Highness, did you know you had several spots on your sherwani?' He did not reply but that evening appeared in the same jacket – with even more spots; the impertinence had been reciprocated.

When his subjects came to see him on ceremonial occasions, they had to present a gift to mark the event, called a nazar. Even the poorest would be expected to hand over some token and for the noblemen it had to be a gold sovereign. Moreover, 'He always knew who should be at the palace and who had made themselves scarce.' Once safely at home, his subjects dreaded the clattering arrival of a carriage with two horses, and turbaned servants carrying a silver tray. This would herald a gift from the Exalted One's table, usually some dates or buffalo milk, which meant a gift in return: the correct expression of gratitude another gold sovereign. Some were anxious because towards the end of his life his food was kept in a dirty old meat safe which was a landing strip for every manner of Deccan fly.

His daughter, a bony embittered creature, was a spinster because of the superstition that if she married the Nizam would die. She would stand and swing the bags of gold and silver behind her father's chair.

But he did in his time arrange clever marriages for his two sons. The Prince of Berar, the eldest, was paired with the daughter of the last Caliph of Turkey so that the Nizam's grandson would be directly descended from her ancestor, the Emperor Harifa the Faithful.

It was a double wedding at the Caliph's villa in the South of France in 1931 because his redheaded niece, Princess Niloufer, a sweet-faced beauty, was being married at the same time to the Nizam's second son, Prince Muzzam Jah. The two stocky brothers had won their brides against bidding from the Shah of Persia, King Faud of Egypt and King Feisal of Iraq. The Caliph, who fled to Nice with almost none of his treasure, was virtually kept by the Nizam; thanks to his wealth a whole string of Turkish relatives never again had to worry where the next kebab was coming from.

The wedding photographs show two apprehensive, unsmiling Caucasian brides in day dresses and garlands. They are seated, ankles decorously crossed, their diminutive grooms standing behind them in elaborate headdresses. The Crown Prince is leaning on his sword. He had boils and had been having difficulty walking.

Princess Berar, who liked to paint and write poetry, had all the hauteur of a European aristocrat and found life almost intolerable in Hyderabad. Her husband was pretty typical of a bad Indian Prince; as Commander-in-Chief of the Hyderabad

Army, he cultivated a military swagger but only succeeded in looking like an imitation major.

The old man had three wives. The first of them, Dulham Pasha Begum, was thought by one British ADC to look like a little old rat, whether she was driving round Hyderabad in purdah or staying in the Savoy for ten months at a time.

After Independence, the Nizam became more apart and gently eccentric. He would shuffle round the backstreets of Hyderabad in disguise with a muffler round his mouth. Towards the end of his days, when he had become a recluse, he gathered about him a band of tramps and village women. In Hyderabad today there are some strange wild-eyed creatures who hang around the old palace, with white inbred faces and watery eyes.

None of the children of his concubines can be moved on and they add to the sad and overwhelming sense of inertia and decay. At one time the old Nizam was rumoured to be supporting as many as 14,200 dependants. He was an opium addict and stabilised himself on about eleven grains a day; but he made sure that the women in the harem were given the same so they would all be on a high together.

The drain of the huge trust-funds he had established, coupled with the demands of his still-legion dependants at a time when the Indian Government was clamping firmly down on princely incomes, brought the old Nizam to his bony knees. How much of his problem was real and how much the eccentric acceptance of poverty was hard to gauge: certainly the world laughed when he said he was broke.

He became withdrawn, a recluse, a pathetic figure, only too aware of the humiliation for Hyderabad which despite its mainly Hindu population had regarded itself as a leader of Islam, guardian of the international Moslem ethic. At the end of his days he was living on 7s 6d a week and said he could not make ends meet. He was knitting his own socks, sleeping on a humble charpoy, living on rice and lentils, bargaining with stallholders over the price of a soft drink, rationing biscuits to one each at tea, and smoking cheap local Char Minar cigarettes. Though like many mean people he appreciated other people's better brands of tobacco and would take four or five cigarettes from visitors and store them away for future use. A steady companion was a pet white goat chewing on a turnip.

One of his economies, in 1956, was to disinherit his decadent eldest son, who did little except smother his hair in pomade, play polo, shoot tigers and chase women round his Palace of the Mangoes. 'A lot of worthless wenches,' thought the old Nizam, hardly in a position of strength himself. He made his grandson, Prince Mukarram Jah, his heir.

Hyderabad is still famous for its pearls and its Golconda Fort, but today in the Chow Mahalla, one of the prettiest of palaces, an old servant with a filthy rag pads around with gabbling gums and eager eyes. He takes a desultory swipe at an exotic screen with its cheerful mixture of scenes from the birth of Christ and the English hunting field. There are corridors of wardrobes; a faded grey topper fell out of one, the blue label by Thomas Townend, Hatters, Lime Street, Est 1778, still bright. There was a crumpled pearl-button patent shoe and 39 suitcases full of tailcoats, desolately open, as if Ascot week had suddenly been cancelled.

The custodian, Colonel Jawad Husain of the 19th India Division, got up from the chaise-longue and banged his pliable palm on the keys of the old piano, but nothing came out except dust. He is particularly proud of the bathroom built especially for the visit of Queen Mary in 1911 with its five taps fitted with scent sprays. Recently four American girls touring the palace took their clothes off and jumped into one of the marble baths; the old Nizam must have stirred in his mausoleum.

When the present Nizam was born in Paris, one of the grandfathers sent a telegram to his mother, saying, 'I hope he is a little snowball like you.' She replied: 'No, he is a little sootball, but I love him just the same.' He was named Mukarram which showed a certain restraint because other children in the family were called Princess Windy Loo; Princess Pinkie Poo; Princess Dinkie Doo and Prince Doodles.

This 'baby sootball', grandson of the richest man in the world, warns that if you address an envelope to his home in Australia using the title His Highness, the chances are he will never get the letter. 'Please,' he insists, 'just address it Mr V. M. Jah.'

Prince Mukarram has settled on a vast sheep station called Murchison, West of Kalbarri, 650 miles from Perth. Now married for the second time, to an Australian girl, he loves the abrasiveness of Down Under democracy. 'I respect Western Australians more than anyone else. They shake my hand, say "Hi Jah, how're yer doing?"'

But he cannot ignore his uneasy heritage and goes back to India twice or three times a year. His Australian friends would double up with laughter if they could hear their Indian 'mate' being reverently addressed by old palace retainers in Hyderabad. 'After kissing the Threshold of Your Throne', would produce a lot of ribaldry.

'Jeez Jah' and 's'trewth' the shearers would say as the monotone goes on: 'Great and Holy Protector of the World, Shadow of God, Mighty Holder of Destinies, Full of Light and Most Elevated among Creatures, the Exalted, May God's Shadow Never Grow Less, May God Protect your Kingdom and Your Sultanate, Most Respectfully I beg to submit . . .'

Educated at Harrow and Cambridge, where he read History, the Prince was also at Sandhurst and was commissioned into the Royal Engineers, serving in the Territorial Army. During this time in England he liked nothing better than visiting his friends when they had no furniture and everyone was sitting on orange boxes. He would just drop in and say 'What shall we do this evening?' and they might go to a bistro or the cinema. He hates smart places like Annabel's, would much prefer to listen to modern jazz in Ronnie Scott's. A strict Moslem, he does not drink but loves music and danced until the small hours at a May Ball.

As the grandson of the last ruling Nizam of Hyderabad, Prince Mukarram Jah could never speak directly to his grandfather, and he was too frightened of the old man anyway. The Court Chamberlain would take the boy and his brother to the old miser's apartments in his palace, King Kothi.

His Exalted Highness, his droopy moustache and lower lip

stained with pan juice, would sit in tattered camelskin slippers, a grubby sherwani hanging loosely around his tiny 5 foot 2 inches frame, and stare intently at his grandson. 'How is senior prince doing at mathematics?' he would ask Ali Pasha, a courtier, in his high-pitched voice. His grandson, home from Harrow, would respond: 'Tell my honoured grandfather that I am working my hardest.'

Ali Pasha is still at the palace, a thin man with elegant hands and married to the daughter of one of the Nizam's more celebrated concubines. The Nizam would give a thin metallic laugh and puff on one of his cigarettes. 'The Nizam spoke to me directly only twice,' his grandson recalls. 'Once he said, "How is your mother?" and, another time, "Have some more."'

The present Nizam, who is happiest in dungarees, fixing a lorry or a car, feels the title 'prince' has become meaningless. 'If I call myself Prince Jah, I become like Duke Ellington,' he says.

Every time the Nizam comes back to Hyderabad, the city seems a little more neglected. Doorplates have been sold, and gardens once like the Tuileries have become rubbish tips. But the white Char Minar Arch with its four towering minarets is a wistful reminder of its original airy elegance and, in February, there is almond blossom everywhere. However the sulphur dioxide smell from the chemical works does not settle well over Madame Sleek's emporium for the genteel dresser or the Hyderabad Sip Shop for the thirsty, and certainly not if you have popped into the Ich Dien Ice-cream parlour. The splendour of the past is now a memory. There were great plans to turn at least part of the royal palace into an hotel; nothing has happened. Hyderabad could do with a glossy hotel as those who stay in the Ritz, a former royal fort, find its name is misleading.

The chauffeur leaves Hyderabad behind; its graffiti: 'Down with American Imperialism' and 'Down with Soviet Imperialism', chides both super-powers. The car swings by the lake with its bank of poinsettias, past airy, well-designed houses, some pure thirties, Great West Road. The present Nizam's house is high on a hill called Banjara, which means barren land.

This Moslem Prince who has lived in palaces all his life has built a modern house with a huge expanse of glass which could belong to a double-glazing millionaire in Hampshire. Called Chiraan, which means light, it is high-ceilinged, looks unfriendly and is heavily guarded because the Nizam is obsessional about personal security. There have been two attempts on his life, so he now has Yemeni bodyguards as tough and unswerving as any Gurkha. They hover around even when he lights the barbecue on the patio. They worry when he goes to the mosque every Friday and invites people back.

There are forty servants, who have hardly anything to do because he is rarely there. They dust his piano, the French furniture, the gold mirrors and the Nizam's study with his favourite reading: *Bygone Days in India* by Douglas Dewar, *The History of Don Quixote*, and Boswell's *Life of Johnson*; *Reader's Digest* and Wilbur Smith bestsellers. The house was decorated by his former wife, Princess Esra, in a light and airy style, but still there is an exotic smell of incense. In the 300 acres of grounds, there is a mosque, a swimming pool and early rosebuds.

The present Nizam also likes to go into the old town, driving his jeep within the city walls, where the poor are crowded together in the crumbling grey of rickety houses with their dash of Grecian blue in the shutters. His ADCs can hardly keep up as he nippily darts through the teeming mobs, wearing his blue dungarees, among the stalls of coconuts and chillies and carts piled high with grapes and bananas; but all he wants is spare parts for his trucks.

The Nizam's wife says that although her husband is incredibly generous, she hates it when he listens to sycophants in India: 'I sometimes wonder. I think he listens to them when it suits him. It is the one thing I dislike, and I can't get used to people saying things to him which are ingratiating; it is abhorrent to me.'

He became disillusioned in 1972. Mrs Gandhi had taken away the privy purses, so he decided he would look round the world to see where he might settle. Two doctors who had been good friends at Cambridge had gone to Australia.

But when his plane touched down in Perth at 2 am he turned to his aide and said, 'If this is Perth, let's go on to Sydney.' However, he was persuaded to stay a night and booked into the city's Transit Inn. The Nizam loves to tell you how he went for a walk at lunchtime and thought Martial Law had been declared because the streets were so deserted.

His first marriage, in 1960, was to a 21-year-old Turkish language student, Esra Birgin, in a Kensington registrar's office. The daughter of a research chemist, and educated at Lillesden girls' school in Kent, Princess Esra had a pale-skinned formal grace and a flair for interior design. She was appalled when her husband decided he wanted to settle in Western Australia. Rugged life as a grazier's wife, hearing the roustabouts bellowing 'Jah' or 'Charlie' whenever they wanted the Nizam, outraged her strong sense of dignity. After ten days, she flew back to Hyderabad and then to London.

When Helen Simmons set eyes on the Nizam, with his pale skin and Che Guevara moustache, she thought him incredibly handsome: 'It was love at first sight, he had such great presence.'

The daughter of Irish–Scottish parents, like hundreds of other Australian girls she left home at twenty-one and went to Europe. She did all sorts of jobs, first as a nanny and then in the drama department of the BBC, which she loved. When she went back to Australia an architect with whom she had worked invited her to dinner. 'I have this friend,' he explained, 'who is an Indian Prince.' 'Sure,' said Helen with a little laugh.

The Nizam, son of a forceful, remote mother, liked Helen's refreshing lack of snobbery. He had been on his own in Australia for four years; he had built roads and dams on his sheep station and had lost a great friend, an Indian who was crushed to death when a bulldozer he was driving overturned. He was lonely, shy and introverted.

They fell in love, had picnics at his beach house, idyllic days at the farm and went to the cinema a lot in Perth: 'Barkat is a film buff – he'll watch anything.' Impressionable, open-minded, she became a Moslem and was given a magnificent diamond ring. They had a Moslem marriage when she was eight months pregnant with their first son, Alexander Azam, born in 1979.

The birth of this son convinced Princess Esra that she must protect the inheritance of her own children. During the divorce proceedings the two women had a chilly session in Perth. The Nizam thought they should meet. He left them alone together in the sitting room, tiptoeing away like many a husband, innocently thinking that the women in his life would get on like pals at the golf club. They could not be more different, Princess Esra with her green eyes and slightly imperious air and the emotional, cuddly Helen Simmons. The meeting was not a success.

The Princess's lawyers acted swiftly in their dealings with one of the world's richest husbands. Having secured all the agreements she needed, she returned to Europe, to have fun doing up houses in London and California and to become a friend of Princess Michael of Kent, another foreign beauty trying to make a crust in England.

She enjoyed this friendship, and so did her mother-in-law, until her name was dragged into stories about the aspiring Austrian Royal's relationship with J. Ward Hunt, cousin of the oil tycoon, Nelson Bunker Hunt. And all because she had lent Princess Michael a house she owned in California. But any hint of scandal could be very damaging to Princess Esra, whose decent alimony is paid by custodians of the Nizam's wealth. With Moslem rectitude they would frown on the slightest impropriety.

Helen Simmons became the Begum of Hyderabad at a civil ceremony in Perth at the age of thirty-one. The bride wore a blue jersey suit and put a spray of fern in her hair. They both wanted a daughter, but had a second son. She tried hard to look after the Nizam's two children by his first marriage, a stunningly beautiful daughter called Shekyar and his heir, Azmet: 'We have our ups and downs. When they are with their mother they have a very social life, but we don't have anything like that in Australia, and they get a bit bored.'

For an inexperienced girl brought up in the Australian

countryside, dealing with the Byzantine intrigue and jealousy
within Hyderabad's Most Exalted Family gave her a nervous
breakdown and migraines which only hot lemonade seemed to
cure.

Whether she is at home in Perth or in a smart rented apartment
in Mayfair, the Princess likes to wear a white tracksuit which
makes her look like a baby in rompers. It is a face without
deviousness, large emotional eyes, blonde-pink baby skin and
soft Hollywood starlet curls which are tied with a white ribbon.
Toenails are varnished bright red, and she wears lots of gold
rings and chains. 'Radiant One' is her husband's Moslem name
for her, although he uses the Indian name, Ayesha.

After three years the Nizam took his new wife to Europe and
Hyderabad. Some of the courtiers liked her for trying to speak
Urdu, for tending the roses and for wearing silk Moslem harem
pants and loose tops, but then she is the sort of girl who likes
to wear kaftans and flowing clothes, to flatter an ample figure.
As a Western woman, the young Begum found it leaden
socially. 'In India at a party or a dinner, you can sit for an hour
and not a word will be said . . . I am quite shy. I don't speak
the language and find it hard to make the initial move, and they
stare a lot. We are taught that that is rude and it made me feel
uneasy.'

Unsophisticated at the time of her marriage, she had not
appreciated the restrictions on her life as a good Moslem wife.
After eleven years together, there is just a hint of boredom in
the air at Havelock House, their home in Perth. Princess Jah,
who insists you call her Helen, has a new gravity. She is a
wealthy woman, but not acquisitive. She has a weakness for
shoes and bought fifteen pairs in London.

Her day starts early with a swim, then breakfast with the
Nizam: he is very traditional 'coffee and croissants'. He works
on the land; they have lunch. She is a good cook, French mainly,
but as a strict Moslem, smoking and alcohol have little appeal.

Helen says that the Nizam 'still finds it difficult to accept the
freer side of my life. People are only too pleased to tell him
things, that they have seen me around town – "Hey, I saw

Helen in a club." I like to zip around in my Triumph Stag, but as a Moslem, he finds it hard to accept that I should go out on my own and have men friends – just platonic.'

It is sad for Helen Jah that so many of her old friends have dropped out of her life. 'When I married, a lot of them simply disappeared; they could not cope.' When a holiday in Europe without her husband was suggested, the Nizam was shocked, then agreed only if 'a ladyfriend came with me'. None of her girlfriends were free or had the money. In the end an old family friend, a large Australian called Richard, wearing a trendy cardigan and cords, accompanied the Begum to Switzerland where 'we just ate chestnuts in the street' and to London. 'He is like a brother to me.'

The Nizam claims he is not a wealthy man in Australia; although he is a multi-millionaire much of his wealth is locked in Hyderabad and he is still a prisoner of his past. There are not hundreds of hangers on, but thousands, and 836 members of his family have sued him for one reason or another.

The Nizam is extremely withdrawn and hates anything which puts him in the limelight. And yet his wife was moved by the way he spoke to a crowd of several hundred thousand in India: 'It was wonderful. He was born to it and deep down he still thinks of himself as a Ruler.'

⚜ 19 ⚜

Terrific Reception

QUEEN VICTORIA was fifty-six when she became Empress of
India in 1877. She learnt Hindi, employed Indian servants,
entertained maharajahs at the Palace and forbade her courtiers
to refer to them as 'these Injuns' and 'black men'. The Queen
was also extraordinarily enlightened.

Courtiers were secretly appalled as they watched the rise of
a young Indian attendant, known as the Munshi. The Queen
thought Abdul Karim had a 'fine, serious countenance' and got
him an English tutor. He wore a scarlet and gold turban, medals
and a cummerbund, cooked Indian dishes for her in the home
she had given him at Frogmore and read private papers relating
to India. This was intolerable to the Household, but the more
they intrigued against the Moslem attendant, whom the French
called Le Munchy, the more the Queen relied on him. She
loathed their 'race prejudice' and said they were simply jealous
of Munshi to whom she gave the title of Private Secretary.

Queen Victoria never went to India, but it captured the royal
imagination. She was charmed by the Gaekwad of Baroda's
wife, 'a pretty little thing', in pale blue satin and scarlet and
gold veil as she presented her five children, four boys and a
daughter, Indira. The Queen looked down and asked which
was the little girl. They were all wearing white pyjamas, brocade
and gold caps, and looking back solemnly at her. One of
the boys stepped forward and solemnly nodded, 'I am, Your

Majesty,' but the Queen, sensing the joke, glided off behind the little band and spotted Indira's telltale pigtail.

Entertaining another Maharajah, Queen Victoria noticed at a Buckingham Palace banquet that he was lifting up his finger-bowl and drinking from it, and promptly did the same. She deplored the attitude of some of her people in India and told Lord Curzon, when he was going out as Viceroy, to beware 'the snobbish and vulgar, overbearing and offensive behaviour of our Civil and Political Agents'. But she appreciated the fruits of Imperial conquest.

When the British seized the Punjab in 1849, the Queen was presented with its Koh-i-Noor diamond and also its owner, a boy with beautiful eyes, the twelve-year-old Maharajah Dhuleep Singh, son of the Lion of the Punjab. He was shipped to England; the treasury had been ransacked at the palace in Lahore and a white Council of Three had taken over the state.

The boy was given an English guardian who taught him English manners. When he was summoned to Buckingham Palace, dressed in brocade and a silk turban, he was able to make a pretty speech thanking the Queen for saving him from assassination at his former court in Lahore. 'This thought,' the Queen piously confided in her journal, 'reconciled me to having had to despoil him of his Kingdom.' Dhuleep Singh became a plaything at the palace, like a beautiful tiger cub. Bright, full of gaiety, he was painted by Winterhalter. He learnt how to dance, became a Christian and enjoyed English country pursuits, which led to his downfall and final poignant indignity.

He was twenty-five when he bought Elveden Hall in the flat lands of Suffolk. The villagers liked him and called him the Black Prince. Red willows and beech circled a lake. The hot-house was filled with peaches, grapes and nectarines, the orchard with damsons. The shooting was good enough to attract the Prince of Wales. In one season the bag was 9,600 pheasants and 9,400 partridges.

The 'Black Prince' designed a hall in white Carrara marble like the Taj Mahal, where local landowners warmed their legs in tweedy knickerbockers and drank brandy-and-sodas. The

Indian servants were particularly exotic in that fecund, root vegetable countryside, gliding noiselessly about the drawing room with its Indian mosaic floors and ceilings of glittering stars in their blue and green livery.

Dhuleep Singh married a Christian, the illegitimate daughter of a German merchant and an Abyssinian girl. Queen Victoria was godmother to their first son, Victor. A popular and generous host, he entertained too well and became heavily in debt. He was getting £40,000 a year from the East India Company but claimed that he had never been paid his full pension. He sold jewels and silver but still his creditors pressed. In a rage Dhuleep Singh, who now called Queen Victoria 'Mrs Fagin' behind her back, vowed he would recover the Koh-i-Noor diamond and also his state in the Punjab.

In an acrimonious exchange, the Queen reminded him that she had always taken a maternal interest in him, from the time he came to England 'as a beautiful and charming boy', and had treated him like her adopted son. But Dhuleep Singh was desperate and with revolution in his heart, set out for India. He was stopped at Aden by Indian government officials and compelled to confine his protest to giving up Christianity and becoming a Sikh again. Restless and ill, calling himself 'Sovereign of the Sikh Nation and Implacable Foe of the British Government', he tried unsuccessfully to interest the Tsar in his cause. But in St Petersburg he seemed a fat, excitable playboy rather than a dedicated, cold-eyed revolutionary. Disconsolate, and now a widower, he went to his villa in Nice. He had heard that Queen Victoria was having a spring holiday in Grasse in 1891, enjoying her sketching and writing up her diary.

In an impulsive moment he travelled to Grasse, where a richly melodramatic reunion took place between the chastened Prince and his Empress. 'Pray excuse and forgive my faults,' Dhuleep Singh blubbed imploringly. But she became alarmed when 'he burst out into a most violent fit of crying, almost screaming'. Seeing he was truly contrite, the Queen, who could be warmly sentimental, took his hand in hers, and soothed 'the demented Maharajah'.

'The Black Prince' died in Paris in 1893. He was buried in the churchyard at Elveden and estate workers carried the coffin, as they would any popular squire. The Prince of Wales sent a wreath with the message, Auld Lang Syne.

The Queen guarded India jealously. But the Prince of Wales managed to escape his mother and his wife, Princess Alexandra, for a riotous six months in 1875–6. He shot elephants and on one day bagged six tigers before lunch. He disapproved of the 'disgraceful habit of officers in the King's service speaking of the inhabitants of India, many of them sprung from the great races, as "niggers".'

Showered with gifts, a silver bathtub, a gold bed, gold crowns hung with emeralds, gold and silver swords, necklaces, bracelets, he travelled in barges shaped like swans. Shaded by gold umbrellas, he walked on carpets of pearl and turquoise. The little Gaekwad of Baroda, aged nine, was so weighed down with a mass of jewels when presented to the Prince of Wales that he looked like a 'crystallised rainbow'.

There was a comic charm about some of the welcomes, touching in their efforts to get a flavour of Victorian England. The Prince passed under a triumphal arch of palm leaves where ten nude children, meant to look like angelic Protestant cherubs, had been daubed with whitewash, given wands, floppy gold wings and curious reddish wigs. They held a 'Welcome to our future Emperor' sign.

In Bombay on the Prince's thirty-fourth birthday there were banners with the lyrical message for the Queen, 'Tell Mamma we are happy'. The old lady in black bombazine in Windsor was happy too when HMS *Osborne* sailed home low in the gunwales with the weight of gifts from her imperial children.

The Prince of Wales's worldly zest for pretty women, parties and hunting endeared him to the Indians, but Kate Strachey, wife of Sir John Strachey, Lieutenant-Governor at Allahabad, dreaded the arrival of 'the horrid Prince'. She was horrified by the drinking. 'Between seventy and eighty dozen of champagne in a fortnight and fourteen dozen of soda water a day.' But her tune changed and 'charmed by the Prince himself' she thought he had the gift of extremely pleasant manners. Her surprise at the courtesy of one of the Royal Family shows just how above themselves some of the British in India had become.

As for his suite, they lived up to her worst forebodings. Lord Alfred Paget was a 'horrible coarse-looking man who drinks brandy and water all day and is called "Old Beetroot" even by HRH, who descends to silly coarse jokes on occasions.'

His son, the future George V, was a much more earnest royal visitor. He went to India in 1905 as Prince of Wales and later with Queen Mary in 1911. They both enjoyed India, succumbing to the beauty of Mysore, that elegant city of princely design with its ice-cream palace of white columns, cool shades of pistachio, gold-tipped fly whisks and marble lamps shaped like lotus flowers. There is a smaller palace like a wedding cake and in the temple a holy man in a rose-coloured shift smashes a coconut and daubs sacred red powder on the visitor's forehead.

George V was as dismayed as his father and grandmother had been by the more puffed-up members of the Raj. During eighteen weeks in India covering 9,000 miles by train, car and carriage, he was struck by the way in which 'all salutations by the Natives were disregarded by the persons to whom they were given'. He considered 'Native States' an 'outmoded . . . offensive' term for the princely states and that the rulers should be treated tactfully as equals rather than inferiors and school-boys. He wondered why the Princes could not be members of any clubs frequented by Europeans. This painful distancing by skin colour could not be overcome until 1947, when strongholds of white supremacy like the Willingdon were taken over by Indians who have kept the chintz armchairs and still read *Country Life*.

In Calcutta a retinue of Talukdars, hereditary landowners on sturdy, woolly ponies waited at Government House, touchingly anxious to give a good welcome to the son of their King-Emperor. As soon as they saw the Prince of Wales appear with his entourage, at the top of the steps at the porticoed entrance, these tigerish little warriors put their heads down and, with hunched shoulders galloped their ponies up and down the steps at a terrific rate. The Prince of Wales tried to look inscrutable, but as the Talukdars eagerly pranced up the steps again, could hardly keep a straight face. He waited until they turned for the downward prance, then had to go inside to a private room where he shook with laughter until the tears ran down his cheeks.

In 1911 George V as King-Emperor was in India for the last and grandest Delhi Durbar. Delhi became a magnificent tented city for the Durbar which is the Persian word for a court gathering. To the imperialists, looking at these magnificent 40,000 tents of red, aquamarine and chrome yellow spread across the Delhi plain, the sun catching the silver mirrors in the great canopies, the Indian empire had a glamorous aura of security. Each princely canopy was different. The tent of Ranji, the ruler of Jamnagar, was studded in oyster shells, symbols of his seaside state in Kathiawar. The King's camp alone was spread over 83 acres of dusty red plain, its 233 tents complete with marble fireplaces, carved walnut and mahogany panels, gold dinner services and crystal lamps.

A crowd of 100,000 gathered in the tented city; many simple villagers had come to celebrate the Coronation of a man they assumed must be a god. George V did not disappoint them although his State entry into Delhi lacked the grandeur they expected. He had ignored the advice of the maharajahs who urged him to enter the city by that symbol of imperial rule, the elephant. The King-Emperor should sit in a gold howdah on a stately elephant with bright vermillion flowers on its forehead, covered with gold embroidered crimson silk trimmed with gold tassels, with gold on its tusks, great silver gilt bells and gold anklets, they advised. Instead he tittuped into Delhi five days before the Durbar on a docile dark brown horse and wearing a white pith helmet.

But at the Durbar itself the King-Emperor made up for it in majesty. In that still heat, a misty pink haze over the plain, he sat with Queen Mary on gold thrones sheltered by scarlet and gold umbrellas while courtiers in dark blue velvet carried jewelled gifts to them on gold trays. The King was also wearing quite a few jewels in his new Imperial Crown of India, which twinkled with sapphires, rubies, emeralds and diamonds.

Not that many in the crowd, villagers, skinny boys in white cotton clinging to trees and chewing pan, girls of twelve with their babies, knew much about Garrard, but they had paid the Crown Jeweller's bill of £60,000 for that crown, and they marvelled at their gift every time the King inclined his head, gently acknowledging another offering. Then the Crown, which the King wore for three long hours, was whisked back to the Tower of London 'for safe keeping' as soon as decently possible.

As the Indian Princes paid homage, *The Times* reported, 'the poorest coolie . . . stood fascinated and awed . . .' by the King's staring solemnity and Queen Mary, upright, not moving a muscle, a dignified great white Queen. 'She looked for all the world like the Jungfrau, white and sparkling in the sun,' the diarist Chips Channon thought. They gazed out at a sea of turbans, yellow, crimson, blue and fuchsia all rippling like festoon blinds. The King was moved to describe the Durbar as 'the most beautiful and wonderful sight' he had ever seen.

First to acknowledge his King-Emperor was the Nizam of Hyderabad. Then, in order of priority, Baroda, Gwalior, Mysore and Kashmir walked to the throne, presenting their gifts like biblical princes in formal brocade coats and carrying jewelled swords. Their necklaces were crescent moons of diamonds and pearls, with one large ruby or emerald alone in the silk folds of an ice blue turban like the evening star.

The Maharajah of Baroda turned up wearing simple white cotton trousers and coat. Instead of bowing before the golden dais he waved a stick jauntily at the King and, defying all convention, turned his back on his monarch when returning to his seat. There were cries of 'Shame, shame, hang the traitor' when this moment was shown on jerky film in London's Scala Theatre.

The Maharajah of Indore was rather over confident. He, too, had a stick, gold with jewelled insets and a handle carved out of a single ruby. He walked up to the dais twirling it but then he slipped and fell, a crumpled heap of brocade and silk, and the stick was shattered.

The Light of the Hindus, the Maharana of Udaipur, was a highly respected ruler and seen as the last real monarch in India. He was anti-British, had been offered a seat alongside the King but had refused. A tall, impressive man with a white cleft beard and curling moustaches, he dressed in gold spun satin robes but gave a cursory bow and he, too, did not reverse away from the canopied thrones.

Later he had to be persuaded to accept the highest honour the King could give him, the Grand Commander of the Star of India. He complained that the sash and jewels were the sort of thing his humblest peons wore and put it round his horse's neck. Asked why he was given the honour by the British, he would explain, drolly, that they had been grateful he had not seized Delhi when they were busy with the First World War.

The relationship between the King and the maharajahs was mercurial. When he was in England for George V's Silver Jubilee, the Maharajah of Patiala asked if he might visit the King at Buckingham Palace. Patiala had been a huge success in London. He got tremendous cheers, a splendid exotic figure in the royal coach with its six greys, cantering back from the Jubilee service at St Paul's. On the morning of his 11 o'clock appointment with the King, the Punjab prince was still fast asleep in his suite at the Savoy at ten o'clock. His beard was hanging loose, which his Sikh servants knew would take ages to comb and tuck under his ceremonial turban; an hour at least. But Highness seemed in no hurry and shouted terrifying abuse at anyone who dared mention Buckingham Palace.

A steely message came from the King's Private Secretary, Sir Clive Wigram. The Maharajah was already an hour late and at the palace unpunctuality has always been seen as one of the most heinous crimes. Worse than swearing, being drunk or even kicking a dog. But Patiala was unflustered and merely sauntered into the sitting room and sat down to play cards with four of his favourite wives. His courtiers dared not show any anxiety so stood and smirked.

There were several more telephone calls. Eventually, perfumed and turbaned, Patiala ambled to the hotel lift and left
for the Mall at 12.30. Instead of taking an ADC with him, he
ordered his personal Palace physician to accompany him. A
testy Sir Clive Wigram was waiting at the palace, so taut with
anger at the insult to his King that he refused to shake the
Punjabi's hand. The King was in the Audience Chamber and
barely on simmer, he was so furious.

But before the monarch could explode, the artful Patiala
suddenly became a pitiful sight, tottering about, weakly clinging
to his doctor's arm. 'Your Highness, His Highness had a throm-
bosis on the way,' the Maharajah's doctor, Colonel Narain
Singh, explained, 'and we nearly lost him.' The King, who was
kind at heart, was immediately touched by such loyalty and
solicitously guided the Maharajah to one of the regency striped
sofas.

There were other little incidents, unintentional slights. Who
knows? When King George V and Queen Mary went to stay
at Gwalior, the famous silver train carried drinks round the
table with all sorts of delicious bowls of food and rich spicey
brown sauces. The Maharajah controlled it and, by pressing a
button, made it whistle every time it came to a standstill.
Unfortunately, on the night of the royal banquet, it braked
suddenly and toppled into the King's lap.

When Queen Mary was about to have a stately bath, the vast
marble creation fell through the floor at the *moment critique*. But
Gwalior, a vivid character who liked to wear his turban at a
jaunty angle, a cascade of pearls and diamonds and a scarlet
caste mark on his forehead, got away with it. He called his
children George and Mary and persuaded the King and Queen
to be godparents.

Everywhere the Queen went, she remained serenely regal in
the heat, unmoved even if she sensed a mosquito in her toque
or when roughly joggled by a bullock cart. In Agra on the road
to the Taj Mahal, she saw dancing bears and monkeys. Today
a pink and white shop selling nothing much has a coveted 'By
Appointment to the late Queen Mary' sign over its door. Close

by another sign proudly announces 'Over 14,000 abortions'. In a city which still has a centre for lepers, bicycle rickshaws park in Agra's financial district, where one building carries the slogan, 'India's largest bank for the smallest men'.

When Edward VIII went to India as Prince of Wales in 1921–22, it marked the beginning of the end of Royal India for both visiting and indigenous Princes. Several incidents were to flaw this royal tour. David, as his family called him, was aware that the cry for Independence for India was no longer a whisper, that this was not the right time for a royal visit, but the King insisted. At the beginning, however, it looked like being another golden royal tour, as the Prince sailed into Bombay in HMS *Renown* at dawn on 17 November 1921.

There was a white pavilion, pinnacled and domed, on the shore and nearby they were still finishing the Gateway to India which had marked his parents' visit ten years before. A far more glamorous figure than his father or grandfather, blond, articulate with a hint of the playboy, the Prince of Wales began well. 'I want you to know me and I want to know you,' he said. But the one person he would not be allowed to get to know was the most significant Indian of all, Mahatma Gandhi.

Lord Reading, who was Viceroy, had appealed to the King to prevent a meeting with Gandhi. And as the King always assumed that his heir was up to something silly, he immediately forbade it. The Prince was deflated and his visit was to be plagued by hartal, a Hindi word used by Gandhi for civil disobedience. Gandhi said afterwards that had he received the Prince's invitation, he would have accepted it. 'There would have been no civil disobedience. He would have appealed to our hospitality. We should have been obliged to receive him as our guest.' Nobody knows. Indians have an exaggerated sense of hospitality but Gandhi was, as Sir Woodrow Wyatt remembers, a 'very mischievous man . . . a lovely man and a very funny man'. During the months leading up to Independence, as harassed aides sweated in pinstripe suits, Gandhi would disarmingly announce, 'I've been applying my aged loyal brain to this . . .' and, as Woodrow Wyatt says, 'Then I knew we were done for.'

The Prince of Wales sent a telegram to the King: 'Terrific reception, riots involving 400,000. 300 dead.' His tour irritated him from the start and he infuriated the British Raj. The kindest thing they could say was that 'he was a charming schoolboy but behaved like a retarded adolescent'.

On the surface, there were all the trappings of a royal tour. In Bombay, then an airy city of minarets, cupolas and Victorian Gothic buildings, he watched polo, went to a garden party on fashionable Malabar Hill where there was a soft breeze from the sea. That night he went to a ball and announced, 'I will dance with a girl, not too tall, but the prettiest girl in the room will do.'

Well-bred English girls fluttered, but the Prince found many of them dull. 'There was always a list of wives of senior officials he was supposed to dance with,' one commentator said. 'These worthy women would be told, "you are number 3" and be thrilled to the marrow bone at the thought of dancing with HRH. But not a bit of it, he would catch the eye of some bright young thing and off he'd go. He put his foot in it all over the place.'

He was due to present his grandfather's Prince of Wales Cup, the top polo trophy. It was a high point in the season, with the best polo in the world. The Indian Princes whose teams had eliminated the British Cavalry were sitting on a dais beside an empty throne waiting for the Prince of Wales. The teams were lined up and beginning to get hot and bored. Aides bustled about. Eventually the Prince was found at a side ground where he was having a knock-up game with some ADCs. When reminded respectfully that he was meant to be presenting his grandfather's cup, 'I can't be bothered,' he replied.

British officials, red in the face, insisted. Still he looked sulky. 'You can't not,' they expostulated. 'These are your subjects. Hell's going to pop if you don't.' Eventually he agreed but was angry and, instead of sitting on the throne, walked down amongst the crowd and sat on the ground with them. 'But, sir, you can't sit with the coolies.'

'But I will,' he replied. 'I like it here,' and looked calmly at the fraught viceregal aides.

His great-uncle would have been proud when Prince Charles was in India just before his engagement in 1981. He visited Mother Teresa in Calcutta, who took him by the hand and made him say her favourite prayer. He was not pleased when the British High Commission laid on a Rolls-Royce for his visit to a village of Untouchables, where he gave his guides the slip and went into a hut which had not been expecting the future King of England. Sixty years apart and a willingness to break barriers in both.

Prince Edward went pig-sticking in Jodhpur, got off his horse and was rebuked by Sir Pratap Singh, the Maharajah-Regent, who told him to get back in the saddle smartly. 'I know you Prince of Wales; you know you Prince, but pig certainly does not.' A vivid character, Sir Pratap also ordered the Prince of Wales to bed early before another dawn attack on the pigs.

He drove across the desert to Bikaner, where the Maharajah wore the white buckskin breeches, pale cream tunic with gold braid and scarlet turban with crests of silver, the uniform of his Bikaner Camel Corps. The camels did a march past in time to the music of the band, their crimson trappings moving rhythmically to each lurch forward as the troopers swayed in the Royal salute. That night fakirs danced like dervishes around red coals and then trampled on them before putting on saffron robes and bowing to the Prince of Wales. Another man did a barefoot dance on the tips of swords. There was a brief stop at Bhopal with enough time to bag three tigers, a panther, one cheetah and two deer.

There were several anxious moments while the Prince of Wales was in India. Once when he was staying in a palace the lights fused in his suite. Immediately equerries surrounded his room, wrapped in towels and clutching .45 revolvers, expecting a freedom fighter to spring from the crystal chandeliers.

But there was a real danger when he went to the North

West Frontier, where there had been disturbances in Peshawar.
Nobody went into the city unless escorted. The Prince had been
expected to arrive by open carriage but at the last minute the
Governor, Sir John Matthey, and Sir Cecil Kaye, Director of
Central Intelligence, arranged a car. There was a huge crowd
and agitators were shouting anti-British slogans so nobody
could hear the Prince's speech. It was decided that for safety he
should go back by a different route.

The Prince protested: 'Certainly not, you are making me look
a coward, as if I am showing the white feather.' They insisted
and he childishly retaliated by refusing to attend a huge parade
planned for the next day. At this point the Governor exploded.
All his pent-up feelings during the Prince's visit erupted: stories
of his tiresomeness, the squash courts built for him which had
never been used, the girls he had never danced with, all had
filtered up to the Frontier.

'Look here,' Sir John said, turning on the heir to the throne.
'Not one of us cares a tuppenny damn what happens to you
. . . you can be dead tomorrow or in five minutes for all we
care.' The Prince gazed back at him, his huge eyes fixed on
the apoplectic figure, plumes in his ceremonial white helmet
waving furiously. 'What does matter is that I go down the drain
and so do a whole lot of other people: Sir Cecil, the police, the
Viceroy, all going to be smashed because of you . . . all our
careers on the line because you refuse to see sense.' The Prince
of Wales was icily silent and was not seen again for several
hours.

He reappeared at teatime, a ritual at the same hour in England
or on any dusty patch of grass on the North West Frontier.
Lady Matthey was sitting under a tree in a pretty cotton dress,
coolly pouring tea.

There was silence for a minute or two and out of the corner
of her eye she could see the Prince kicking the turf about.
Eventually, with that distinctive angular walk of his, he joined
her, sat in a wickerwork chair. 'By jove, Lady Matthey,' he
said disarmingly, 'your husband does talk straight to a feller.'

Starvation and Dark Days

A DOBERMANN PINSCHER was savaging a servant's hand, grey smoke was belching out of the 2 o'clock train to Agra. Her Highness, the Begum of Oudh, was 'At Home', sitting straight-backed, imperious and aggrieved in the waiting room of New Delhi Station where she has squatted for thirteen years. Invitations to meet her are sent, on creamy parchment paper embossed in gold, from HRH, The Begum of Oudh, The Ruler of Oudh in Exile, State Ending Road, New Delhi.

It had not been easy to find her. Instead of palatial gates swinging open, the springless car bumped down a dirt road past the pink turban of a young Sikh peeking out from underneath a 1920s Ford as he tinkered with the ancient car. Then across a piece of rough ground, used as a car park, to find the correct side door.

On the station platforms nobody seemed to have heard of Her Highness, Shehzadi Wilyat Mahal, head of the deposed House of Oudh. Guards played cards on Platform 1 and, in the superintendent's office, four clerks sat marvelling as a fifth dipped his chappati into a tin of ghee. A ticket collector eventually waved towards a large red waiting room once used by the Viceroy but now sealed off from the railway's other property and accessible only from the car park.

The car stops and the Crown Prince, 24-year-old Ali Riza, appears in trendy navy tracksuit and sneakers. He has intense, staring eyes and a sprouting beard. Angrily he orders the driver to leave. 'You come into the Kingdom of Oudh alone.' The driver skids the car around in his anxiety to get away and gratefully races back to the depot of Rajiv Taxis: 'We stand for integrity'.

'Once we had twenty-seven Dobermann pinschers and Great Danes,' Prince Ali explains, 'but our enemies have poisoned many of them. I have a hatred of the outside world, it is mean and cruel.' The remaining twelve Dobermanns, thin and restless as they run round inside the wire surrounding the waiting room, seemed to be doing a grand job. One growled viciously at the Prince who moves swiftly like an athlete on springy heels.

It was like being in a rather menacing *Alice in Wonderland.* Suddenly there was another outburst from Prince Ali: 'Do you hear that?' He is in an understandable fury as blackish smoke puffs from the train and announcements from the railway tannoy compete with blasts of Indian music. 'I have grown up with this, oh the noise . . . the music!' He holds his hands to his head.

They have no electricity, water or light and about five ragged servants. One of them, a small boy in a Congress hat, fans the Begum but grows forgetful and accidentally hits her on the nose, receiving a fierce look for his pains.

The Prince was twelve and his sister, Princess Saheena Mahal, fourteen when their mother huffily refused the Government's offer of a house in Lucknow, because it was suburban, and came to live at the station. 'Can you imagine a queen living in a bungalow?' she retorted dismissively. Not that you ever have direct speech with the 53-year-old Begum. A question is put to her and her son or daughter will repeat what the Begum has said. 'This is known as royal refrain,' the Princess explains.

A strong woman, the Begum, with an air of pained dignity and melancholy, wears a black sari with a diamond clip and sits grandly on a raised platform in the stark room, which has a few old paintings, hunting shields, potted plants and a very worn Persian carpet spotted by monsoon rain. 'When you are royal it does not take much to live majestically,' the Prince says, and he is serious, daring you to smile. He hates daylight. 'I love sleeping,' he explains.

He travelled to England once to hand in a petition at Buckingham Palace. But the vital years of his life have been spent fighting for the House of Oudh and they have clearly had a profound effect upon his mental attitude. He talked wistfully about his childhood. 'I had an English governess, ah, Miss Marchant taught me everything. It is so sad.' He has a Moslem intensity and complains that no Hindu prince has ever been treated in the same way. 'Oh, if only Lord Mountbatten were alive. But we will rule our kingdom; we are not going to bow.' They believe their Moslem faith has helped. 'We are Shiites, used to suffering and mortification, the ladies of Oudh have always stood strong.'

Like so many people passionate in the belief they have been wronged, they have boxes of letters from the Begum to the Government of India and Buckingham Palace with references to the 'guilty conscience' of the Queen. They hold her great-great-grandmother Queen Victoria responsible for the family's distress.

The grievance stems from the confiscation by the British of the Kingdom of Oudh and the deposing of a rather exotic ancestor, the fifth and last King. Lucknow, the capital, had been an intriguing city of muddy streets, minarets and royal mosques, of poetry and music, of beautiful courtesans and the best roses in India. Tigers, cheetahs and hunting-leopards lay tethered and listless on the grass.

It was a city which attracted adventurers from all over Asia. An eighteenth-century French soldier, Claude Martin, built a boys' school which looked like a palace with gargoyles, Corinthian columns and oriental arches beside a lake. Under the archways of the homes of the feudal aristocracy in the old city, merchants sold carvings, gold and silver brocades and jewels.

King Wajid Ali Khan, who came to the throne in 1847, was clever but utterly debauched. When asked by the conscientious English Commissioners if he might cut down on the number of women in Farhat Bakhsh, the aptly called 'Delight-Giving' Palace, he tore up the letter and ordered ninety more concubines for the harem that same day.

He wore robes like an English king, drank great quantities of champagne, composed verse and emptied the treasury after two years on the throne. His great ambition was to be the finest drummer in Oudh. He walked at the head of processions during Moslem festivals banging a madal, a double-ended drum, with his hands, to the bafflement of his people who were getting poorer and poorer.

Wajid Ali Khan kept 25,000 pigeons and flocks of pelicans who hopped about on spindly legs. Peacocks perched in the trees looking down on their dissolute monarch in his decaying little kingdom. He was totally gullible, under the influence of sycophantic eunuchs, mistresses and wives, making the fatal mistake of never facing up to a call from the British Resident. The excuse was always made that Highness had taken medicine and could not see anybody for ten days.

He was ensnared by tricksters and by the Chief Singer at the palace. He was lured to meet a celebrated dervish, who would take him to the King of the Fairies, who would cure his palpitations. Jewels and money changed hands in the Lucknow bazaar. But the hoax was discovered when the tubby dervish collapsed through a canvas ceiling where he had been masquerading as the voice of the healing Fairy King.

An English residency surgeon, Dr Bell, sternly reported that the King was weakened by 'excessive indulgence in sexual pleasures'.

The Queen Mother, who had known better days in Oudh when her husband was alive, had no influence with her depraved son. Sir William 'Thuggee' Sleeman, who toured Oudh in 1849, suggested in his scathing report that all the 'fiddlers, singers and eunuchs' should be kicked out and that the East India Company should administer Oudh in consultation with the Queen Mother. Nothing quite so considerate happened. In 1856, the King was deposed unceremoniously and the British seized this wayward kingdom.

It was the end of a medieval era and an engaging, outrageous dynasty which blended style with decadence. There was a lot of emotion in India about the arbitrary seizing of Oudh. Sir Alfred Lyall talked about 'the scandalous cant with which we tried to whitewash the transaction' in a letter home. Sleeman warned that 'the annexation of Oudh would cost the British more than the value of ten kingdoms and lead to a mutiny of sepoys'.

His words were prophetic. The next year saw the Indian Mutiny or India's First War of Independence and the siege of the Lucknow Residency, ironically built by Ali Khan. Indian troops had been inflamed by the Governor-General's orders that they should serve abroad. The sepoys, mainly proud Rajputs, argued that any strict Hindu who left his native land automatically became an outcast. It is not an argument which seems to have deterred migration more recently. When a new breech-loading rifle was issued in 1856, there was a mischievous rumour that the new cartridges were greased with animal fat. Though it was in fact neither, the uncertainty as to whether it was cow or pig fat, which would have defiled Hindus or Moslems, meant that all sepoys became equally disaffected.

The aristocracy and the exiled House of Oudh felt little sympathy with the British after the high-handed treatment of Ali Khan the year before. Many sided with the rebels, who were not only besieging Sir Henry Lawrence and his British garrison in the Lucknow Residency but had also mutinied at Meerut, shot their officers and marched on Delhi. The uprising was not put down for several months. It was the beginning of Indian Nationalism and the end of the East India Company. The Crown took over and in her proclamation Queen Victoria gave the assurance 'We shall respect the rights, dignity and honour of the native Princes as our own.'

In 1911, the Begum's grandmother, Zamrud Mahal, appeared in an ostentatiously tatty sari before the Prince of Wales and said she would never accept money for the loss of land and property. The family struggled on until 1947, when Nehru, who was sympathetic to the Begum, gave them a house in

Kashmir. To add to their misery this was burnt down and they moved to Delhi so they could more easily petition the Indian Government.

Only in India could you find a long-running struggle with such faintly comic overtones. The Begum is indulged, though she has no hope of ever recovering her ancestral palace in Lucknow. It is now part of the All-India Institute of Medical Science. But the authorities have not been too insensitive. The Begum and her children have been offered a lodge in one of Delhi's acacia forests. Bat infested it may be, but 'Malcha Mahal' has a semblance of royal style with its verandahs overlooking desolate acres. It is near the Delhi polo club on the Sardar Patel Road and was built by the Moslem King Ferozeshah, but for years was overrun with snakes, lizards and rats.

Still this was an offer the Begum could not refuse. In 1985 an eviction order was served and she agreed to move to the forest. At least it is a palace of sorts, though her servants face a half-mile bicycle ride each day for water. The family are not destitute though they are selling off Persian carpets and jewellery. But the lodge is a far cry from the original dream of being restored to a family palace in Lucknow in Uttar Pradesh.

Historians say that the Begum has a genuine case. The British had no legal justification for seizing Oudh; it was merely being mismanaged. Nevertheless it is unlikely that the Begum and her children will ever get anything better than that slightly spooky forest lodge.

There are no marriage proposals for the Princess. In India you are old for marriage at twenty-five. Her brother Prince Ali, whose nerves are obviously frayed, has a simmering watchfulness and says aggressively, 'We have no friends, none of the Princes want to know about us.' But then his mood becomes gentle and poetic: 'I have known starvation and dark days, but I have dreams and once I walked on diamonds.'

◀ 21 ▶

Does the Dark Fella
Speak English?

THE AMIABLE and attractive Maharajah of Cooch Behar, who
later married English model girl Gina Egan, was staying with
Lord Monckton at his home in Ightham, in Kent, one summer.

The family had a cricket ground and 'Cooch' as they called
him, had been invited to play in the annual match against the
village. Over tankards of ale outside the timbered pub, shaded
by apple blossom, the talk was of a needle match for sure.

A balmy day, the ground was like clipped moss. Lord Monckton had won the toss and went in to bat. The Maharajah was a
bowler and so was only at nine or ten in the batting order. But
as the innings progressed and there was still no sign of his guest,
Monckton began to grow anxious. 'Anyone seen Cooch?' A
young lad was sent to the village to try and find the Prince,
perhaps he was unwell or was exploring a few charming Kentish
oasthouses. Cooch Behar was eventually found in the village
pub. The young lad came back from his errand, pink in the
face, and reported to Lord Monckton that he had found His
Highness in bed upstairs with the landlord's daughter.

Cricket was quintessentially a game of empire and thoroughly
middle class. Rudyard Kipling was acerbic about 'flannelled
fools' at the wicket but they were the men who ruled India,
decent and honourable. It was not a hot, sweaty game like

football where you might have to tackle a member of the lower classes, and it was manly. The Raj, normally pale and grey-looking in India, had an aura of nobility in their cricketing clothes. The sight of a fair-haired young bowler running towards the crease stirred the hearts of Princes and administrators alike – the epitome of Young England. It symbolised 'fair play' and Indian Princes today talk like public school housemasters about 'sticky wickets', 'playing the game' and 'straight bats'.

'Cricket is a game invented by the British who, not being a spiritual people, had to have some concept of eternity.' The Maharajah of Baroda, who, in leaner days, was a first-class cricketer and whose voice is heard with the BBC experts at Lords, likes to be provocative. As a young man, he learned to bat for his State on a cossetted wicket at the palace at Baroda. In his golden, athletic days – he had also been a national junior tennis champion – the Gaekwad's highest score in first-class cricket was 99 and he still regrets the casual stroke that denied him a century. Later he became Manager for the Indian Test Tour of England and President of the Board of Control for Cricket in India.

When a little portliness crept round the waistline, the cream-flannelled legs moved languorously to the commentators' box. Happy droning afternoons were spent at Lords, chiming in with the reassuring English voices of Brian Johnston and Christopher Martin-Jenkins, enjoying conviviality and the homemade cakes sent in by adoring women listeners. Some of his best friends are cricketers, robust characters like Keith Miller in Australia and the slightly less ebullient but well-rounded John Arlott, who always called him Prince.

The first time an Indian cricket team was seen in Britain was in 1886. It was fairly elementary cricket and hardly a curtain raiser for the glamorous 'Ranji'. Unfortunately the Jam Saheb of Nawanagar, Ranjitsinghi, did not play for his own country. He was one of the best cricketers India ever produced, including the Pataudis, Kapil Dev, India's captain, and Sunil Gavaskar.

'Ranji' arrived in Cambridge in 1892, not as a dilettante

student but having passed into Trinity. He took rooms above the Dorothy Café in Sidney Street, where the jeweller, the tailor and the man from Purdy called to do business. He thought nothing of booking the whole of the University Arms for his friends for a night. Undergraduates referred to him as 'Smith'.

He gained his Blue and soon became the 'Prince of Cricket' to the world. He played for England and captained Sussex for five years. A stylish and classic bat, by 1897 he was fifth in the national averages, scoring 1,940 runs, and was chosen for the English team for Australia. He never seemed to have an 'off' season: between 1895 and 1904 he exceeded 1,000 runs every year. Three times during this decade he scored more than 2,000 and he celebrated the turn of the century by exceeding 3,000 in both 1899 and 1900. The ten-year spell saw him top of the batting averages in three years, second in 1903 and third in three years.

His eye was remarkable. He once took four stumps, set three of them up and, using the fourth as a bat, proceeded to cut and glide every ball to the discomfiture of one particularly conceited fast bowler.

He was a dapper, exotic creature who could bring a crowd to its feet as he sauntered down the pavilion steps with his distinctive swinging walk, trailing his bat, slender and light beside the more robust white cricketers. There was the familiar lackadaisical pose at the wicket, silk shirt buttoned at the wrist, flapping round his body like a sail, a relaxed elegance and speedy grace. Ranji, as a cricketer and a prince, was the first Indian really to fire the imagination and had just as much appeal as Ian Botham today, with his expensively highlighted hair. Ranji's constant companion was Popsey, a slightly moth-eaten parrot who was with him for forty years.

Foreign names were a bit unusual then and his proper name, Ranjitsinghi, was too much for one fan, who shouted 'Ramsgate Jimmy'. The crowd called him Ranji and rated him with their English gods of cricket, W. G. Grace, Archie Maclaren and C. B. Fry.

'Does the dark fella speak English?' Ranji heard one spectator with a cravat bark at another. This cultivated ruler of a small state with a 13-gun salute smiled. Nobody would have heard much about his home in the Kathiawar peninsular, a stretch of land on the West coast about half the size of Ireland, which became famous for producing not only India's greatest cricketer but also Mahatma Gandhi.

Ranji was a sensation, but he was not strong. He suffered from asthma and was a poor sailor so cricket tours were a misery for him. In London he stayed at either the Kensington Palace Hotel or the Grosvenor. By 1907 he needed some peace and rented an old friary in Sussex which belonged to Lord Winterton. He restored it with all a foreigner's enthusiasm, filling the old stone 'stews' with trout. He had 15,000 acres altogether, rich with duck and the pheasant he had specially reared.

Dr Grace brought a team to play on the newly laid pitch at Shillinglee and that night glasses were raised to 'the three greatest living cricketers, Grace, Ranji and Archie Maclaren'. When Ranji was hosting a dinner part he wore English clothes but an astonishing waistcoat with jewelled buttons or eight black pearls, brilliant amongst the drab black. Sir Arthur 'Skipper' Priestley, a former cricketer and an amusing companion, was a frequent guest at the Jam Saheb's palace in Kathiawar. Sir Arthur was an enthusiastic gourmet who relished the good food at the palace, but on one particular day Skipper came bounding in for lunch at one o'clock to find his host sunk in gloom, no wine, no oysters, just black bread, water and a few chapatis. His face fell. There had been a death at the palace, the Jam Saheb explained.

'But isn't it unusual for a guest to be required to fast as well as a host, Ranji?'

The Jam Saheb looked mournful. 'Sorry, Skipper, it was a very close relative.'

Sir Arthur rose, hungry but dignified, and said he would return to Delhi at once. He left the dining table and ordered his servants to pack, but suddenly heard roars of laughter from the dining room. Mystified, he went back, to see dozens of oysters and a bottle of Chablis just opened. The two old friends made

TOP: The Maharajah of Baroda's second wife, Sita Devi, is helped into her necklace; the diamonds of this suite once belonged to Napoleon

ABOVE: An appealing little Prince Sayajirao, only child of the Maharajah of Baroda's second marriage, was adored by his mother. Friends could not bring themselves to tell her about his death in mysterious circumstances in the south of France in 1985. She has been in a coma for some years and is cared for in her house in Paris, once the scene of so many exotic parties

LEFT: The Maharajah of Baroda, who succeeded in 1939, was sometimes compared to George V because he tended to be equally solemn. But there is a flicker of a smile during a visit to Nevada when he meets two showgirl 'lovelies'

ABOVE: This is a rarely seen photograph of the Maharajah of Jaipur's second wife, who was ousted when he fell in love with the glamorous Gayatri Devi. Here they seem happy at Bognor, and the heir, master 'Bubbles', is at the wheel of a baby limousine

LEFT: The Maharajah of Jaipur, the great polo player, with his third wife Gayatri Devi, who was believed to be one of the ten most beautiful women in the world, and Jagat Singh, the only child of their marriage

BELOW: The Maharani of Cooch Behar was a legendary beauty and a spirited personality

TOP LEFT: The Maharajah of Bharatpur's four sons in formal brocade; the *dhurzie* (dressmaker) seems to have miscalculated the arm-length of the second youngest prince – he and the youngest are still in their Daniel Neal button shoes

TOP RIGHT: In the palaces of India, baby princes and princesses had their own uniformed *chaprassis* (orderlies) who pushed the prams for the nannies

ABOVE: The Jaipur royal children in bonnets, coats, white ankle socks and shoes similar to those worn by the Queen and Princess Margaret when they were young. Here they look at the Palace hounds. The jackal was the prey in India, rather than the fox

LEFT: Nannies found life at the palace in Jaipur quite pleasing, being rowed by a dignified servant or riding in the early morning

ABOVE: The Maharajah of Patiala, Bhupinder Singh, was a splendid and imposing figure in his ceremonial jewels. LEFT: He was a frequent visitor to Paris and London where he favoured fashionable co-respondent shoes and Savile Row tailoring. To Englishwomen, he was an Arabian Nights figure. In his heyday he liked a virgin a day, but in old age cut down to one a week. The British thought him amusing and flamboyant but were forced to ban him from Simla where he became overexcited

BELOW LEFT: In Europe the Maharajahs often fell for English girls. The engaging Maharajah of Cooch Behar, seen here with model girl Gina Egan at Alfredo's in Rome, later married her and took her back to India. He fell from a horse and she spent his last years nursing him when he was incapacitated. The Maharani never remarried and is known in the family as 'Aunty Gina'

BELOW: Part of doing the season in London was sitting for a portrait. Here the Maharajah of Cooch Behar poses for artist Frank Hereford. The Maharajah is in pale blue and was in London for the Coronation in 1937

ABOVE: The Maharajah of Kapurthala, Paramjit Singh, in London in 1960 with the wife he loved best, an English girl called Stella Mudge. His father forced him to marry a second Indian wife and have a son

RIGHT: As Crown Prince of Kapurthala with his sophisticated, French-educated first wife, Indian princess Bindra on a voyage round the world. The marriage ended when she was unable to produce an heir

BELOW RIGHT: The present Maharajah of Jodhpur's father was an enthusiastic magician. Here he is performing his 'fire from water' trick before nearly 600 members of the Magic Circle

BELOW: The Maharajah of Jodhpur with his second wife Sandra McBryde, a nurse from Scotland who became a Hindu when they married in September 1948. Miss McBryde was known as Sundra Devi

LEFT: The Maharani of Jaipur had a spellbinding effect in the villages when she went campaigning as a candidate for the right-wing Swatantra Party

ABOVE: The Nizam of Hyderabad (left, with plumed turban) chartered a Constellation to take him to Delhi for a Governors' Conference in 1952. The Maharajah of Patiala looks preoccupied at the head of the table, while the Prime Minister, Nehru, nearest the camera on left, appears less gloomy than the princes

CENTRE LEFT: The Maharajah of Bikaner is mobbed by supporters as he leaves the Supreme Court of India in 1970. The Court had overruled the Presidential Order which stripped the Maharajahs of their privileges. But a year later the princes lost everything

BELOW: The princes formed their own trade union. They met in Delhi in 1924. In the front row the Viceroy, Lord Reading, is seated beside the Maharajah of Gwalior. Third from the left is Alwar, legs crossed. Third from the right in the front row is the Maharajah of Kapurthala

ABOVE: The Nizam of Hyderabad, one of the wealthiest men in the world, wore the same old muffler and greasy hat in spite of pleas by fastidious British advisers

RIGHT: In his youth the Nizam wore jewels and brocade, was handsome, cultivated, a poet and fond of pink champagne. He ascended the throne in 1911 and grew more and more anxious about his money

CENTRE RIGHT: The present Nizam's first wife was a Turkish student. Princess Esra could not face life on a ranch in Perth and the couple divorced. The Princess, who is a friend of Princess Michael of Kent and actor Sean Connery and his wife, has not remarried and lives in style in London and California

BELOW: The old Nizam disinherited his profligate son and made his grandson Prince Mukarram Jah his heir. The present Nizam has chosen to live in Australia where he is known as 'Jah' and has married a bonny Australian girl called Helen Simmons. They have two sons

BOTTOM RIGHT: Marriage between Indian princes and European girls could be companionable and successful. Here the Maharana of Udaipur and his second wife Annabella have a giggle at the Ajanta Caves in Bombay in 1964

LEFT: This rose-stoned fortress tinged with royal blue was first captured by a Gwalior ancestor, Madhav Rao Scindia, in 1784. It had a spectacular and strategic view which spanned north India to the south. Seized over the centuries by Muslim invaders, squabbled over by Moghul Emperors and their generals, occupied briefly by Jat chieftains and by the British until 1885, when it was finally returned to its rightful owners, it reflects some of India's turbulent history

RIGHT: The Maharajah of Gwalior, Madhav Rao Scindia, who succeeded in 1886, was popular with the British because he 'modernised' his state. For ceremonial occasions, as here, when he is receiving the Viceroy, Lord Reading, he wore his traditional Maratha hat

BELOW: This is one of the three palaces owned by the Gwalior family. This marble extravaganza, Jai Vilas, was built at great speed by Maharajah Jayaji Rao between 1872 and 1874 in time for a visit by the Prince of Wales. The architect, Sir Michael Filose, an Indian army officer, pandered to the Maharajah's love of gold

their peace. This princely joke, childish and yet mocking, had the Jam Saheb chuckling for days.

The Princes often knew when they were being exploited but kept up a veneer of languid indifference. Ranji found that he was sometimes used by people claiming an old friendship dating back to some obscure cricket match, who would come and stay for weeks at a time. But he was wise and saw through the cadgers and spongers. He escaped in 1924, buying a castle in one of the wildest and most beautiful parts of Ireland.

Ballynahinch Castle in Connemara gave him everything he dreamt of, good fishing on a perfect lake and all around him a protective chain of dark blue mountains dotted with very few thatched white cottages. He had naturally supple wrists and often landed a sea trout at dusk when everyone else had given up. The Irish liked his Indian staff and in turn the Jam Saheb employed the locals, sixty for the fishing alone. The standard of living improved in the village. It is traditionally desolate countryside, its wayward beauty captured so well by Paul Henry, the Irish artist who specialised in the west. Ranji had a fine art collection including a few Landseers, some Peter Lelys and a de Laszlo of Gladys Cooper, an actress he admired enormously.

The Irish took to the Jam Saheb. Irish and Indian humour are alike. He enjoyed visits from the local priest and promised to send his nieces to the local Kylemore convent. He was a popular figure also with the County and had a catholic collection of tweedy friends, including Lord Westmorland, Lord Londesborough and the Duke of Beaufort; he was always a welcome guest at house parties and shoots.

His career as a cricketer ended dramatically on a Yorkshire grouse moor in 1915. Ranji noticed that his neighbour in the butts was shooting quite wildly and remonstrated with him. Pellets were coming dangerously close as the man grew even more reckless, constantly bringing his gun round and shooting down the line. Five minutes from the start of the shoot, Ranji was hit in the face. He was rushed to Leeds Infirmary where doctors removed his right eye.

'I have been unlucky,' the Jam Saheb told the doctors stoically.

After the accident, he wrote a touching letter to his guardian, Major Berthon. Describing the accident, with true British understatement, as 'this unfortunate episode', he thought the Major would be pleased to know that his charge had been able to keep 'absolute control'. He added, 'I behaved in a manner you would like.' British grit brought consolation.

The King was moved, 'Dear Friend,' he wrote, '. . . to think that you who have made such wonderful use of your eyes should now be deprived of the sight of one of them . . .' Purdey, who made 301 guns in 1901 for Edward VII alone, later built one for Ranji with a special cast-off stock so that he could bring it to his right shoulder and use the left eye. Today it takes three years to build a Purdey and prices begin at £15,000.

From then on Ranji always made sure he was photographed on his left side. He never married, and when he lost his eye was at particular pains to find a convincing glass one so that neither his mother nor his servants in the palace in Kathiawar should know.

'I am the proudest man in England,' the Jam Saheb remarked as he watched his nephew at the Oval, another starry cricketer K. S. Duleepsinhji, whom he had coached from the age of eight. The boy was to make a century in his first Test Match against the Australians. When he thought Duleepsinhji had not done well enough in a Test Match, Ranji sent a cryptic telegram: 'Go and play tennis with Betty Nuthall.' The message had meaning only for uncle and nephew. But he himself had to put up with criticism when he got fat; critics taunted him with 'The Jam Saheb is forty, the Jam Saheb is fat . . . the temple bells are calling him back . . .'

When Ranji died in 1933, there were all sorts of tributes. There was talk of the Jam Saheb's seventy-two centuries in first-class cricket, 'supple dusky legerdemain'; and of how a strange light out of the East was seen on English fields when he batted. It was his shirt which some remembered most, how it rippled in the breeze, others, the ease with which India's greatest cricketer won a match for the MCC against Yorkshire with a second innings of 157 scored in three and a half hours.

Lord Salisbury's patronising thoughts about the great cricketer reflected the popular view of India: 'Here was a black man playing cricket for all the world as if he were a white man.'

Another princely cricketer was the Maharajah of Porbander. 'Natwarsinhji' captained the first All India cricket team when it came to England in 1932. They were glamorous figures arriving muffled up against April weather in Humphrey Bogart hats, or turbans and belted Crombie overcoats. But England won by 158 runs. The Indian Test team could well have done with another of its great homegrown cricketers, 'Pat', the Nawab of Pataudi, a Moslem prince. Two years later, 'Pat' – his proper name was Iftiquar Ali Khan – was scoring a century for England against Australia in his first Test.

A true sportsman, he was unhappy and uneasy when he became embroiled in the unsavoury row about leg theory during the 1932–3 tour to Australia. He did not approve of the captain Douglas Jardine's obsessional preoccupation with winning by bodyline attack on the Australian batsmen and went back to India before the tour ended. His son, the present Nawab of Pataudi, has always resented the suggestion that his father was dropped for slow batting and came home in a sulk.

Pataudi was a Ruler and a dedicated cricketer coached by Frank Woolley; he was not going to brawl publicly with the distant Jardine, preferring to keep a cool distance when the bodyline tactics nearly caused an international incident. He later captained India in 1946 and was described as a 'genial and subtle captain'. He died at forty-one from a heart attack when he was playing polo.

His son, now the Nawab of Pataudi, known as 'The Noob' or Tiger, star captain of India's cricket team from 1960 to 1975, was once rather cross with his father. He was seven at the time. They were playing in a cricket match together and the junior Noob had cupped his hands to catch the ball.

'Suddenly I saw two other, larger hands appear over my head. My father made the catch instead, saying: "Well, I can't trust you at the moment."' But the boy had already bagged his first tiger, though he had been told he should just pretend to shoot. This was early coaching of a boy who became a legendary batsman.

The Noob, who likes to be a bit flip, appears looking un-shaven, wearing a polo neck, says he hates watching cricket and is slightly bleary-eyed after a late night in Delhi, smoking constantly. He is married to film star Sharmila Tagore, a relation of the poet Rabindranath Tagore. 'We just met, and got married without any arrangement,' and they are a social couple. He pretends to dislike the playboy image, but it is difficult, he has always been used to a great deal of adulation.

He does not share the trendy view of his contemporaries that Europe is 'old hat' and that America is the place for his son. He loved his time at Winchester and Oxford, 'had a great time though I was kept terribly short of money.' He has a remarkable mother, the Begum of Bhopal, who has represented the tiny Moslem state of Pataudi in parliament. She is one of several formidable women in the Bhopal dynasty who have ruled effectively in purdah, wearing the burkha and giving orders from behind the bamboo curtain. Mother and glamorous daughter-in-law get on, sharing a large house with a big lawn and a vegetable garden in a leafy smart part of Delhi.

Once the youngest Test captain, the Nawab was an intuitive player who moved in a graceful and catlike way, unselfconscious and uninhibited. Old Wykehamists still remember how Geoff Hodges, the Headmaster's Assistant, would tour the grounds when he was playing, intoning: 'Hulloo, hulloo, Pataudi one hundred,' until it became almost a schoolboy stock imitation.

Another old Wykehamist, Tommy Cookson, remembered directing a film at Winchester and casting the Nawab in the role of the villain. 'We just let him get on with it. He was not camera shy at all. He turned the last sod over the grave, took off his trilby and made the sign of the cross with it and mooched off with his two sidekicks . . . his 45 seconds worth just about stole the show.'

But he has never shown emotion in public. In 1961 when he was at Balliol he and some friends who had been playing cricket all day against Sussex went to Brighton and had a Chinese meal. The wicket-keeper Robin Walters then offered to drive the five friends back to their hotel in Hove in a Morris 1000. It was such a balmy July night that three of them decided to walk the last part of the journey. 'Come with us, Pat,' they called, 'it will do you good.' But the Nawab was feeling tired and decided to ride back. He clambered into the front passenger seat in time to take the brunt of an oncoming car which crashed into them head-on.

And those strange mischievous gods who ruined the Jam Saheb's career, took away Pataudi's sight. His right eye was ruined by splinters of windscreen glass and he too has a glass eye.

Six months later he was chosen for the Test series against England. He was twenty-one when he took over the captaincy of India. 'I was an unqualified success,' he says solemnly, and explains with that shell of supercilious humour, that the secret of his captaincy was his ability to outguess his most formidable opponents and win the toss thirteen times in succession. 'I claim definite supremacy.'

Nowadays he edits a magazine called *Sportworld*. He has a nice line in self deprecatory humour and likes to tell the story of how he was walking in Delhi with his fiancée when some schoolboys appeared. 'Oh, do you mind,' the Noob whispered, 'this will only take a minute. They will want my autograph.' But the boys ignored him completely and, looking adoringly at the film star on his arm, held out their autograph books to Sharmila Tagore.

Shortly after Pataudi had lost the sight of his eye and while he was still at Balliol, he played 'the most thrilling innings' against the West Indian touring team in the Parks. 'He was on for about forty minutes and made 45 effortless runs, playing Hall and Griffiths, the fastest bowlers in the world, off the back foot because he couldn't see the ball soon enough to play it off the front.' But only his friends will tell you about such tigerish extraordinary courage.

22

An Oriental Intrigue

'YOU ARE GUEST OF HIGHNESS?' inquires a cheery, rosy-cheeked chauffeur at Udaipur airport. Yes, but who knows which Highness? This Sungod dynasty, India's oldest family, like the Duke of Norfolk's in England, is locked in the most unseemly squabble ever known in its impeccable history of fourteen centuries.

Since the death of the Maharana Baghwat Singh in 1985, an intrigue of Byzantine extravagance has unfolded, rocking the wild hyacinth on Lake Pichola as his two sons fight out the succession. The only thing the brothers share now is a name. Both fell out with the autocratic father at different times, but the elder, Mohendra, was disinherited and lost out to Arvind his younger brother. Yet the title Maharana, 'Light of the Hindus', which is much more distinguished than maharajah, rests with the eldest.

Udaipur, a city of white marble palaces and an enchanted mother-of-pearl lake, seems serene. The palace looks deceptively innocent, heavy with the scent of tuberoses at dusk, giving no hint of the drama and intrigue behind the dark green louvred shutters.

'Ya,' says the chauffeur, as he hops into the back seat, 'the old man is my driver, madam.' Almost everyone has a servant in India. Intruding on the peace again, he asks, 'You are knowing the *Octopussy* of James Bond?' In his international English, he explains that the Lake Palace has been the location for another Cubby Broccoli film with Roger Moore as the hero, a matter of great pride.

The old Maharana was one of the first of the Princes to turn his palace into an hotel. 'It's not so bad being an hotel keeper,' he would say wryly, adapting to commerce. Later he was disillusioned and when he queried the staff's electricity bill they walked, or rather rowed, out. They grabbed the gondolas leaving guests stranded in the middle of the lake, but they gamely waded ashore as the water was low and the crocodiles comatose. Normally gondoliers in grey wool jackets with Nehru collars swish in canopied boats from the marble steps of the Lake Palace Hotel to the shore.

The road to the City Palace is busy, the old gentleman with white handlebar whiskers who has taken the wheel seldom exceeds 5 mph. Even sugar cane carts and camels saddled with sheafs of green coriander are going faster. A Tara lorry decorated with storks and lotus flowers hoots at girls with diamonds in their noses and sacking round their bodies, splitting rocks at the roadside. Black goats hurry into the yellow mustard, a holy man in a pink loincloth sits under a tree with his books and spectacles.

High on a hill is Shivniwas Palace where guests of His Highness – the Queen, Jacqueline Kennedy and the Shah of Iran – stay. It is under the wing of its parent, the shimmering and creamy seventeenth-century City Palace, where the marble balustrades are warm in the late afternoon and the hibiscus turn a deep pinkish purple. The royal hunting lodges are silhouetted on the skyline above the lake in the Arvalli Hills. Only a few stark palm trees are left; the villagers have cut down the forests for firewood, and the tigers and panthers have become royal trophies.

There is a crescent of royal suites in the guest palace with crystal furniture and Belgian chandeliers. The doors open out onto a clear blue marble pool with a Greek key design and brass handles gleam in the mouths of lions. Luscious green parakeets whoosh by like a curtsey in taffeta to pick sugar lumps from a tea tray under an umbrella by the pool.

Two vultures hover over a balustrade. In an upper corner of the vast City Palace sits a grieving Maharani. This cultivated, Bikaner princess who was a superior catch for the Maharana never goes out. Her sons have made her sad; she takes the side of the eldest, Mohendra. She was lonely long before her husband's death. The Maharana had married an English girl, a colonel's daughter. The two women never met though they lived underneath the same golden domes.

The second Maharani of Udaipur is known in Gloucestershire as Mrs Singh. She lives at Winchcombe with her widowed father in a house where the garden is overrun with butterflies and flowers each summer. London friends intimated you would be in no doubt that she was the wife of an Indian Prince.

Taut, with the alabaster prettiness of Japanese blossom, a sweet smile and almond brown eyes, Her Highness, Annabella Singh of Mewar swished into Browns Hotel dressed in cream silk with a Gucci trim of green and red and a briefcase full of animal welfare work. It would be unwise not to call her Your Highness and her writing paper has the title in gold on the back of the envelopes. Sitting up straight, extremely self-possessed, she is very much a princess.

She grew up in the Far East, studied ballet and Ninette de Valois felt she had great promise. But she was always restless and found the wandering life attractive: 'I never had roots.' It was when she was staying in India with friends that she met the Maharana, at Mayo College, and thought him 'a most interesting man'. Taken by her cool serenity and that eastern stillness, he offered her a lift back from the Ajmer Hills.

Soon afterwards she received a call in Bombay, 'We are getting married,' the Maharana told her. 'As I say, one did as my husband said.' They married in a Registrar's Office and, back in Udaipur, went in the Maharana's Rolls to the shrine of the family god, Eklingji, on a winding country road. 'My husband explained that it was the custom to remain celibate for a year, after the blessing, but only if I wished. I said I thought the blessing was enough.'

Like many other Western wives of Princes, she was not taken

as seriously as she imagined at the palace. She lived in strict purdah. 'I never went anywhere, except to the hospital and the cinema once. I worked in a turret in the palace. I learnt a little Hindi which the servants did not understand, typed, listened to classical music and read a lot. My husband was in a completely different part of the palace during the day. I missed green grass most, every time they cut the lawns in the courtyards, I loved it.'

Annabella left her turret long before her husband's death. He was travelling a great deal, giving high flown lectures on Hinduism in New York and enjoying the company of an Indian girl.

Mohendra disapproved when his stepmother came back to Udaipur wearing a white sari, the colour of mourning, with bright red lipstick after the Maharana's death. The family always resented her. If Annabella was aware of these waves, she remained cool and gracious. Her bangles are gold, but her traditional glass wedding bracelets were ritually smashed when she became a widow.

In common with other separated English wives, dogs and cats have become her life. She seems relaxed and happy, loves her work with the RSPCA and her canardlytels. An unusual breed, some kind of duckdog perhaps? 'No, no,' Her Highness laughs. 'They are my "can hardly tell" dogs, my lovely mongrels.'

Her stepdaughter, Princess Yogeshwari Kumari, 'Everyone calls me Sweetie', has taken the part of her younger brother, Arvind. She is married to a senior policeman. 'Father, we always called him Papa, was twenty years ahead of his time. He let me marry a man who wanted to earn his living, though of course he was of princely blood.'

The Princess in dark blue shawl and dark floral silk sari is quietly watchful. Servants in white leggings bring in silver trays of canapés, far too much for two people. Tandoori chicken kebabs, prawns, scampi with tartare sauce all for 'Highness's guest'. Henry Kissinger is also staying. The beaming chef is brought in, 'Did you like?' As he leaves the Princess says, 'He is one of the older retainers, they work for the family until they actually die off.'

Young, shrewd, a little sad, the Princess says, 'We have nothing left except priceless French furniture,' and points to chairs with gold arms carved into bird shapes, mirrored chaises-longues with rose satin covers and exquisite crystal chandeliers twinkling like rainbows. The million rupee question is which of her brothers will inherit all this?

This old and distinguished family has never matched the other Rajput Princes who made Mogul marriages in solid wealth or comforting caches of jewels. 'We fought the Moguls and none of our ancestors intermarried,' the Princess says, swinging her sari over her shoulder. 'Unlike the Jaipurs and Jodhpurs who do not like to be reminded of this,' she adds sniffily. The grand history of the Mewar dynasty and its resistance to the Moslem rulers has left Udaipur with a legacy of integrity but no money, only 19 guns and 'two lakhs of lazy people'.

In India you talk about dynasties, twelfth-century ancestors, the Emperor Akbar, as if it were all yesterday. When a villager was asked if Queen Victoria ever saw the Lake Palace, he replied solemnly, 'No, she is not coming here yet.'

Two enjoyable days went by with still no sign of either Highness. It was like being cossetted in purdah. Mornings were spent in a pretty blue suite looking down on the life of Udaipur, its gypsies and camels.

In the City Palace museum the funny little lift is shown off with as much pride as the murals of dancing girls among lotus leaves, the frescos of elephants washing in lily ponds and the red and silver mirrored royal bedrooms. There is a gaudy gold and brown cardboard cut-out figure of Sir Bhupal Singh Baduhar, one of Udaipur's greatest rulers whom the British resident movingly described as 'a demi-god'. The palace servant is equally proud of the ceramic white lavatory tiles beside the ancient Chinese and Persian blue, explaining how they were 'all new ting in the 1940s'.

A third morning sitting by the pool when, suddenly, a man comes bounding in with a swashbuckling air. Wearing a beret, a suede zipped jacket, dark glasses and cords, he looks like a bouncy French travel agent. Everyone jumps to attention. 'Yes, Your Highness' . . . 'No, Your Highness.' This is Maharaj Arvind Singh, the younger brother, who is virtually running the Mewar inheritance.

He is tough, cynical but kind-hearted. He says he is not the Maharana and is quite happy for his brother to accept that spiritual garland. He does not bear fools gladly. He laughs when his officious young aide in flared brown trousers, ingratiatingly shooing the pigeons away, tells him some foreign visitors would like to see him at 2.30. 'What, are we creatures in a zoo to be stared at? . . . Pah' and pounds off with his leather handbag after a quick cup of coffee. 'My sister has told me about you,' he says over his shoulder. 'Come to the Ranch tonight.'

The widowed Maharani's Cadillac with a deerskin rug on the floor and curtained windows makes its stately way to the Ranch House about twenty minutes away from the City Palace. This is a modern American style house with stables because Maharaj Kumaror Arvind is mad about horses. Prince and Princess Michael of Kent spent part of their honeymoon at the Ranch and Arvind Singh was one of the first to hear when they were expecting their first baby.

Away from the palace Arvind Singh is much less intimidating, relaxed in blue shirt and jeans. His head is shaved and he has grown a beard, a custom in India for sons after their father's death. 'For six months after our father's death, we must abstain from alcohol, meat and all sorts of things,' he grins. Besides, he is in training for polo. A Great Dane puts her head in his lap; his sister arrives, also much easier and friendlier away from the palace. Dinner is European with potent crêpes suzette.

His wife, 'Bhootie', Raj Kumari Vijayraj, a Kutch princess, whom he married without permission in 1972, is in Bombay expecting their third child. She reads compulsively, is good company and walks the golf course to keep fit. She is no submissive Indian wife, though her grandmother married at the age of nine, had a child at eleven and sixteen more children.

Arvind Singh explains that this third baby was not entirely

their own choice. 'We were happy with two daughters but my father ordered us to have another child so Bhootie was pregnant before he died.'

Before dinner, photographs are passed round of his father's cremation. It is always a shock in India to see the body, a head peeking above garlands of marigolds. 'Father made a good fire, that is a good omen.' Arvind Singh, as he is called in Udaipur, is now very much head of the family and not reluctant to talk about his relationship with his father and the impasse with his elder brother.

He fell out with the Maharana when he left Mayo College and they did not speak for ten years. To show his independence Arvind came to England and began work in a factory in Salford, earning £14 a week. 'I gave my landlady £7,' he says with some pride.

Marjorie Hamilton, a doctor's widow, is a chatty, sympathetic, bird-like creature. She welcomed the pale, trembling young boy at Hale station in the middle of winter. He introduced himself diffidently: 'I am Arvind Singh.' He was so frightened, 'Poor boy, he couldn't speak. He was like someone who had spent his whole life in a convent.'

She remembers how, when he arrived at her vast, red stone manse in a good part of Cheshire, he put his little Buddha statue up in the bedroom and asked her not to introduce him as an Indian Prince's son. His father had been all over *Cheshire Life* once and the gossip columns full of titbits about the glamorous Maharani, his French wife. 'Of course,' Mrs Hamilton shrugged, 'she was not the Maharani at all, just a girlfriend in Europe.'

Every morning Arvind caught the train from Altrincham to go to the clothing factory in the rush hour. 'He hated trains and especially loathed people knocking against him.' In the palace, he had never experienced this sort of human contact except when one of his three personal servants was putting shoes on, and if he got it wrong, 'Arvind said he would give him a kick . . . if he was being annoying.'

After supper in the vast kitchen, with its deep white

cupboards, Mrs Hamilton would spread out coins and notes to teach her model lodger about money. He was baffled. He knew nothing about everyday life and as for buying his ticket for the train, this was something done by an ADC. He was cautious about what he ate; there was always a lurking fear in Udaipur that food might be poisoned. 'Life in a palace must be very hazardous,' his landlady shivered, glad not to be a maharani.

Looking back, Arvind Singh thinks it was a marvellous experience. Unlike many of the Princes, he knows how to earn a living. 'Father didn't send money. He was too proud and I was too proud to ask, but I was very happy and always kept a pound by for tea in the pavilion.' By that time he was playing cricket for Lancashire which enabled him to make lasting friendships. Then he left for Chicago, where he says he washed dishes, changed bedlinen and learnt everything there was to know about hotel management.

He loves England but is critical of British rule in India. 'I am afraid they imposed a style and feeling of being above everyone else and then we were let down with a ratlike bang.'

In the summer of 1985, Mrs Hamilton was at her kitchen window when a Mercedes drew up; it was Arvind Singh, 'Oh so confident, so self-possessed,' she thought. 'What a joy!' In London he is trying to decide on a rented house near Marble Arch but is worried about the noise. 'You see I am used to a quiet place at home,' he says to an unsuspecting agent who knows him simply as Mr Singh.

The two brothers could not be more different. Mohendra, the eldest and new Maharana, is thin at 45, ascetic and precise with ritual handwashing after food. Looking rather stark with his head shaven, he is courteous and intense.

'You have landed up smack in the middle of an oriental intrigue,' Mohendra smiles. It is late at night. After several telephone calls he has been tracked to his house which is called Samore Bagh, down in the valley.

It was an emotionally charged atmosphere in the darkly lit drawing room and there were endless telephone calls from lawyers. Obviously proud of his heritage, Mohendra says simply, 'I am Maharana, but my younger brother has all the documents; now we must fight this in the courts.' Other Princes watch with horrified fascination. There is a feeling that the eldest son would be a good spiritual leader and the younger better at making the palaces more profitable.

Mohendra explains that he took out the injunction against his father, with whom he had 'a love–hate relationship', because he believed he was being badly advised. 'I thought my father was allowing the Mewar inheritance to be squandered.

'Dealers would arrive; there was never any inventory and Udaipur was being stripped. It was very distressing. Father was getting rid of a lot of beautiful things; people simply walked off with the miniatures. Father was very impulsive, he loved entertaining.'

But the Maharana never forgave his eldest son. He made a provocative will just before his death in November 1984, witnessed by his younger son Arvind. On the grounds that Maharaj Kumaror Mohendra Singh was 'living in a world of unreality . . . and not coming up to expectations', he cut him out, barring his heir and also his mother 'from receiving or inheriting any part of the estate'.

To keep calm, Mohendra reads the scriptures, and says he owes his love of reading to his English tutor: 'He was my friend and adviser: because of my education, I can hold myself high in a drawing room.'

He has nothing to lose by litigation, but the need for it causes him concern. Particularly when he remembers how moved he was, immediately after his father's death, at being carried through the streets by an excited crowd chanting 'our Maharana'. He finds the whole thing 'bizarre' and adds, with a slight smile, 'But I have absolutely no ambition to play the evil Grand Vizier.'

Next morning Arvind is striding around Udaipur airport, challenging, assertive, dressed in traditional shawl over one shoulder. Relatives and aides hanging on his every word, he is off to Bombay again to see his lawyers. Just as he is about to board a plane for Bombay, he hears the news that his wife has given birth to a son. 'Oh sir, it is the spirit of your father,' hints a lurking cousin.

The rooms in the City Palace stay locked by the litigants. It is hollow and has a sad, decaying beauty. On the walls of the old zenana there are pictures of Residents and British army officers. Some fleshy indulgent faces, hair plastered down, others quizzical, with plucky smiles, solemn or wryly amused. This battle for succession would not have been allowed in their time. In the middle, there is a painting of Queen Victoria in a cloud of lace. As usual she looks disapproving, as if some impropriety is about to take place. She would not have been wrong in Udaipur.

23

A Little Fling

SIMLA WAS AN EXCLUSIVE little Esher snug in the splendour of the Himalayas, a mixture of viceregal grandeur and anxious middle-class gentility. Lord Curzon found the mid-April exodus to Simla tedious and never came to terms with the tall 'Disappointed Gothic' houses called Fairy Cottage and Windermere, with their Burmese stools and faded chintz, the teashops and depressing churches. He thought it utterly dull, a desert: 'like dining every day with the butler in the housekeeper's rooms'.

This would have shocked those army and Civil Service wives who were being so vivacious in Simla, imagining themselves a huge success in viceregal circles where they might not be so easily accepted once back in the plains. 'Clod-hopping' Collectors and their families were never welcome. Girls in search of husbands were disappointed as flirty army and Civil Service wives, 'grass widows' in wide-brimmed straw hats with ostrich feathers and lace collars, had all the fun.

Other hill stations, Ooty for Madras, Naini Tal for Lucknow and Darjeeling for Calcutta, were pleasant but less fashionable. Simla was chic because in 1830 it became the Viceroy's summer capital when it was unbearably hot in Delhi. It was also a delicious way of escaping the tyranny of the despatch boxes, the social equivalent of shooting in Scotland on the 12th.

The priggish but perceptive Fanny Eden, spinster sister of

Lord Auckland, who became Governor-General of India in 1835, stopped pining for Greenwich when she set eyes on Simla in 1838. She loved the air and the wholesomeness but found the Indian 'dirt and tinsel' distasteful. Yet she was sensitive enough to ask why the hill people in Simla wrapped in their bright yellow and red shawls, who had never seen Europeans before, should be so polite. '. . . I sometimes wonder they do not cut off all our heads and say nothing more about it.'

Instead, on the night of the Annandale ball, they bowed and were bemused by a party of English men and women, eating salmon from Scotland and sardines from the Mediterranean, and praising the chef's St Cloud's potage à la Julienne, while the band played selections from Bellini's *I Puritani*. The men admired the 'ladies', who fretted in case their sleeves were unfashionably tight. The term 'wife' was not polite until the middle of the nineteenth century, so husbands referred to their wives as 'my lady' whatever their private thoughts.

The journey from Delhi was once by bullock cart and tonga. Then in 1903 the creamy Kalka Mail train began. It is still running and looks such a tiny toy for its windy journey up to the terraced hillsides of a now rather ghostly Simla. Only hand luggage is allowed. First stop is for a cow on the line. Children run alongside the train, skipping along the banks, brushing their teeth with bark from the neem tree.

Already there is a tingle of Simla in the air at Barogh, which is the 'half-way halt'. Migrating wives in flower-sprigged frocks stopped here for tea with 'Slaice of Omelate' in the First Class Officers' Rest Room where the brass fittings still gleam. There is a well-polished, decent mahogany table at which a note could be scribbled about something spotted in the Army and Navy catalogue.

The station master is a dignified figure in a grey knitted hat and Nehru jacket. Tall, noble sentries, blankets thrown over one shoulder, stand about attentively as the driver takes out his Parker pen; there is a burst of music and the train is on its way again. Doorstep red houses with green wooden verandahs, called Fairview and Rose Cottage, loom nearer, and lawns once

the scene of hard fought games of croquet are overgrown; but
for memsahibs and Princes and unattached ADCs this was the
start of romance and glamour.

Simla was so English, it appealed to the more exotic Princes.
Normally they moved in viceregal circles, but now they also
met in Simla a whole host of women at parties who had shaken
off solemn husbands left slogging conscientiously in the heat of
Delhi and Calcutta. As Kipling said:

> Jack's own Jill goes up the hill,
> To Murree or Chakrata;
> Jack remains and dies in the plains,
> And Jill remarries soon after.

The Princes' concubines and wives held their own purdah
parties. Molly Hamilton (the author M. M. Kaye) remembered
how well dressed all the women were, wearing nail polish and
fashionably designed jewellery. 'But I remember going to one
purdah party where the wife of this hill rajah was wearing a
chintzy chemise and was very fat. A chaprassi passed by on the
veranda and quite suddenly she left us and went under the table.
We had to lure her out like an agitated cat. She said, "You must
forgive me but I've never seen a man before except my husband.
Feel my heart, feel my heart," and grabbed my hand, putting
it to this very fat bosom.'

Lady Audrey Talbot, a gentle, artistic girl, staying with Lady
Chetwode, 'aunt Star', was not impressed by some of the people
she met in Simla. From the security of her position as the
daughter of an earl, she thought some of them . . . 'so dreadful'.
At a viceregal dance, it was too killing being forced to dance
with a 'frightful young man . . . who talked about the pater'.
Others were worse, 'over polite and attentive, bouncing up to
light Aunt S's cigarette and handing things one can reach
oneself'.

The chief archaeologist for India, Sir John Marshall, and his
wife were 'ultra-refined; she takes tea with her little finger in
the air'. Others made conversational faux pas, talking about

'viscountess so-and-so and the honourable Mrs'. Subtleties of conversation contrived to divide people immediately. It was social death if you failed to keep up when talk at tea turned frivolously to the origin of French words: 'lunatic, my dear it comes from the French . . .' a smattering was enough to appreciate that 'loon = French for moon, d'ye see?'

These hill stations were heavenly melting pots for socially aspiring, flirtatious women. But they were not stimulating intellectual company. Sir Alfred Lyall had nothing but 'contempt for them', ever plunging about on lawn tennis courts, and dancing incessantly with 'les militaires'. He complained that nobody cared about literature. He was right. Books often held nothing more than pressed flowers.

But the Princes were not in Simla to talk about *Antigone*. They hummed Gilbert and Sullivan tunes and enjoyed the shows at the Gaiety Theatre, laughing at performances of *The Road to Ruin*, *Miss in her Teens* and *The Padlock*. Although it was so intrinsically a mixture of Cheltenham and Brighton, the great lure for the Punjab Princes particularly was the skittish dedication to fun.

They looked forward to their white and blue laced invitations, to 'bridge and gimlet' mornings, garden parties, polo, croquet gymkhanas, golf and tea dances. There were picnics in the pine forests, the alpine astringency giving an appetite for fish, cold meat, fruit and duck paste, tea or gin and tonic. One of Calcutta's prettiest girls could eat two pounds of mutton chops without blinking; there were hot cashew nuts and sweet ginger cake for tea at the end of an afternoon's pony-trekking and walking. Tennis at Viceregal Lodge was in the shadow of Simla's highest mountain, the Silver Bangle, where light English voices carried across the snowy valley: 'Oh well played, Henrietta.' They skated on the ice rinks and galloped into the Mall for mango ice cream and apricot sherberts at five. Near the church, there was Simla's Scandal Point for gossip about flirtations and romances.

Rickshaws were like necklaces strung across the hillside in Simla whenever there was a Viceregal Ball. Only the three

top people, the Viceroy, the Commander-in-Chief and the
Governor of the Punjab, were allowed cars and carriages in the
Mall. For everyone else there were rickshaws, although even
here there was a distinction. For the aristocracy there were red
rosettes on the rickshaws and the panting scarlet-liveried coolies
ran straight to the private entrance. It was white roses and the
public entrance for everyone else. The arrival of a 17-stone
general's wife 'flaxen wigged' was always a little slower; her
coolies were known as the Faith Team for their ability to move
mountains. There were fancy dress galas, like the one in 1886
at which girls such as Miss Gough were a huge success, 'adorable
in white with swansdown and little pussy ears . . .' and the
Viceroy, Lord Dufferin, dressed up as an Arab making 'all the
ladies positively swoon'; even his wife did not recognise him.

Champagne flowed; there was smoked salmon and whitebait,
partridge and pheasant; and in the valleys the most delectable
wild strawberries, apricots and cherries. And a missionary called
Stokes had introduced the apple to Simla, including the red
Richard; it really was just like being in Kent.

Those were the days of doeskin gloves, ball gowns of black
silk, parasols of lace; memsahibs spent their days sketching or
sitting on verandahs in bamboo chairs under hanging baskets
of flowers, gossiping about dances and new faces. They amused
themselves by selecting new hats and pretty silks and idly
watching the butterflies and bright red and blue birds.

The Maharajah of Patiala loved Simla. He was a sensation, a
superb dancer, a sexual athlete, sophisticated and, unlike some
of the Princes, did not think that if an English woman danced
she must be a nautch girl. His retinue of 1,000, including wives,
mistresses, secretariat and stables, would move to his Simla
palace for six months of partying, tennis, excellent cricket and
royal hunting. But there was a strict code of behaviour which
he failed to understand, carried away by the floss and frivolity.

On his sixtieth birthday, celebrated in Simla, he was given a
present of four concubines. Handsome in a novelettish way –
six feet tall, swashbuckling, with gleaming black thigh-high
boots, a long red tunic and white bucksin trousers, he was never

inscrutable. He had a waxed curving moustache and vivid staring dark eyes, and he made the poor ICS – Cecils, Henrys and Philips – look moistly pink and insipid. The memsahibs might have tittered about this 'Favoured Son of the British Empire', but in the fantasies of at least a few he was a tiger of a man.

At lunch in Viceregal Lodge, Patiala once ate three poached eggs and rice, four thick slices of mutton and vegetables, two large helpings of chicken curry and plum tart. He made Lady Chetwode angry, not because he confided that once he had liked a virgin a day but now could only cope with one a week, but when he sent for her chef. The Commander-in-Chief's wife was outraged. She was accustomed to sycophantic requests for her 'toothsome' recipes.

The Maharajah bought three properties in Simla, giving these stucco, stockbroker houses dull, unimaginative names which were fashionable at the time – The Cedars, Oakover and Rookwood. In 1891 he built Chail, a 20-roomed palace, and with its powdering of snow, a welcome wooded retreat after the heat of Delhi and the Punjab. He hoped it would rival the Viceroy's house. Chail is twenty-eight miles outside Simla, high on a hill above sweet-smelling pine forests full of deer and vivid birds. There are two unusual pink stone sentry boxes, narcissi on the well-kept lawns and a scattering of white wrought-iron tables and two large white cherubs with jet black hair. One of the royal gardeners, Laxmi Ram, hands you a flower as he always did in the Maharajah's day. This was where Patiala – Sir Bhupinder Singh 'the Magnificent' – gave the best parties in Simla, where couples drank Sidecars and smoked de Reske cigarettes leaning against curving staircases, and tunes were played on the grand piano and sesame wood fireplaces were ablaze with pine logs.

If Patiala was addressed properly, the word 'sri' had to be inserted 108 times, but he graciously waived this formality while in the hills. He was a fine cricketer, a good shot and dogbreeder. But women were his downfall.

Curzon, with his unswerving sense of propriety, was particularly outraged when he found his own wife, Mary, had succumbed to the sensuous pleasure of being wrapped in a crinkling silk sari by the Maharajah of Patiala, who excitedly fished out his best jewels and covered her in rubies, emeralds and diamonds and heavy gold ankle bracelets.

The Maharajah also bought a cluster of pine cottages down in the woods for his ADCs and secretaries. The palace is a hotel now, and Indian honeymooners covet one of the cottages. It is decorated in appalling taste, red candlewick bedspreads, red satin hearts with purple arrows and pictures from the Kama Sutra and of the erotic carvings at Khajuraho. Newlyweds, expected to match the pouting goddesses, archly smiling, legs wound saucily round the waists of their warriors, get a drink on the house. This is Lassi, a gentle yoghurt and milk drink which is hardly an aphrodisiac, but the groom may get a glass of milk with almonds and saffron.

'It was all such fun when we were young and blonde and had admirers; it is all gone now. We used to go to parties, now all we have are cupboards full of Russian fur coats.' Two maiden memsahibs, Irene and Dorothy Heysham ('we date back to William the Conqueror') are living on a hillside in Simla, 'hanging on' in a house called Dunloe with a kindly bearer who cooks for them. They have high singsong voices, but remember putting flowers in their hair, drinking champagne and dancing at Viceroy's House. 'In those days Queen Victoria had to approve a marriage,' they add, as if explaining their single state.

Viceregal Lodge, once filled with teak and walnut furniture, is rather neglected now. Once Nehru, Jinnah, Gandhi and Mountbatten met here in a high room overlooking Simla's orchards of apples and cherries; 'our wallies' a local says gesturing towards the sweeping landscape below which looks like Switzerland. 'It makes me absolutely sick to see this house full of smelly Indians,' Lady Pamela Hicks once heard a corseted memsahib say to another on the staircase of the Lodge. It is shabby now, the gold and white of the doors grubby, but the names embossed on Burma teak endure and there are a few portraits left of thin-nosed vicereines. The staff all used to wear imperial scarlet and each guest had eleven servants. Now it is a worthy Institute of Advanced Studies. A slightly sneery Indian academic shows the English visitor out.

The Maharajah of Patiala was shown the way out of Viceregal Lodge and Simla by the British. He had become overexcited by the number of seemingly available young women and misunderstood the atmosphere. When the Viceroy was enthusiastic about 'a damned good little piece of stuff', he meant a breed of Burmese pony, ideal for the Hill Station. The Maharajah was banned by the British on charges of making 'immoral overtures' to an Englishwoman; they never allowed him into Simla again.

Now newlyweds from Delhi dance in the snow at the Maharajah's Palace and pose for the photographer, who says, 'Be a maharajah and a maharani for a day.'

❧ 24 ❧

Nothing but Grief and Heartache

THE PRINCES became commoners on 1 January 1972. Misters now, never Maharajah, Maharana, Nawab, Nizam or Jam Saheb again. They lost their titles, their privy purses and their privileges. Hundreds of servants wept and went back to their villages. There was no money to pay them, so no more salaaming or reverent stroking of Highness's feet. Life at the palace would never be the same again.

Their masters shed tears too. They grieved; no more gun salutes. That harmless, noisy way of flattering the Princes, invented by the British, meant so much, especially to the top five, Baroda, Gwalior, Hyderabad, Kashmir and Mysore, who all rated 21 booms. The money was not important to them, they were wealthy in their own right. Those guns were the indelible symbol of their superior rating in the Indian peerage.

'Every time I came to London, I was entitled to a 21-gun salute and to be met by the Queen at London Airport.' The former ruler of Baroda, Mr Fatesinghrao Gaekwad, is droll about the implications. The Queen would be chasing up and down the M4 constantly as there is hardly a day an Indian Prince does not arrive at Heathrow. The former Maharajah does not hanker for lost privileges, but at the same time puts it succinctly, 'How would you feel if someone tried to remove your clothes?' He went on to become an industrialist. Others were ambassadors for their country, Jaipur in Madrid and Jodhpur in Trinidad.

But for many, not particularly resilient, educated or worldly in terms of survival, it was a blow from which they would never really recover. As the Maharajah of Benares, a spiritual leader, said: 'No Prince could be happy, it was too late to become businessmen.'

For them the money mattered most. It may have seemed bizarre, shades of Tsarist Russia and the Dauphin's France, that 277 maharajahs should have been on the pension list in this adolescent democracy of starving millions. The Maharajah of Mysore was getting £144,000 a year tax free. As it happens he was an ascetic man who did good works. The Barodas, Jaipurs, Travancores, Kashmirs and Patialas each got £90,000.

The Princes argue that this was nothing much in terms of what they had 'willingly' given up at the time of Independence. In 1948 they sacrificed two-fifths of India. Half accepted compensation, the other half trustingly chose what they believed to be the more enduring privy purses and privileges.

That civil list, based on the revenue of their former kingdoms, cost the Indian Government two and a half million pounds a year. 'It wouldn't,' the Maharana of Udaipur remarked bitterly, 'buy every Indian a picture postcard.' At the bottom end of the scale, one Prince, the Rajah of Katodia, got only £10 a year and went to work on a bicycle; he was a clerk in Gujarat. He never accepted invitations unless sent the fare first.

The privileges included free water and electricity, free medicine, immunity from legal action, armed guards and their own red State number plates. They were allowed to fly flags, had special police escorts, were able to import their gin, whisky, brandy and anything else from abroad free of import duties and, finally, were entitled to full military honours at their funeral.

Defying Mrs Gandhi the Princes formed a union, the Concord of India. They appointed the rarified Maharajah of Dhrangadhra, with his Oxford English, as their Intendant General and convenor. Sophisticated, rather grand and very precise, a £22,000 privy purser, he seemed the ideal imperial father to put their case.

But this was no pushy, militant union, with Dhrangadhra pushing back his silk hat and saying, 'Look here, brothers . . .' He did not have to tell them that they were sad figures, scapegoats for royal India and a hated imperial past.

They met in Bombay, sometimes at the home of the Nawab of Palanpur, at others in the Imperial Hotel. They talked nobly about the greatest hardship being the loss of Izzat, their self-respect. They issued beautifully bound, embossed brochures setting out their views called 'Breach of Faith'. First the British had broken faith with them and now one of their own.

Some had been good Rulers, enlightened and caring. But just as in 1947, when they were living in fantasy land and unworldly, now they were bewildered by the new thrusting socialism. In December 1970, late at night, Parliament voted to reduce the Princes to the rank of commoners and for the abolition of the privy purses and privileges. The President was dragged out of bed to sign the order. The Princes went to the Supreme Court pleading it was against the Constitution. They lost.

Two maharajahs actively supported Mrs Gandhi, the Maharajah of Kashmir and the Rajah of Suket, both of whom thought the princely institution an albatross. They were called the Pink Princes and tried to act as go-betweens with Congress. Four dowagers, Gwalior, Jaipur, Jodhpur and Bikaner, were in the right-wing Opposition, disliking Mrs Gandhi's stern socialism. Nine Princes, including Kotah, Baroda and Gwalior, had been elected members of Parliament.

But the Congress Party was re-elected in 1971, and any chance the Princes had of surviving vanished. They were as vulnerable as the deer they had tied up between two lighted posts to be pounced on by a tiger at viceregal shoots.

Mrs Gandhi was in her lair, almost replete after the over-whelming election success, a strong Prime Minister again. She had gone into the Indian villages and attacked the Princes: 'Go and ask the maharajahs how many wells they dug for the people in their states when they ruled them, how many roads they constructed? What did they do to fight the slavery of the British?' Now she waited, drily amused, as the Princes, one by one, came to see her. They called her Madam. She twiddled with her sari and politely inquired of the elderly Maharajah of Dewas Junior, a kingdom made famous by E. M. Forster in *The Hill of Devi*, if he had any thoughts on the formalities. 'Madam,' he said, 'if I am told I am to be executed tomorrow, it's really of little moment to me whether you use a hemp rope or a gold chain. Please suit yourself; the methodology is of small consequence.'

Mrs Gandhi, educated at Girton and filled with fresh idealism, saw most of the Princes as a medieval frivolity, a joke. She had promised the Left that they would go, but the people had not been baying for the maharajahs' blood. India has never been an equal society and Communism has never had the success one might expect in India except in Kerala, which has the country's highest literacy rate. Strong faith and fatalism seem to sustain a people who have every reason to be resentful.

But the Prime Minister had a regard for some of the Princes and listened to them. The Maharawal of Dungarpur, a highly respected elder, was one. He tried to explain to her that she was being high-handed. 'I told her, "We are not begging." Mrs Gandhi sat fiddling with her thumbnail.' He imitated the gesture. 'I then said, "What you are doing is totally wrong."' Complete silence; still fiddling with her nail and without looking up, the Prime Minister said with a slow smile: 'Come again, Your Highness.' This was too much for Rajasthan's longest serving Ruler. Drawing himself up to his full height, he looked down, meeting her cool abstracted stare. '"Your Highness!" I said. "I am nothing of the sort. It is a poor compliment. I am afraid that, thanks to you, I am His Lowliness."'

Even some of the union meetings in their hour of crisis lacked the fervour of a united, wronged brotherhood. One Prince brought a new toy to a meeting in the dingy hotel room. It was a tape-recorder but would not be used to take minutes of their restrained, gentlemanly discussions. A shoeless royal bearer padded in silently, so as not to disturb Highness's important meeting. He had carried in the ungainly machine and frantically tried to make the plug fit securely in the wall-socket. But it was too loose. 'Bearer,' called the Prince, toying with his glass of whisky, 'stand with your foot against the plug.' The servant put his bare foot against the plug in the wall and, with an amiable smile, wedged it for over an hour standing on one leg. Western pop music and a few old paso dobles and cha-cha-chas soothed his master and his two princely friends. The Princes lolled back in their chairs, eyes closing with scampering memories of 'terrific parties'. It was the eve of their execution, New Year's Eve 1971.

For some it meant relative poverty, like the impecunious earl who was asked if perhaps he could economise by cutting down on his staff. 'How on earth could I manage with less people?' was his reply. Well, perhaps he could let the pastry cook go. He was appalled. 'Can't a fella have a biscuit with his tea?' They were a generation not accustomed to work although they resented being caricatured as decadent spendthrifts.

The Maharana of Udaipur, who had once called Mrs Gandhi 'Little Sister', wrote to her wryly recalling her promise there would be no hardship or humiliation for the Rulers.

The formidable Begum of Bhopal, now seventy, is outspoken. 'What is all this talk about ostentation and glamour? Maybe a few, but why all this portraying of the Princes in a light of opulence and easy living?'

She sits perched on a low divan, legs curled underneath, in the hall of the large house in Delhi which she shares with her son, the Nawab of Pataudi and his film star wife. She is impressive, worn, smiling at her grandchildren. Bedrolls come flying in; some of the family like to sleep outside on the verandah. Her son is with friends, drinking beer from a silver tankard before a log fire in the drawing room which is very chintzy, the coffee tables covered with long-tailed silver pheasants.

She had a remarkable grandmother, the Begum of Bhopal, who ruled effectively from behind a purdah curtain.

'The Princes gave up everything for the good of their country,' she says, 'and it is not easy to give up power. Now all we get from these people who are lording it over us with their inferiority complexes, is contempt. Ah, India is such a mess!'

It had been harrowing for her. Fugitives from the Union Carbide chemical plant disaster in Bhopal had made their way to her house in Delhi, one man almost blind. The Begum had taken them in. 'You see the average villager still has a great deal of loyalty to his Ruler, the good Ruler.' She was tiring. A servant went by. 'Of course, we had hundreds of those,' and when he had gone added, 'they bred like rabbits. We didn't need them but we gave them food and a home.'

The relationship between the Princes and their servants is often comical, a game which both enjoy. At Bikaner, Dr Karni Singh, the Maharajah, is a roly poly figure in pinstripe trousers, navy cardigan and silk cravat. He is followed everywhere by a devoted covey of servants who look solemn as he sneezes every time he goes near the paintings. One carries a notebook, another lifts the sheet covering each picture. 'Aagh, white ants,' says the Maharajah, an Olympic sportsman. 'Make a note.' Headshaking by the servants as if this is the most noble instruction they have ever been given. They smile indulgently; nothing will be done, the ants have been feasting for years. It costs money to restore paintings.

Nobody except his daughter goes into the vaults any more because they are frightened of snakes, not rats. Father and daughter are trying to create a gallery dedicated to Earl Mountbatten and are searching for photographs, menus and letters. Rats are sacred in Bikaner and have their own white temple, dating back to the plague in 1934, which is always floodlit. It is auspicious to let these ageing grey white rats run over your feet.

Bikaner was one of the great states, with its dusty rose palace rising up out of the inhospitable desert, and its Camel Corps. There are warm, chatty letters from King George V and Queen Mary, clocks from the Tsar's palace in Russia and photographs of grandfather Bikaner, the great Ganga who was at the Treaty of Versailles. But now, the ex-maharajah says, 'We have nothing left, no more boodle; it has been nothing but grief and heartache. My mind is adjusted now to the plastic cup; that is all that matters.'

He and his wife live in one room in the palace, eating at a card table. Guests are entertained in a vast room of gloomy drapes and mahogany furniture with carved garlands of roses. The Maharajah fusses, 'How can it be all right? Once you would have had French food on a gold dinner service, three hundred at a sitting, now hardly one.' He fishes out an old menu with the Bikaner crest, peers at it. 'Ah, Consommé Colbert, Filet de Pomfret.' Brown eyes fly to the date as he recites other delicacies like a litany of saints. 'American Rognons Swann, plats de Bikaner, Havana cigars, monogrammed cigarettes for the ladies.'

The Maharajah grew nostalgic for the old tunes played by the eight-piece Bikaner orchestra: '"Chant of the Jungle" and "Lonely Feet" – my wife and I, once we danced from city to city in Mexico and on round the world.' In the car, he drives fast. 'Belt up, you are precious.' There is a fair bit of deprecating tongue-in-cheek humour. He was, after all, in politics for many years.

His father-in-law, the Maharawal of Dungarpur, has a more robust attitude although his palace, sitting beside a small temple by the water's edge, is distinctly crumbling. 'I am trying to keep it up with distemper,' the Maharawal says like a tired housewife.

If interior designers were allowed into the palace to give it a facelift with Indian fabrics, it could rival the golden palace on the lake at Udaipur. But commerce is not innately in the heart of this 78-year-old man who also enjoyed a political career: 'I was Speaker with Madam.' He has given up hunting now, but still paints well, landscapes mainly.

It is a palace of glittery marble courtyards, snow white in the sun. Inside, rooms have a thirties flavour; twin beds with canopies and gloomy green curtains, paintings of peonies, a Patience Strong picture of an English thatched cottage smothered in a horseshoe of roses, a lake in Donegal covered in mist. There are jaded pink sofas and, on the desks, old inkwells and a couple of sheets of embossed writing paper. It is as if one of the Raj, a *Daily Telegraph* reader, had just popped out rather unexpectedly in 1947, but would be back.

The Maharawal rattles round the palace. The glasses were a bit dusty, but the fifteen servants can only do so much. 'Once there were sixty but as they die off, I can't replace them.' You sense again the same smiling devotion between servant and ex-Ruler. He met his Sikh washerman when he went to Nairobi; he is still a big game hunter.

'This dhobi invited me to his home. "Come," he said, "eat." Well, there was a stuffed chicken and a bottle of whisky on the table. I was faced with this on my own. Nobody was sitting down with me and so I said to the family, "I can't eat all this on my own," but the Sikh smiled, "What you leave, we eat." He is a very rich man now.'

The Maharawal talked movingly about the unceremonial handing over of his land in 1972.

'This is how it happened in my case. It was indicated by the Collector of Dungarpur to my private secretary that all the maharajahs should hand over on a certain date. I should meet him to do this.' Knowing Indian bureaucracy, there was a vision of this distinguished figure waiting at the palace gates to hand over his inheritance or sitting in the Collector's office for hours, while clerks looked for his papers, unlocked a safe, and brought out a packet of damp Nice biscuits for tea.

It was too much to expect, a final indignity. Once the owner of 30 cars, 100 horses, 5 elephants and now left with a bare 120 acres, the Maharawal declined the invitation. Sitting back in his chair, left arm stretched out touching a chutney jar on the table, he did what he had always done:

'I sent my man.'

25

Sinister Beyond Belief

THE PRINCES had a childlike sense of fun. The Maharajah of Gwalior loved giving his British guests poached eggs which were made of stone, long-stemmed glasses of sparkling lemonade contained Eno's Fruit Salts, sandwiches were made with pink flannel rather than ham and cigarettes and cushions were constantly exploding.

The Maharajah of Bharatpur, Kishan Singh, who bankrupted the state by the time he was twenty-eight, dealt with affairs of state every Sunday evening over cocktails. Memos from the British Resident, plans for tax reform, pathetic pleas from his people, all in buff folders tied with red ribbon, would, at a nod from 'Highness', be sorted into two piles by his favourite woman from the harem for that particular night.

More drinks were poured and the maharanis and concubines, flushed and skittish, would pretend to be very solemn as the Maharajah walked to the desk. With a flourish he would daub a mark on a top paper on the left-hand pile and ignore those on the right. The private secretary would bow reverently at his master's Solomon-like judgement; the following week, he might sign the right-hand pile. This Mad Hatter approach to justice let villains go free while the innocent suffered.

When a British Political Agent asked for a map of Udaipur the Ruler ordered that he be sent a wrinkled dried popadum, which he felt should give the Resident as good an idea as any of the layout of the 12,915-square-mile state. They had their favourite little sayings: 'A slow train is best, you get more value for money.'

Matters of state never interfered with serious pleasure. Some Rulers presided ingeniously behind heavy curtains, lolling on rugs, smoking and canoodling with favourite beauties. It was understood that as the Cabinet meeting went on, silence meant the bill was rejected. It could be disheartening for an ambitious minister, who could not tell when the figure behind the curtain had slipped away, irresistibly drawn to the zenana.

Aides were too frightened or too sycophantic to cross them. Fawning at its classic best was the polite applause of Khande Rao's courtiers every time he passed wind or burped. Courtiers stood round his bed waiting as the Ruler woke up. Yawns, sneezes, wind, were all greeted by 'Excellent, Your Highness' or 'that was a fine one', heads shaken in wonder. When he yawned they snapped their fingers to ward away flies. They looked anxious as he closed his mouth: this was one of the few things a servant could not do for the Ruler. If any unfortunate courtier sneezed it was protocol to suspend him and everything shut down for the day, lest Highness catch a chill.

Rulers got endless pleasure dreaming up jokes and planned them for hours, ignoring more pressing needs. One European guest staying with Ranji, the famous cricketer, had not been on a panther shoot before. As soon as he saw the panther, he was told, he should fire, immediately throw away his rifle and run. Hundreds of beaters, servants and bearers were in on the joke.

'There, I saw its ears move!' One of the beaters pointed to the bushes. The guest eagerly pulled the trigger. After a volley of shots, he flung the rifle away and leapt whitefaced to safety. A beater came back from the jungle to the clearing with a stick smeared with blood and on it a bit of black fur:'Your panther, sahib,' and servants gathered round humble and admiring. The Jam Saheb congratulated his guest and took him to the palace for celebration drinks. The servants then hoisted the model panther on to a cart – brushing at the chips newly made in his clay flanks.

The Maharajah of Junagadh loved dogs, preferring them to people. He was also devoted to his three hundred lions roaming round the scrubland of the Gir forest. He had a pack of eight hundred dogs, each with its own room with a telephone and a servant. The cost of their upkeep was at least £5,000 a year. They had a proper, white-tiled hospital with an English vet. If he could not save them there was court mourning and the musicians played Chopin's funeral march.

Only the Viceroy, Lord Irwin, refused an invitation to the wedding arranged between a royal golden retriever Bobby and a Junagadh pet called Roshanara. A number of ruling Princes and well-connected guests arrived with the groom's party. The Nawab and 250 dogs in jewelled brocade were at the railway station on caparisoned elephants when Bobby stepped off the train on to a red carpet flanked by a two-legged guard of honour and a military band.

Roshanara's fur was gleaming from a silky shampoo. A great favourite with the Maharajah, she was scented and jewelled in an ornate coat and necklace and carried to the Durbar Hall on a silver palanquin. The Maharajah sat solemnly on his throne, it was as if a favourite daughter were getting married. The groom wore gold bracelets round his paws, a gold necklace and an embroidered silk cummerbund. Unlike other dogs, excited and bewildered by fancy dress, Roshanara and Bobby stood unblinking in their finery. After the wedding ceremony, conducted by priests who dared not refuse, there was a wedding breakfast for the couple and the Ruler's guests.

After the consummation of the marriage, Bobby was sent to kennels. His bride spent the rest of her life on velvet cushions in an air-conditioned room, pampered and fed titbits by her master. Dog weddings became highly fashionable.

In Simla, the Maharajah put his dogs into evening dress and sat them in rickshaws to annoy the 'Raj', whose airs and graces he resented. The women were infuriated, often feeling a dog's breath on their pale powdered faces as the rickshaws jostled for space on the way to Cecil's Hotel for a dance. The Maharajah had a stormy meeting with the Viceroy and promised to keep his dogs locked away. He had to agree but waited until there was a ball at Viceregal Lodge and then ordered his servants to round up every crazed, lunatic pi dog in Simla. He set them loose in the grounds and was rewarded by the sound of horrified memsahibs shrieking like peacocks.

The Moslem Maharajah was forced into exile after Independence in 1947; he had tried to cede to Pakistan but failed. He protected his animals, but not his throne, and was forced to flee to Pakistan as his country became part of India. He took with him three wives and four dogs. He would have taken a fourth wife but she had forgotten one of her children and went back to the palace and the private plane took off without her.

The Maharajah of Bharatpur never travelled without his statue of the god Krishna; a seat was always booked for the deity. Announcements at airports all over the world would warn on the tannoy that the flight would shortly be closing:'This is a last call for Mr Krishna, who still has not checked in.'

Maharajahs played impish tricks on one another. They were always exchanging virgins, pearls and elephants. One impecunious young Ruler, selling a dozen dancing girls to a Parsee millionaire, at the eleventh hour slyly slipped in three grandmothers, keeping the three youngest and most nubile for himself.

These lovable, foolish antics of the Princes were enjoyed by the British even if they were sometimes the victims of salt in tea or blotting paper biscuits. It was an indulgent relationship. Some Princes had a droll, self-deprecatory humour. The very dark-skinned Prince of Taluqdar liked to wear a grey dinner jacket: 'If I wore a black one nobody would notice me,' he enjoyed telling other guests at Government House. One maharajah mournfully pretended that his favourite wife, the senior maharani, was far from well. Only a telegram of sympathy would cheer her up, he told the Viceroy's wife, Lady Reading. It was quite untrue.

They gave girls elaborate gifts. After a stunning performance in *Oh Kay* Gertrude Lawrence was invited to join one of the Nizam of Hyderabad's sons for supper. She was thrilled when she found a gift from her host, a gold kidskin evening bag, and was intrigued when she pressed to find that inside there seemed to be several little hard jewel-like objects. Longing to see whether they were garnets, diamonds or pearls, she waited until the men were having cigars and brandy, and hurriedly opened the bag to find nothing inside except 'horrid' betel nuts which Indians like to chew and which turn the gums a very angry red.

There were other, more decadent Princes. The Maharajah of Alwar was so hideously cruel and sadistic that he made the Marquis de Sade look like Noddy. He was sophisticated, and clever.

Marvellous to look at, in a brocade coat stiff with embroidered pink roses and an old rose velvet cap, he could enchant the Vicereine and her guests with his talk of Hindu mysticism and the transmigration of souls. Only hours earlier he had been ordering widows and babies to be tied up at the palace as tiger bait. Described as a man 'sinister beyond belief', his favourite amusement was seeing young boys dragged between two bullock carts across rough tracks.

A malevolent humour and irritation with one of his lascivious brothers-in-law made him play a savage trick. The man was drunk and had been annoying the Maharajah all evening with his slobbering lechery as he repeatedly requested a beautiful girl for the night.

Eventually Alwar said he could have the best girl in his harem but was not to speak to her and could only make love to her in the dark. A girl was ordered and sent to his brother-in-law and the lights in the palace went out. After the lovemaking, the palace blazed with light as the power was suddenly switched on. It was then the man saw he had made love to his sister, one of Alwar's wives. They both committed suicide.

Alwar was smart and, bored by his lack of real power, he adopted a religious pose, calling himself Raj Rishi, the Royal Teacher and Holy Sage of the Domain. This apparent Hindu fanaticism and extreme sanctity was a way of needling the British. Respect for the cow in Hindu mythology meant, he explained, that he never touched leather and always wore gloves of black silk or chamois. He refused an invitation to stay with the Viceroy in Simla because naturally he could not sit in hide armchairs. But Lady Reading was so keen to have the witty, decadent prince at her house party, she had all the leather furniture covered in chintz. The Maharajah arrived in a Rolls-Royce upholstered in tapestry.

He humiliated other vicereines. Lady Willingdon's acquisitiveness was well known, but the devious Alwar publicly insulted her. Like Queen Mary, Lady Willingdon was notorious for her habit of admiring *objets d'art* and then expecting the unfortunate owner to offer them as a gift. She was a great collector of jewels and even accepted a cinema from one of the Princes.

At a viceregal dinner party in the early thirties the Vicereine admired a diamond ring Alwar was wearing. He handed it over to her but showed no sign of offering it as a present. Lady Willingdon put it on, stretched her fingers out: the guests were full of admiration – but eventually she had to hand it back. There was further humiliation as Alwar told the waiter to fill his crystal glass with water; he dipped the ring in it, polished it painstakingly with his napkin, removing any trace of contamination left by white viceregal flesh, and put it carefully back on his gloved finger.

When he was invited to Buckingham Palace in 1931, he announced that he would not shake hands, even with King George V or Queen Mary, without his gloves on. Queen Mary was furious, but kept his name on the guest list as he was a delegate to the Round Table Conference in 1931. He arrived. At the vital moment, the disarmingly dazzling figure in beige satin studded with diamonds and dark green velvet turban pressed a switch so that his gloves shot off mechanically for the quickest of handshakes with the Queen. Underneath, he was wearing another pair of fine, transparent gloves.

His fellow Princes were scornful of this contrived piety and went to enormous trouble and expense to play jokes on him. The Maharajah of Bharatpur, expecting Alwar at a family wedding, deliberately sent a Rolls-Royce with elegant calf upholstery to meet him, the footman and chauffeur also in a riot of leather jackets, breeches and gaiters.

The Maharajah of Bikaner, who thoroughly disapproved of Alwar, was giving a party at Mount Abu, one of the hill stations favoured by the Princes, and did not invite Alwar. In almost biblical fashion Alwar sent his servants out three days before the party and they bought up all the food for forty miles around. Alwar then saved Bikaner, who had no food for his guests, by inviting them to dine with him.

An astrologer who made the journey from Bombay to Alwar was clapped in jail as soon as he arrived. When the bewildered soothsayer was brought before the Maharajah he complained bitterly about his inhospitable time in a filthy prison. But he was laughed at for not being able to predict his own fate.

But a Savile Row tailor played a joke on Alwar, who had 4,000 suits and 2,000 walking sticks. Summoned to the palace in Rajasthan, he heard the Maharajah complain that a button was not set quite right. The tailor sighed and shook his head: 'It will take a very long time to put this right, Your Highness.' The Maharajah gave an expansive wave, told his ADC that the man from London should be given the best guest suite, an elephant, a Rolls-Royce and a selection of beautiful girls. The tailor bowed and took the jacket with him, stitched it in two seconds and spent weeks on tiger-shoots, touring Jaipur and enjoying the Taj Mahal. He was given a generous gift and left for England lucky to have escaped one of the Maharajah's favourite tricks. He liked to invite beautiful male guests to touch the ornate silver candelabra in the middle of the dining table; but as soon as they leant across, manacles shot out and trapped the wrists of the unsuspecting young men leaving them in a vulnerable plight.

Every time Alwar was about to be dethroned because he had gone just too far, he would go to England and find a way of dining with Edwin Montagu, Secretary of State for India. At his expansive and enlightened best, he would talk knowledgeably and sensitively about the role of the British in India. This usually worked and for many years his file in Whitehall was favourable.

In the end it was his cruelty to animals and not his sly insults or even the orgiastic murders which finally disaffected the British. His pederasty was well known. He had four wives, but was always surrounded by boys and young men between the ages of ten and twenty, dressed in rainbow silks; the older ones, he said, were part of the Alwar army.

He brought about his own downfall when he got into one of his purple furies at a polo match. He had played badly, blamed the pony, poured petrol over it and set fire to it in front of a horrified crowd, including the animal loving British. There had been rumours of black magic, all sorts of beastliness; now, before their own eyes, was the intolerable evidence of cruelty. Alwar was deposed in 1933 and exiled to Paris with twenty-five servants where he lived on port and brandy until he died on 20 May 1937, upset because he had not been invited to George VI's Coronation.

Even his funeral procession was bizarre. His body was brought back to Alwar – a last glimpse for his unfortunate people. His gold-plated Lanchester with its ivory steering wheel was driven through the streets and propped up in the back against gold brocade cushions was the Maharajah, in dark glasses, elaborately dressed – and wearing gloves, sinister even in death.

26

Absolute Heaven

THEY WERE the privileged ones, well-connected 'gels' who spent a winter season staying in India with their influential and well-born relations. Letters home to the shires, 'Darling Mummy, I danced with the Viceroy, he's frightfully good looking,' made no mention of the early signs that the great imperial days in India were nearly over.

The crumbling, creaky Raj was strangely resistant to change, and political nuance, anyway, meant nothing to Lavender Christie Miller, Joan Wetherell-Pepper, Penelope Chetwode or Lady Mary Clive, sister of Lord Longford. These viceregal daughters, their cousins and friends, short-haired girls in tweed jackets adopting extravagant 1930s poses, thought 'our' India was life at its best: picnicking in Simla, racing in Calcutta, polo at Quetta and dancing in Delhi. Young men were either Sir Launcelot or Sir Galahad and dhurzies worked from morning till night from *Vogue* patterns making 'evening dresses split to the kidneys at the back. It was boop, boop de boop all the way . . .' A season in India was 'absolute heaven'.

They came out by flying boat. First to Paris, then to Brindisi, on to Athens, staying at the Beau Rivage in Alexandria, flying low over Jerusalem and looking down on the pearl towns. 'Everyone came out to see us, it was such a lark. The steward would come out and say, "Mustn't land in Baluchistan, not very friendly," and then we'd fly very low over Delhi' – looking to those young eyes like a picture by Corot.

These few were not to be confused with the 'fishing fleet', those middle-class girls on the look out for husbands. 'One never moved in those circles.'

'It was that lovely time between coming out and marrying,' recalled Lady Audrey Morris, another daughter of 'good family' and a niece of Lord Chetwode. As Commander-in-Chief he was almost as important a Lord Sahib as the Viceroy. His daughter Penelope had fallen in love with an impecunious young poet who came down to dinner in fancy dress. The Chetwodes were trying to stop the marriage and had even gone so far as to choose an ADC, Randall Plunkett, whom they hoped might deflect Penelope from marrying this peculiar fellow, whose name was John Betjeman – in vain.

Lady Betjeman, at seventy-seven, had sturdy legs, a little girl face with a short grey fringe of hair and lived on top of a mountain in Herefordshire, riding a Welsh cob into Hay to do her shopping. She disliked the social side of India at first. 'I had been dragged away from Florence and art, I hated tennis parties, so I sulked at first. But it was such fun.'

They rode out from Delhi early in the morning, often with the Viceroy and Commander-in-Chief, onto a plain whose summer colour was deep cayenne; in November it became yellow with mimosa and flowering tamarinds. They ate picnic breakfasts by ancient tombs and the horses tried to eat the hollyhocks. They rode back past the fields of turquoise blue linseed still glistening with dew.

Her cousin Audrey was very excited watching the King's Birthday Parade, when 'Both Uncle Philip and the Viceroy reviewed the troops. The white topees and ceremonial red uniforms looked lovely in the sun.'

There was always an ADC around. Geoffrey Kellie was a bit of a card, 'awfully suave, he once locked an Indian in a train, got off at Calcutta and left him.' Lady Carnworth was shocked at first by the way the young subalterns drank and hit their servants, laughing wildly. 'I mean, at home, they would never do this to their valets or butlers. One young subaltern kicked his bearer until the servant just turned his face to the wall and died.' What a jape!

It was a heady life for many of these young men, fresh from public school and regimental service, suddenly given valets and butlers, enjoying as much hunting, polo, brandy and champagne as they could take, especially for those with respectable but frugal backgrounds.

Lord Curzon deplored the behaviour of some of the 'inferior class of Englishman' he came across in India who felt they could batter a black man to death because he was 'only a d-d nigger'. But India, with servants always bowing and dragging their dusters obsequiously across the floor, pandered to any inherent cruelty or bullying instinct in a young subaltern.

The Princes were hospitable, stylish hosts. The Maharajah of Kashmir, a genuinely generous man, was not brilliantly clever but not naïve. At one of his parties he noticed, with the barest flicker of an eyelid, a young subaltern scooping up a bottle of champagne, putting it in his pocket and chortling with his chums when he got outside.

The Maharajah went to the butler and said icily, 'That gentleman seems to like my champagne. Please take two bottles and put them in his car.' Then he called for his ADC and said in a peremptory way, 'Find out who the fellow is and make sure he never comes to my house again.' The poor 'fellow', realising he was going to be banned from one of the loveliest palaces and some of the best parties, shuffled back in, backed up to the table, took the champagne out of his pocket and put it back among the rows of Veuve Clicquot. But it was too late. What was one bottle beside ten dozen in silver buckets with white napkins ready for pouring into long-stemmed crystal glasses?

Known affectionately as 'Hari Singh', Kashmir was not usually prickly. He was popular with the Raj and gave good lunch parties at which the guests, including the impeccable young girls, condescendingly thought 'he was just another jolly wog'. They were rather shocked when Lady Willingdon kept putting her arm around him. There was a 'darling baby in a gold cloth'. This was Karan Singh, the present Maharajah, and because Sir Philip Chetwode has just been made a Field Marshal, they gave him the child's teddy bear. 'The baby must have been furious.'

It was sometimes very difficult to keep a straight face at one of the palaces, where the Princes were very taken with a new fangled cocktail shaker from Fortnum & Mason shaped like a donkey. 'You can imagine where the drink came out of and it was very difficult as one was not the kind of girl who could guffaw.'

The roly-poly Maharajah of Bithur, Nana Sahib, was a good host to the British. Food came from Fortnum's and it was thought 'frightfully amusing' when pudding was served in a soup plate or one was given a hand towel instead of a napkin. Some of the Princes were over-anxious hosts. When Lord and Lady Reading visited the great cricketer Ranji in the Punjab, the crested programme detailed an early morning train stop when a cow would be 'freshly milked – without noise' for the Viceroy's 'bed tea'.

Well-born young girls still remember that the terror of being summoned to Government House to see the Viceroy was much worse than being presented at Court. 'Before meeting the Vicereine trays of white gloves were passed around. You curt-sied five times. There were meticulous rules. One never spoke about the "British Raj" but of the British Empire and turbans were always called puggarees, the Hindu word.'

These young girls sang for their suppers. One wrote, 'I quite enjoy society because all the men one sits next to are "bigwigs" and frightfully interesting. Then after dinner you sit ensconced in a chair and an ADC brings people up to you to talk to. But only for five or six minutes, then someone else is dragged along.' Although only about twenty, they were always put at the top table by birth alone. They sat through 'endlessly boring princely banquets' which went on for hours and would have been enjoyed more by people twice their age who worked in India but had never been inside a palace.

The ADCs were chosen for their silken ability to steer the Princes to HE at the right moment. Randall Plunkett sometimes became rather irritated, grumbling loudly when he was told off for allowing the glamorous Maharajah of Jaipur to sit for rather too long with the bewitching Ma Cooch, the widow of the Maharajah of Cooch Behar. 'Why didn't you move them on after ten minutes, it was the most frightful faux pas.' But he merely boomed back, 'How should I be expected to know their stud arrangements?'

When Mrs Keppel stayed with the Linlithgows, she held court sitting under a portrait of King Edward VII and fussy aides were appalled. But Lady Linlithgow insisted, 'Leave her there.'

The tedium was lightened occasionally by the unpredictable. Ranjit Singh, Jam Saheb of Nawanagar, was a travelled, sophisticated, round man with an English mistress. It was a 13-gun state, of small importance, but this paled beside the Maharajah's jolly personality. In the middle of a formal dinner guests were astonished when the great diva Clara Butt climbed to her feet and gave a powerful rendering of 'God Save the King'. There was something extraordinarily comic about this deep contralto voice ringing out over the desert. She sat down as suddenly to continue spooning up her carrot halva.

Lady Birdwood still has a cherished invitation for her eighteenth birthday, sent by her favourite Maharajah. When he asked her parents and herself to tea at the palace, the Maharajah also wanted to know, since it was an 'auspicious occasion', whether she wanted to play tennis or 'see prostitutes dancing'. 'It was charming; he knew only the proper name for them. They were the nautch girls, the cabaret artists, the entertainers who danced at weddings and parties. Their dancing was incredibly boring and they were fully clothed.' So many of the Princes had a sweet gaiety which could be enchanting and childish.

At tennis parties, the Maharajahs wore long skirts which they would tuck up and gather about them to run to the net. Once, when about to start a game of doubles, one of them said, 'Oh dear, there is a stool on the court,' using this quaint English almost out of a medical dictionary.

Joan Wetherell-Pepper, now Lady Carnworth, was leaning

against her tiny Fiat at a polo match in Calcutta when there was a gasp from the crowd. One of the players had fallen heavily from his pony at full gallop. She heard an army wife reassuring a friend, 'Don't worry, my dear, he's only a gunner.'

A shy and serious girl, she was watching polo when she was drenched in champagne. The Maharajah of Baroda had thought she was looking far too prim and emptied the bottle over her fair hair. She was not prim but preoccupied. She had fallen in with a very fast, social, polo-playing set and in her sensitive way thought it all reminiscent of Madame Récamier. 'I blame a lot of those women. They drifted round gardens and swimming pools with literally pints of gin; they drank like fishes, wandering around in their nighties half dressed – it was all very Happy Valley. I thought they did a lot of harm.

'Many of them did nothing but drink, spend their time at the hairdressers and have their nails done, being frightfully blah. They did not see the poor or the dust and even up country in a desolate grey cantonment they would suddenly brighten, 'My dear, this is Ascot week,' and then shout at the servants. Some were quite dreadful. I heard one say in a Prince's hearing, "I loathe coloured skin." But he heard her and when he shook hands with everyone, gave her his unclean left hand.'

Lord Linlithgow was appalled by the colour bar and told his son that he thought it extraordinary that the British had any friends in India at all. He always insisted that his daughters and their guests danced with the Princes. 'But it was difficult in Calcutta as young things when we all wanted to go on to the Three Hundred.'

This was where they could dance under a canopy of scarlet flowers on a teak floor below the Gul Mohr tree. When it was cold, couples snuggled inside at small tables lit with pink lampshades, mellowing the sepia-coloured walls. They shouted 'Oh Fuzz, more,' when the Filipino drummer shouted, 'That's arl.' There was genuine Russian food, blinis and Chicken Kiev, prepared by Boris Lissanevitch, a vivid character and formerly a cadet in the Imperial Russian Navy.

Even a 21-gun prince was barred by the colour of his skin

from accompanying an English girl to any public place other than the cinema. Nor could Indian Princes ever ask the girls staying with the Viceroy or Commander-in-Chief to dance (except under Lord Linlithgow). 'They could only dance with inferiors, tutors' daughters . . . We thought of them as panto-mime figures in brocade, not always frightfully clean, grubby cuffs showing under dressing gowns . . . that sort of thing.'

Indians were rigorously excluded from all British clubs. The Three Hundred, like the Tollygunge and the Saturday Club, shut its doors on both Indians and pets. In the 1920s Ranji, as part of his cricketing laurels, was welcomed to exclusive clubs all over the world and was a member of the Marlborough. But the Gymkhana Club in Bombay turned him down. Later he was asked to join but replied, 'Stick to your principles.'

The Gymkhana Club in Delhi, with its wickerwork chairs on the lawns, is where nowadays smart Indian families meet for buffet curry lunch on Sundays. It is quite unchanged inside, still the same vast library of English classics bound in burgundy and dark green leather: the ideal place to spend a somnolent hour with a pink gin. A waiter standing in the centre of a pillared ballroom with a marble fireplace at each end looks like a ballet dancer with a tray of soft drinks. 'It is just the same as the Cavalry Club,' a member said. Well, almost, except outside there was a cart of tomatoes and huge white radishes which would just not be allowed by the traffic wardens in Piccadilly.

Lady Betjeman thought that although Indian Princes would have liked affairs with lady sahibs, they did not allow their women to flirt with anybody. Any hopeful Prince tiptoeing along the corridor to Penelope Chetwode's room would have been lucky not to trip over her gazelle, Rupmati, tied to her bed.

Severely thoughtful, never a wasted word, enjoying academic work in her tiny flat off the King's Road, Lady Birdwood smiles thinly at the fictional Daphne Manners in *The Jewel in the Crown* who had a relationship with an Indian. 'I can tell you that I would have been a contemporary of Daphne Manners, and no girl of good family would have become involved with an Indian. That sort of behaviour was for landladies' daughters.'

❦ 27 ❧

The Saddle is My Home

HIGHNESS IS AT his desk. It is Saturday morning so the Chairman of the Baroda Rayon Corporation is wearing a red check shirt and shorts. The red telephone – 'the hot line' – is bleeping, a bearer brings in a glass of Complan on a tray with a Mappin and Webb silver spoon. 'Is this strawberry flavour? You know it is my favourite.' The servant grins.

The call is from his sister; it is followed immediately by another asking if he will host a party for UN delegates and a third inquiring if Prince Philip may land his plane at Baroda.

Silver fish dart around a tank and glamorous long-haired girls smile out from perspex photograph frames. Alongside Irving Wallace's *The Nymphs and Other Maniacs* and Tolstoy's *War and Peace* there are several dictionaries and the Baroda family motto: 'the saddle is my home, the saddle is my throne.'

The Maharajah of Baroda, very much a man for all seasons, was able to make the transition from prince to politician and industrialist with ease. He is one of the few Princes to unshackle himself from the past. He founded the successful Baroda Rayon Corporation in 1956. He is a chameleon. In London, it is cashmere sweater and herringbone trousers, or a suit when he goes to see Prince Philip at Buckingham Palace to talk about wildlife in India or saving the pheasant in Thailand. But he is equally at home in the white khadi and shawl, handspun, handwoven, to meet a political group at his bungalow in Delhi which is far from ostentatious and where stoppers have trouble keeping the bathwater in.

The office is light and airy on Bombay's Narriman Point, near the celebrated Air India building with a view of the bay. 'Come out to Number Ten,' he says, leading the way with a copy of Chamberlin's, down the white wooden steps from the glass doors onto a green terrace. You get an immediate whiff of the city's hot, humid air and down below cars swishing along into Bombay's flashy skyscraper hotels on the peninsula.

The Maharajah was educated in the palace at Baroda by an English tutor: 'Well, he was a Kiwi really,' and relishes the formality of giving his two Christian names: 'Malcolm Arthur Young. I owe him my love for English literature.'

In 1951, when he was twenty-one, he went up to Cambridge but was abruptly forced to return to Baroda to succeed his father, who had lost the title because he had challenged the constitution in the Supreme Court. Some thought old Baroda a bit of a George V figure, but the resemblance was limited to a daunting physical presence.

He fled to Europe with his second wife Sita Devi, an exotic spendthrift who had a ruby-studded cigarette holder and took Paris by storm. When they left India she made sure she had some good Baroda jewellery in her luggage, which was auctioned off to maintain her Beluga Grey lifestyle.

Although they were simply Mr and Mrs, the Maharajah liked to be addressed by his title. He owned three houses in England; they stayed in Claridges, had a box at Ascot and strings of thoroughbred racehorses, almost winning the Derby with My Babu in 1948. They invariably stayed at the Waldorf in New York, flew about in his well-equipped personal Douglas DC-47, wintered in St Moritz, all the food and wine in their Paris apartment came from Fauchon, the French equivalent of Fortnum & Mason. His wild spending earned him the profound disapproval of the Indian Government.

Sita Devi and the former Maharajah were divorced in 1956 and she moved to France with their only child, the ten-year-old Prince Sayajirao Pratapsingh Gaekwad. He was made a ward of the

French courts to make sure his father could not whisk him off to India. 'Princey' was outrageously indulged by his mother, who always defended him, emphasising how hard he worked and that he never got up later than three in the afternoon. She herself never appeared before about two o'clock and certainly would not stir from her suite until six or seven for cocktails; it was a rare evening when she did not give a dinner party.

For a while the Maharani reigned over Paris, not a city which is easily impressed. She was known as 'Becky' to her friends and lived in the best part of the city, although she also had homes in Grosvenor Square and Florida's Palm Beach. Her cutlery was gold and she had 900 saris and 400 pairs of shoes, bought in New York. She had a capacity to surprise even worldly film star friends like David Niven, arriving at his house in the South of France in a Baroda-crested white Rolls-Royce lined with red velvet, the door held open by her black chauffeur in a gold-braided white uniform.

Mother and son swept into night clubs, she swathed in furs with four strands of enormous pearls, he, almost as beautiful, in shirts open to the navel and skin-tight velvet pants. One hostess was cut off the Maharani's list because Dom Perignon was not served and she once flew from New York to London because she could make the telephone connection from there to India.

In 1959, she moved to Monte Carlo and became a citizen of Monaco. But this did not protect her from a swingeing tax demand by the French government sixteen years later for £60,000 based solely on her bills for dinner parties, hotel and nightclub accounts. Her expenses in Paris then averaged about £150,000 a year. Her bad luck peaked with the death of her adored, spoilt Princey on 8 May 1985. He was found at Cagnes-sur-Mer in Southern France with his throat cut at a villa called 'I Love You'. Police suggested suicide, but investigated the possibility of a homosexual murder or drug trafficking.

'Some thought it was none other than my humble self,' the Gaekwad told friends, and for the sixth time in his life had the 'rather dubious distinction and vicarious pleasure' of reading his own obituary.

After the divorce, his father, the ex-maharajah, became a sad figure in London, often on his own, drinking a pint at Paddy Kennedy's pub, the Star, in Belgravia or staying in the family apartment in New York. Jackie remained close to his father and will not be drawn about his flamboyant stepbrother or the antics of his stepmother. 'It is better not to get involved,' he says, rolling his eyes. His stepmother lies prone in her Paris flat, paralysed by a stroke, and friends dare not tell her about Princey's death.

The present Maharajah may appear dilettante but he has been serious about politics since he was a young man and joined the Congress Party in 1956. He had just been round the world by car, covering 25,000 miles in five months. When he got back from the trip, a delegation was waiting for him in Baroda headed by the Mayor. 'They said they had decided I should enter politics. "Look," I said, "politics are dirty, it's the last thing I want to do." "You have to," they said. "Don't I have a choice?" I asked. "None," they said,' Few could have resisted. 'The warmest feeling in the world,' says this man who appears to have everything, 'is to be really wanted.'

In Delhi, Nehru advised him: 'Go back to Cambridge.' '"But I have been there for ten days," I replied.' He became a highly regarded young Parliamentary Secretary for Defence, as V. K. Krishna Menon. Later he joined the State Cabinet as Minister for Health, staying in politics until 1980. Now he is having a battle to keep his Government house, which he has enjoyed since 1958. But he is a wily operator and has suddenly discovered that the Government still owes him money for a plot of land.

His brother, Ranjitsingh, is now an MP, 'keeping the burrow warm'. 'As he is an artist and classical singer I have suggested he should sing his speeches in the Lokh Sabha – why not?' The Gaekwad's youngest brother, Sangram, is his managing director at Baroda Rayon. 'I call him my damaging director.'

The chairman still travels compulsively. Once his passport described his occupation as Ruler, then politician, more recently as industrialist. He would really like it to say conservationist. He never stays anywhere longer than three weeks at a time, then he is off again 'to save the California otter, my dear'. In 1985 he clocked up 165,053 miles around the world. He almost spends more time in the air than on the ground.

It was a bad year with four spells in hospital. Even lying on a sofa covered with an eiderdown and far from well, he has presence. He is proud of a hospital identity tag worn with gold and copper bangles and the Shastri sacred thread. These threads are never removed from the wrist or seen in public.

After a few pleasant, introspective days sitting in the sun in his garden in Delhi, watching the green tail feathers of parakeets busy in the yellow jasmine, he recovers and begins to feel stifled. 'Nair,' he calls the pleasant-faced South Indian who has been his patient, devoted secretary for years, 'book me on that flight to Minneapolis.' His doctors would have a fit.

He has four secretaries already but is about to set up an extra office to deal with conservation work. He was converted when he saw a tiger shot in slow motion on film. Hours are spent now trying to save the Hawaiian Goose and, he says hopefully, 'also the girls on the beach in Honolulu'. The tall agreeable Mr Khoth, the senior Bombay secretary, is sometimes put on a flight to London when well-spoken English secretaries are not available. 'I have not been able to find even in England a perfectionist of the sort I need until recently,' he sighs. In the past secretaries had to track down baby crocodiles at Harrods which the Gaekwad popped in his pocket for the journey home.

Enigmatic, shrewd and unpredictable, he thinks many of the Princes unworldly and easily hoodwinked. He is perhaps over-cautious. Sir Richard Attenborough had been promised backing for his film on Gandhi and was bitterly disappointed when the Gaekwad pulled out. 'Such a long time elapsed from the start of the idea, I had to renege,' he explains.

Distant and princely at times, he has a way of saying 'Thank you' which brings conversation to an end.

On the other hand, when he spotted the film producer Judith de Paul at Charles de Gaulle airport, thinking her 'delicious wrapped in furs' he backed her film on Mountbatten starring Nicol Williamson. Then he arranged permission for her to shoot scenes all over India in places like Viceregal Lodge and the President's palace forbidden to greater film makers.

He has no heir. His wife, a Jodhpur princess whom he married in 1950, died of cancer in 1984. They were apart for years but remained friends. She was a pilot who flew solo at thirteen, bred dogs and was a stylish horsewoman. He loves being teased about getting married again, and purrs as a succession of women flutter and coo over him. He quite likes to stir a bit of jealousy and says he can always tell when women are going to make a scene: 'they start drinking fast'. He is difficult to buy a present for, being far happier to receive a large Easter egg with a Playboy bunny tail on the black and white box than a gold swizzle stick. He likes to make the gestures; a word from him opens doors all over India.

He loves London, though he was mugged by skinheads outside the Six Bells public house in Chelsea. He even likes the high rise buildings in Park Lane; is amused by the pinks, the orange and the purples of the punk rockers. 'It is the most alive city. My idea of fun now is a small dinner party with good conversation. I am anglicised to the extent that I use the weather for conversation.' Then, lapsing into a comic English accent, he says, 'What a dreadful day – frightful,' and, even more clipped, 'Yes, isn't it *sticky*?'

There is not an evening when he does not have an invitation to dinner or a cocktail party but he quite likes staying at home to write or to read poetry. For him it is fun to amble to an Italian delicatessen in the King's Road, Chelsea where he can buy homemade cannelloni. 'Indian Prince has to do own cooking,' he winks, parodying the tabloid newspapers. He heats it up and with a big china leopard from Harrods for company enjoys watching his old friend the Indian actor Sayeed Jaffrey in a series on television about two Indian restaurants. 'Princes can be very lonely,' he says. 'It is part of their self-preservation.'

He is no longer seen so often at Annabel's, where once a sweating Indian in check trousers came up from the kitchen and the Maharajah fell on his neck: 'The son of my gardener,' he explained to his puzzled Sloane Ranger date.

He cooks well. At country house weekends, hostesses are delighted when he volunteers to do Sunday lunch, and he always has his little joke: 'Aha, how to curry a flavour.' He says he plans to teach actress Stephanie Powers a few dishes. Raised eyebrows, amused, 'What? . . . It is our mutual interest in wildlife.'

He is rarely indiscreet though in a news letter which he sends to friends around the world there is a tongue in cheek revelation that in 1984 he had become a member of the Mile High Club with a Lufthansa stewardess while crossing the Atlantic. He seemed equally to enjoy sliding down the shute in an emergency landing.

He is such a frequent traveller he can order the film he wants before a flight; or upgrade the former Labour leader Michael Foot, whom he spotted crammed into economy with women and babies on the flight from Delhi to London after Mrs Gandhi's funeral. 'I had a word with the commander,' and was grieved that his native airline had not recognised a VIP.

There are two men on his staff who do nothing but meet him at airports in India. In Delhi it is Mr Italia, a commanding enormous character with a hectoring but kindly manner who swoops and weaves his way around Delhi airport cleaving through Indian officialdom. In Bombay, it is Mr Ahaizi, a white-bearded jolly gnome who looks like Santa Claus. He is not too young and has been seriously ill with heart trouble, but he enjoys the job although he complains that 'Highness' insists on carrying his own luggage: 'he will not let me carry his case, I keep telling him he must take more care of himself.' Neither of them is very fit but in India there is no lack of porters at any airport.

The walls of the Gaekwad's office in Baroda are lined with airline certificates. One from Japan says in flowery language: 'Having entered the ethereal realm of the sun, the sky and the moon while spanning the Pacific, Fatehsingh Gaekwad has crossed the International Date Line and thus jumbled yesterday, today and tomorrow.'

Home is where he happens to be at the moment. As he says, 'I can always find the saddle even if nowadays there is no throne.'

❧ 28 ❧

Commandeering
Precious Coupés

'HOW MUCH IS THAT ONE?' The nondescript looking man in a
Mayfair car showroom pointed to a Rolls-Royce Phantom II
Tourer.

The young salesman, hair oiled, gleaming white shirt and
formal suit, was rather off-hand. He was not too pleased to be
spoken to so abruptly by this Indian person who was now
opening the door of the limousine and running his hand along
the rich, creamy beige upholstery. So he replied in that toffee-
nosed way of salesmen who wonder how one has the effrontery
to even ask the price of something clearly above one's station,
'Two thousand, six hundred and forty-seven pounds.' (The
equivalent Corniche Convertible today costs £92,995.) Then he
continued to pace up and down the glass showroom, looking
out for a 'toff' who could afford a Rolls.

He was quite taken aback when the Indian barked, 'Fetch the
manager.' He turned on his heel with a petulant shake of the
head. The manager appeared. 'Sir?' he asked, sleek, accommo-
dating. 'I will have every one of these,' the Maharajah of
Bharatpur said quietly, pointing to the Rolls-Royces, some
cream, some white, some with canopies, great silvery chrome
radiators, smoked glass, wide running boards and trim gleaming
mahogany. 'But there is one condition. This young man escorts
them to India.'

The scarlet-faced young salesman could not believe his luck. A great beam spread across his face. 'Thank you, Your Highness. It would be a great honour.' He was the envy of the showroom.

On the voyage he looked after the cars like an old nanny. He polished them and visited them every day. When he got to India, these dignified 'rollers' were driven at stately speed across the Indo-Gangetic plains. The young salesman had read all the travel brochures but he ignored the delights of the palace's famous bird sanctuary, where in the early morning on the lake, even the branches of the trees form bird shapes. He worked for days to give the Rolls a final, loving valeting. Then the summons came. His Highness would inspect his order.

On the appointed morning the splendid cars were arrayed in front of the palace, gleaming, engines revving, the salesman bursting with pride. The Maharajah came out onto the steps of the palace and, with a perfunctory nod, shrugged and told his ADC, 'Arrange for these cars to be taken away; they will be used for municipal rubbish.' There was a throttled wail from the salesman. How could he ever tell his boss? He had just been taught a most expensive lesson.

Within India the great princely journeys were done by train. Each maharajah had his own palace on wheels with musicians, concubines and servants as part of the entourage. The Jodhpur saloon had an ornate blue tapestry bedhead and royal blue carpets. Mysore had curtains of embossed damask, a handsome mahogany bed and chairs covered in gold floral velvet. All had silver door handles; filigree racks; teak louvred shutters; porcelain soap dishes; carved lotus flowers on the ceilings and rosewood bureaux; brass ridged bells like half lemons shone from the dark wood for podgy jewelled fingers to summon a dancing girl, sweetmeats or a glass of champagne.

At night, as the Frontier Mail, the Bombay Queen and other great trains raced authoritatively between Bombay and Delhi, the royal coaches, creamy white or rich maroon, were puffing comfortably along the branch lines. Servants in high twirled orange turbans were lighting the little chandeliers in the dining

car, spreading white tablecloths and laying out the monogrammed porcelain dinner service.

Beside the track girls in ruby red saris threaded with gold
held their babies close, diamonds in button noses, and looked
steadily at the Princes without envy, contained within a natural
grace and that Indian acceptance of caste and 'karma' – their
fate.

As the trains drew into stations, the maharajahs languidly
lifted a slat of the louvred shutters and often gave a small
sigh. Once more they faced another greeting with garlands of
marigolds and jasmine, caparisoned elephants, fluteplayers and
snake charmers.

These trains have traditionally been ideal for royal trysts and
were perfect for trundling from one palace to another. From
Jodhpur to Jaisalmer in the desert, drinking tea from silver
Georgian pots as the sun turned the rippled sand dunes of the
old caravan traders desert way into a deep amber rose. But
the British always insisted that the Rulers should have only the
narrow-gauge line, not the broad. This meant they could never
move great cantonments of troops; and when the full-size lines
had to run through their states, there was an English railway
manager in charge, though the Princes were allowed to levy a
small tax. In India today, the railways still have romance with
11,000 trains carrying 10 million passengers a day.

In 1947, Mountbatten worried about the Mahatma's safety
after Independence, in his miserable hut with its mud floor. 'My
dear Lord Louis,' remonstrated the poet, Mrs Sarojini Naidu,
with outstretched hands, 'you will never know how much
it has cost the Congress Party to keep that old man safely in
poverty.'

She, too, was devoted to Gandhi and explained wearily the
sophisticated public relations effort needed to keep her spiritual
leader in the style to which he had become accustomed. This
ensured that a third-class compartment was always available on
the railway for the Mahatma, his followers and his goats. He
never knew that the whole crowded carriage at the Hooghly
Station was actually full of planted Congress Party members.

Lord Mountbatten, who had a good relationship with Gandhi and once described him as 'an old poppet', was deeply moved when Gandhi was assassinated, feeling it as a personal blow.

The Princes' craze for travel abroad began with Queen Victoria's Jubilee in 1887. One prince arrived with 200 servants, 50 family attendants, 20 chefs and 1,000 packing cases, 10 elephants, 33 tame tigers. For hedonistic Highnesses anxious to escape from the beaky watch of the British Resident, a trip to Europe was the chance for a little frivolity. Racing at Ascot; polo; a suite at Claridges, the Savoy, the Ritz; visits to Lobb and to Cartier's the jewellers and night clubs. The British frowned on these junkets, so the maharajahs argued that they had to have urgent political talks in Whitehall or escort their sons to Eton.

They usually travelled abroad with the entire court, wives, concubines and a tame leopard. They gave gold watches to anyone who had done exactly as they ordered, booked a train or a whole hotel for a party. Sometimes in grand hotels in Italy, the Villa d'Este in Como, Italian families would be sitting around grandmother, all sipping tea and looking like a Winterhalter painting, when a huge Indian party would burst into the lobby, taking over the hotel.

Travelling in the 1890s was rather like an upmarket house party, all the same people doing the European Grand Tour. During the Nile Season of 1895–96, passengers had a blue-bound programme with gilt pages for the tour. They could see at a glance whether they were being joined by the right sort on board the *Rameses* . . . At the top were the Barodas, the Archbishop of York was going too, the Nawab of Rampur and Lord Charles Thynne, and they would be personally conducted by Thomas Cook, a temperance devotee who refused to take couples who were not married.

His men were expected to deal with every eventuality. The Maharajah of Baroda, arriving on a specially chartered steamer to join a cruise in Naples in 1905, insisted on taking over the entire Hotel Royal. His party included cows and sheep which had to be accommodated in the tiny garden. The beds were removed as the royal party preferred their own air mattresses. The servants milked the cows and others killed the sheep in the garden and served up Lamb Mughlai.

When the Nawab of Rampur got to Rome in the 1930s he demanded a performance by the Military Cavalry School because he had a bet 'with one of my friends in Italian equitation'. The General was somehow persuaded to send telegrams to all the officers who were on leave, and five days later they were in Rome giving a superb display. The Nawab was 'so well satisfied' he gave the twenty-five cavalry officers gold watches.

The wonderful quality of the Princes was that unpredictable Mad Hatter touch. One Maharajah landed in Italy with his suite of forty-five, expected flowers, red carpets and military bands but also insisted that he should be taken to see the King, Il Duce and the Pope. Victor Emmanuel and Mussolini were out of town so he settled for Il Papa. The Maharajah wanted to serenade the Pope, so the Sistine choir went along and sang the Vatican anthem and then some Indian ditties.

When the Princes arrived at Victoria station with their monogrammed luggage, in winter even the baby princes in arms wore full-length white mink coats. Waiting for them there was always the reassuring Donald White, head of uniformed Staff, resplendent in gold braid. The original man from Thomas Cook's, the travel agents, he was known as the uncrowned King of Victoria and was renowned for his imperturbability. He even spoke a little Urdu which helped him understand the Princes' every whim. It might be moving the Maharani of Baroda's cutlery from Grosvenor Square to Neuilly, getting a steward to take it on the night sleeper to Paris; or commandeering precious coupés on the Golden Arrow. The Princes, miraculously, always got what they wanted; other people who had made bookings earlier were simply eased out.

Until 1948, a special division of Thomas Cook was called the Indian Princes Department. Then after partition someone complained so it had to be renamed: 'Princes Section – India and Pakistan'. The girls at the Princes' Desk thought many of the maharajahs lovable father figures. If ever they came to the

Berkeley Street office with its glass domes and marble floor, they created a gorgeous flutter with their courtliness, their exotic rings and beards.

By the 1970s there were no longer the old-style maharajahs, instead there was a new breed of prince, the Arab sheikh. But they seemed to lack a certain style. One of the travel girls was summoned to the Dorchester to meet a Middle Eastern prince.

'The room was filled with Arabs,' she recalled. 'Nobody asked me to sit down and they shoved a holdall towards me stuffed with thousands of notes. The Arab prince went on changing his clothes in front of me. I might have been a bit of furniture. All he said, standing in his underpants, was, "You have very blue eyes." '

There could not have been a greater contrast with the aides of the Indian Princes, who arrived at the mahogany counters of Thomas Cook with handfuls of gold sovereigns. In 1948 the Maharajah of Indore's man deposited what was then the enormous sum of £36,000 for travel alone. But at the time Indore was falling in love with a succession of American women and crossing the Atlantic was costly.

Connie Alexander, a well-groomed, unflappable girl of twenty-eight, not long from her home in Blackpool, took the job seriously. She coped with the maharajahs and their families so well that she was given 'gorgeous diamond brooches' and many decorative gaudy elephants and tigers with emerald eyes. Her tasks included chasing to the Louvre to track down a painting; buying a swordstick, which was illegal in London, and getting hold of an American jukebox for the Maharajah of Gwalior, who put it alongside his other treasures. She had to tell the Maharajah of Indore that unfortunately no money could buy Rodin's statue, The Kiss, to take back to India. Others were mad about garden gnomes. They would ring her at all hours of the night.

Telegrams flew between Bombay and Berkeley Square as they waited for the Indian astrologers to say it was auspicious to travel; crews of private planes had to be paid to stand by. Arrangements were made for the shipment of a load of gundogs, some of which died in Bahrain when left in the hold of the aircraft. The Maharajahs of Baroda and Jaipur leased three planes each.

Excess baggage could cause a strike at Tilbury. Only gentle persistence and a gold sovereign or two persuaded disgruntled porters to unload the Maharajah of Kutch's fifty crates of luggage when he was on his way home from Rio where he had been ambassador. But at times the dockers would almost have worked for nothing, there were such vivid, theatrical scenes at Tilbury.

Once, they saw a jacket studded with diamonds thrown overboard by the 'wife' of an agitated Maharajah of Jodhpur as the couple had a blistering row. Then his woman friend, the Scottish nurse Sandra McBryde, whom he later married, refused to come ashore. She stayed in her cabin dressed in her gold sari and twiddling her Indian bangles and for five hours the pantomime went on. Eventually a couple of hefty dockers jumped in the water and retrieved the jacket and later felt the warm touch of a gold sovereign in their palms.

The Princes could change their minds on the slightest whim. One was very taken with a parrot and wanted it to go everywhere with him; on his special train, on the yacht and in the Rolls. Then suddenly he got bored with it and threw it off in Florence.

This treatment was not limited to parrots. Courtiers could fall from favour for the tiniest inattention, for the Princes were like Renaissance Dukes who had never struggled in life. One maharajah on the Grand Tour had left Milan for Switzerland on a special train when it was noticed that one of the royal party was missing. The 'fellow' had been getting on his nerves, the Maharajah explained; he was a relative but he did not want to see him for a while. The unfortunate man had been locked up at Domodossola and only by the silkiest coaxing could the Maharajah be persuaded to part with the key. He relented enough to say the relative could join him in Lucerne.

When he reached Lucerne, the grovellingly grateful relative went to bed, wisely keeping out of the way. But the Maharajah, who was at a Toscanini concert, became enraged. Furious, he sent orders that the unfortunate was to be got out of bed and sent straight back to India. He was put on a train for Genoa. 'Oh, you can send back one of my secretaries too. I saw him asleep on the train.' The two men were put on the SS *Conte Grande* in a double compartment and locked up for the voyage.

The Maharani of Cooch Behar gambled at Le Touquet with her talisman always beside her. It was a tiny live turtle with emeralds, rubies and diamonds embedded in its shell. At the end of the evening, she finally put away her long cigarette holder and swept out in an emerald chiffon sari, her jewels matching those on her pet. The sign for her maid that she had been lucky at chemin-de-fer, or so her children believed, was when her shoes were turned upside down outside the door.

They had houses in the country so it just meant organising a fleet of cars to take the Jaipurs to Sussex or Ascot. Sometimes, special servants would be sent to England ahead. One appeared at Victoria station simply wearing a label round his neck which said 'Thomas Cook'. When his master arrived a few weeks later, he fell down and kissed his feet. Others travelled by seaplane. The flight to India, first class, cost £100, with overnight stops in Rome and Karachi. Deck passages for the servants cost between £10 and £25 each; they just curled up and went to sleep behind the lifeboats.

The Princes had travel crazes and copied one another. One year, they all dashed off to the Bariloche Lakes in Argentina. Perennial favourites were Deauville for golf, Monte Carlo and Le Touquet for the casinos, Cannes for the Carlton and Rome. The Maharajah of Baroda was rather keen on the film star Merle Oberon and enjoyed trips to Hollywood.

Their style fitted in beautifully with the mad gaiety of the years before the First World War, when the King of Portugal gave a girlfriend a pair of snow white mules which drew her along the Strand in a carriage. A Maharajah's wife whose pearls snapped at dinner said, 'Don't bother to pick them up, I can easily get another. I don't want to miss the first act of the play.'

Everywhere the Princes were accepted socially. Women fell at their feet and some of the Princes were dazzling. Jodhpur was very attractive, had wonderful eyes and looked very dashing sweeping along Bond Street in his cloak. He was very keen on magic and conjuring tricks. There were always lots of girls around him with names like Beryl and Dawn. Impulsively taken with three girls he had met in a Mayfair night club, Jodhpur wanted to take them all back to India as magicians' assistants. This did not go down at all well at Petty France, and no amount of influence or bags of sovereigns could get the girls passports as each of them was under age.

Members of Thomas Cook's staff would go to Claridges or the Savoy for their orders. They might be told by a man leaning on a sword, 'Please wait, his Highness is at his natural functions.'

A birthday treat was arranged at Les Ambassadeurs for the Maharajah of Baroda. His present was to be Cupid and throw arrows at a dancer. Each arrow caught her archly unawares and brought away some part of her tinselly clothing until he had no need to throw any more. The five hundred guests got very excited and all wanted one of their own.

The Maharajah of Patiala liked the fifth floor of the Savoy and insisted that the 35 suites should be filled with 3,000 fresh long-stemmed roses every day. The servants slept in the corridors, uncoiling watchfully when merry couples in evening dress swayed past, humming snatches of the songs played by Carroll Gibbons at his celebrated white piano in the River Room.

Patiala, splendid in an apricot turban but Savile Row suit, wore pearl earrings as big as damsons and heavy bracelets. He was as gorgeous as the Maharani. Their arrival could create huge traffic jams in the Strand as twenty Rolls-Royces followed by five truckloads of cricket gear rolled up to the hotel entrance.

'This was just,' the Maharajah stressed, 'a semi-private and informal visit' as he had brought with him only fifty aides, chauffeurs and bodyguards. As this retinue swirled round the beige-carpeted foyer with its bright log fire, ormolu clock and vases of flowers, reception clerks in morning dress, smiling and calm, took charge. The hotel detective supervised and kept a special eye on the jewel cases with their interlocking miniature steel safe.

As the massive Maharajah squeezed into his private gold and scarlet lacquered lift, installed especially for him, housekeepers, valets, chambermaids and under-managers fussed about the fifth floor. There were last bustling looks at the royal suite to make sure that little 'extras' were in order. That the silver bathtub was gleaming, the Irish linen handtowels correctly folded in the marble bathroom, the satin and brocade coverlets in place and the gold-nibbed pens on the delicate Louis Seize writing desks. In the special kitchen on the fifth floor, the Patiala solid silver dishes were being laid out on pink tablecloths ready to be filled with favourite delicacies.

Once for a special dinner party, the Maharajah of Patiala had a sudden fancy for quail out of season. After many telephone calls and telegrams all over Europe, six of these boring little birds were found in Egypt and stuffed with Périgord truffles, the meal ending with pretty elephants and camels carved from ice, filled with pineapple and strawberries with a sprinkling of Kirsch.

Another Prince liked to travel with his concubines and was known as His Exhausted Highness. Wherever the Maharajahs went, whether it was the Château de Madrid in the Bois de Boulogne or the Hotel Gloria in Rio, it was orchids and champagne all the way.

Often long after they were expected back in their states, the British Residents fumed as the time abroad was prolonged. A top courier, Mr Piccoli, had the task of trying to return the Maharajah to Mysore. He met the Prince at Grosvenor House and insisted His Highness had to be in Paris for an important business meeting. Then he would sail to Bombay. They checked into the Hotel Lotti, arranged to have dinner at the Café de Paris and then go on for a last dance at the Scheherazade. Everyone went to the restaurant, but no sign of the Maharajah. Only a great amount of baksheesh revealed that he had left earlier for a certain house in the Champs-Elysées. He was

tracked down, smiling foolishly like an ageing fat Pan, surrounded by giggling girls and drinking champagne.

'We went to the Café de Paris with two Parisian girls; we
started with hors d'oeuvre . . . A minute or two after we sat
down, I noticed him fast asleep with a piece of ham hanging
down from his mouth.' A sharp blow in the ribs revived him,
he got up and danced with one of the smiling girls. Next day
he was on the Simplon Express for Venice with his suite and
the horses and dogs he had bought in Newmarket. Back in
Mysore, he died two weeks later.

A Long Life of Dancing
and Laughter

A SMILING SERVANT carrying a silver umbrella is calling out a haunting chant: 'Maharajah, Maharajah, make way, make way; His Highness is coming.' The Maharajah of Benares, who presides over India's holiest city, is a direct descendant of the god Shiva. He runs up the palace steps; you don't expect a god to look so robust or have a bushy military moustache. He looks well on Ganges water which he has with him wherever he goes in the world. He reads Sanskrit, meditates, is vegetarian, likes classical music, specially the Berlin Philharmonic, was once a good tennis player and hunter, now prefers to exercise his mind with yoga and Indian philosophy. An ascetic prince, he has little time for the outside world.

His son, a spotty shy boy, is being groomed as a god, but at twenty-two he just wants to play tennis and spend time with his friends. He is being educated in the palace where tutors teach him Sanskrit and he studies royal paintings. 'Public schools are only for the élite,' beams the Maharajah in a fetching pink silk hat trimmed with gold and a cream kurtah.

Getting on a flight to Benares, or Varanasi, which is its Indian name, is like trying to get on a plane on the last day on earth. Flights are packed with pilgrims. A smiling Indian Airlines pilot carries a cactus plant into the cockpit. There is a stampede of Indians bound for the place they call Kashi, American tourists and pale young men from the Foreign Office going for a spell

of Sanskrit and to study the treasure of Ayuvedic manuscripts
at the University of Benares. A string of Buddhist pilgrims in
saffron rose robes wearing big coolie straw hats strapped to
their backs are first off when the plane lands.

Every Hindu wants to die in Benares; this is his passport to
the gods, the Nirvana, total peace. At first light, bodies strapped
to bamboo litters are hurried through the narrow streets to
become a crescent of smoke, cremated on a sandalwood fire at
the ghats, the symbolic banks of Mother Ganges, where cows
eat the flowers from the bodies and sadhus in pink loincloths
hold brass pots to the sun and bathe and pray.

Benares is a cheerful city with 140 cinemas. There is a lot of
disease but no epidemics. The people are a bit battered; bumping
against death so often, there is an air of casual solemnity. You
are bombarded with sales chat to buy gold brocade, ivory and
gold. Stalls are selling 'hanging Fancy jhars', 'Varanasi mangoes
very sweet' and tinselly yellow strands. Only the lepers and the
holy men seem not to be in business. The Maharajah is appalled
by the corruption in his city but in the next breath says, 'It is a
most carefree and cheerful city, people are singing and making
money.' It is the way of life in India.

Even the wood for the pyre has a price. An untouchable
caste called the Doms work on a Robin Hood principle. The
Princes and the wealthy have sandalwood and pay about ten
thousand rupees. The poor farmer who has come sixty or
seventy miles by rickshaw past the fields of feathery sugar
cane and ripening wheat can only afford three or four hundred
for twigs.

The eldest son, wearing a white seamless robe, lights the pyre
and incense is thrown on the fire. He walks around the fire five
times to liberate the body from the five elements, water, fire,
air, earth and ether, carrying sacred twigs of holy kusha grass.
Then he cracks the skull with a long bamboo stick to release
the soul. It then goes forward to 'a long life of dancing and
laughter' on the Far Shore. Its goal is where the god Vishnu
sleeps between eras on the waters of the sea of milk and Brahma
broke from a golden egg in his navel at the dawn of creation.

The Doms will rake the ashes for valuables and the family will offer rice balls – pindas – which are a symbol of the soul's journey. If you go down to the Ganges at dawn you feel revived and curiously optimistic about death.

Mothers and wives may have travelled two and three hundred miles by bullock cart or rickshaw to fulfil a dying wish for a husband or son. They are not allowed near the ghats. Afterwards young widows go home to a life of ostracism, the older ones with breasts shrivelled like lemons may go to the convent by the Ganges to sigh and sing mantras, for ever wearing white, the colour of mourning. Near Bharatpur there is a widows' sanctuary which has the marks of blood on the walls where they crashed their heads in ritual grieving, even if their married life had been less than perfect.

Although the widow's ritual throwing of herself on her husband's funeral fire is banned in India, in 1954 the widow of the Comptroller of the royal household in Jodhpur was determined to commit suttee. The symbolic moment came when she cracked her bracelets in pieces, cutting herself off from her caste for ever. It was the moment of no return; her family had tried to persuade her to change her mind as she sat on a bare rock in the arid bed of the slow-moving river Nerbudda surrounded by gloomy dark mango-groves and mud houses. Putting on a special pink robe, she threw herself on her husband's pyre and her ashes were taken to the sacred Ganges.

In a country which is individually clean but collectively dirty, bodies are disposed of quickly by cremation or, if you are a Parsee, you go to the Towers of Silence. Parsees, who escaped Moslem persecution in Persia 1,375 years ago, believe fire and earth are too sacred to be polluted with dead bodies. They leave their dead at the Towers, in Bombay guarded by trees and high walls. Vultures swoop in and pick the corpses dry, leaving only the skeleton on the marble slab. This is finally thrown into a deep well. Years ago you could hear nothing but the melancholy swish of the palm trees and the Arabian Sea beating against the rocks of the western shore. But now Bombay is high rise and it is not unusual for families living in apartment blocks nearby to find a vulture has dropped a bone on their balcony.

Many of the old Rulers seemed alive in the funeral procession, sitting propped up in the back of the car in jewels and court dress. This ensured that there was no disturbing interregnum. The danger was, as a new Ruler of Kutch found out, that a younger brother might be on the throne when the heir got back to the palace after the funeral.

Often the new Ruler sat apart from the cremation. The Maharawal of Jaisalmer did not go to the funeral but sat on a stone throne at the top of the old palace in the fort. At the moment when the fire under the corpse was lit, a signal was made, the state priest put the red tilak mask on the new Ruler's forehead and the drums rolled to tell the people they had a new Maharawal.

The Maharawal of Dungarpur remembers being taken on a silver palanquin to the Palace Durbar Hall the day his father died, 15 November 1918. He sat on the throne. His thumb was ripped open and he became the new Ruler when the tilak of his own blood was on his forehead.

In 1939 the Maharajah of Baroda's ashes were taken to the spot where the Ganges and the river Jumna meet. An English officer, Colonel Carroll-Leahy, was in charge of the little gold urn. He put it on a gun carriage drawn by six horses with a squadron of cavalry as escort:

'I rode in front and we came to the spot; it looked rather like Beachy Head. Over the edge of the cliff appeared two gentlemen in white nightshirts who came up and bowed and said could they take the urn. They disappeared over the cliff to the beach below, where we had a small boat. They would go out to the junction and scatter them there. I said, "Well, I am going to fire a 19-gun salute for you, so when you get out in a suitable place and can keep the boat more or less steady, wave a flag at me and I will start firing my guns." This they did.'

The Maharajah of Benares' ramshackle palace Ramnagar is seventeenth century: a great ivory-cream-coloured fort perched beside the Ganges and refreshingly indifferent to tourists. At the entrance men are sleeping under piles of grey bedding; there is a grubby tennis shoe underneath a paliasse and another guard is plucking his eyebrows with a handheld mirror.

Next day the Maharajah is in a very good mood at the Nadarnsi Palace which is smaller and prettier than the Ramnagar. Outside there is dried grass and a statue of his grandfather covered with a sack. In the hall a white turban hangs on a china hook, antlers are competing with original Christopher Wray lampshades in the Victorian gloom. The ivory furniture and brass bed made for the Queen stand neglected in rooms empty and warm, opening out onto marble balconies where wisps of dried bougainvillaea are chased by the breeze.

When the Queen visited Benares in 1961 she rode on elephants which were caparisoned and wearing crowns. 'I thought,' she said drily, sitting in her canopied silver howdah, 'that only Kings and Queens wore crowns.'

The Maharajah is never seen eating or drinking but enjoys laying on English breakfasts for guests with Cooper's Oxford marmalade on the terrace of the Ramnagar palace. Each new day he has to see a sacred cow when he opens his eyes. When he stayed with the Mountbattens in Delhi, they had to have a cow hoisted in front of his window at dawn every morning.

Offering a seat close to him, the Maharajah, who has a deep challenging voice, seemed anxious. 'Was it true that the Queen and Prince Philip were not sleeping together?' He had been very intrigued by the Queen's lonely plight when the intruder Michael Fagan broke into her bedroom.

Rather than talk about his own family history, his brave ancestor Chait Singh who tried to foil Warren Hastings, the Governor-General of the East India Company, and had to flee from the palace by dhow, he wanted to know about British royalty. He was perturbed that the Princess of Wales might have had virginity tests before getting married to Prince Charles. 'In India,' he said with a shrug, 'there could be no doubt.'

He suddenly got up from his table and went behind an old

blue curtain and there was a sound of dribbling water. 'Highness having juice,' an aide said helpfully.

The Maharajah of Bundi, the winner of the Military Cross for gallantry, left for his heavenly abode at the feet of Lord Mountbatten at Broadlands. 'Chap wanted a last look at his old Viceroy. We had a spot of lunch and he died at my feet . . .' Lord Mountbatten was so taken aback, he telephoned the Queen and started by saying, 'Got Bundi here.' The Queen broke in: 'How nice, do give him my best wishes.'

30

Outshining the Moon

THE PRINCES were the golden geese; today they cannot afford the upkeep of their palaces. They do not have a National Trust, though there is the tentative Indian Heritage Society which has the blessing of Rajiv Gandhi. Meanwhile, all around is decline, goats chewing at banana skins in the dusty doorways of the old forts; the stucco of Calcutta is crumbling but the Victoria Memorial survives, so too do the Indo-Saracenic palaces and Lutyens' Delhi, a pink and perfect example of imperial and classic style.

Britain is the oldest democracy in the world, India the largest, but treasuring English architecture and palaces is not a priority. Conservationists must tread delicately and are anxious not to appear patronising in a country burdened by both poverty and bureaucracy. The pearly marble of the Taj Mahal is turning yellow; there is an oil refinery close on the banks of the Jumna River. A young girl plays hopscotch outside and the visiting memsahibs' lined faces look touchingly vulnerable in the soft light as the guide holds up candles to show the lapis lazuli and flowers carved in the white marble screens. At Bundi, an old night watchman takes a desultory sweep at bat droppings and the walls with traces of the famous green and blue murals are dank and dripping. Huge families chatter and have rice picnics on the dried-up lawns. Ironically, while the red sandstone forts with their secret pearl mosques and blue Persian tiles are in danger, those solid bungalows built by the Raj stand appallingly firm.

Critics say that if the Princes are good for anything, it is as exhibits. Opening your palace to the public in India is not rewarding and owners are penalised, paying heavy taxes. Hordes rush in, sheltering from the monsoon and trampling the Aubussons, so different from our own dear members of the National Trust. There is less reverence in India for old things; familiarity with antiquity is inherent. The palaces which attract the highest number of tourists are Jaipur and Udaipur. In the zenana at Udaipur, a dash of whitewash and cement is slapped on to hold the sixteenth-century balconies together.

They say the world is made up of two kinds of people, those who have been to India and those who have not. You love it or hate it. The British have never stopped caring about India and are moved when elderly bearers turn up at the station to meet them. Administrators who did not like India much when they were there, go back nostalgic for the sound of the chowki-dar, the night watchman shuffling about and clearing his throat, the bunches of basil to keep the mosquitoes away and the babus – clerks hovering with shining eyes, giving a little shake of the head as if your request has been the most wonderful honour and then going off and forgetting it completely.

The forester welcomes you to his mud house with white flowers painted on the walls with as much ceremony as the Rajasthan Prince. In one you drink spiced tea from a terracotta cup, in another it is mango juice from a gold-rimmed glass. Neither will let you go. The poor man says: 'tonight we will get a chicken,' those tiny deprived creatures pecking resiliently at straw shavings killed and cooked at once, adapting brilliantly to crushed spices and slow cooking in a brass pot over a dung fire. 'The problems of India would be solved if they stopped burning the dung,' a warrant officer reported tersely in 1947. His advice was ignored, and at the end of the day villagers sit round these fires which have a whiffy blend of autumn, dried tea and incense.

Royal elephants who once gave way to Rolls-Royces at the

palaces wander into the main streets, called Tolstoy Marg and
Southend Marg, gentle, firm feet plapping along with mahout
and greenery. Gardeners trim the grass verges of India's
Champs-Elysées, the Rajpath, and you are pushed protectively
against a wall in India's holiest city, foot in a pool of suspect
water. 'Make way, make way,' surely the Maharajah is coming,
but it is a sacred cow hurrying along on its own past the gold
temple. It is a good life for a bullock in India.

The Princes' cars were every colour of the rainbow, trimmed
in gold or silver; now they drive Mercedes, Jaguars and white
Italian sports cars. Taxis are trusty old Ambassadors modelled
on a 1954 Morris Oxford. On the road to Jaipur, a boy is
knocked down. The driver gets out grumbling: 'Boy getting
crack. I gave him horn.' They part smiling. There is a snuffling
noise in the boot. 'My dog is in the dickey . . . you would like
to meet?' A huge golden labrador bounds out. 'This dog is
vegetarian, this dog Jimmy. She is most sincere.'

Booking clerks at airports in India are like gods, they hold
such power. If a flight is overbooked, a former maharajah will
always get on, while an official in a magenta turban, white grey
jacket and white moustache, dazzling in the drabness of Delhi
airport, fluttering hands over his beard, apologises: 'They have
failed in their procedure.' But what is an hour or two for a
people preoccupied with eternity? The Prince is on his flight.
The chauffeur will meet him at the airport in Calcutta, the city
where the Indian artist Profulla Mohanti put down a canvas on
the pavement and a ragged thin young man came up to him
and said: 'Why are you using this space? This is where I sleep
and live.'

Madcap is the description the Princes liked to give themselves,
and they fit perfectly in a country where a hotel receptionist in
Mysore, explaining he has no stamps left, says with mournful
eyes: 'It is all exhausted.' Sometimes they can break your heart:
an old man in a boat from the Elephanta Caves throwing crumbs
for the seagulls, food he looks as if he needs himself. Two
venerable gentlemen sitting under yellow eiderdowns on the
platform in Jodhpur watch with detachment an apoplectic Eng-

lishman with red cheeks who shouts: 'I insist I do not make my
own bed!' The royal train has been overbooked; honeymooners
are sharing with widows; but the beauty of India takes away
your rage; and guests of the Maharajah get glasses of champagne
and picnic by moonlight in the desert in Jaisalmer on tandoori
chicken and mangoes.

The Princes never grovelled, and they weathered imperialism
and smiled at the self-confidence of the British. Kipling said
God created maharajahs so that mankind could have a spectacle
of jewels and marble palaces.

Today whether in traditional brocade or jeans and cowboy
boots, there is still a lustre about the last of this quirky heritage.
The Maharajahs have a quality and presence, a rarity value
which shines through, not unlike the neglected diamonds as big
as cherries found in their cellars. Winking and twinkling through
dust and decay, as bright as the sun and outshining the moon,
they are still the children of a golden magical firmament.

Index